HATING WHITEY

HATING WHITEY
and Other Progressive Causes

DAVID HOROWITZ

SPENCE PUBLISHING COMPANY · DALLAS
1999

Published in the United States by
Spence Publishing Company
111 Cole Street
Dallas, Texas 75207

Library of Congress Cataloging-in-Publication Data

Horowitz, David, 1939-
        Hating whitey : and other progressive causes / David Horowitz.
        p. cm.
    Includes bibliographical references and index.
    ISBN 1-890626-21-x
    1. United States—Politics and government—1945-1989.   2. United
States—Politics and government—1989-   3. Progressivism (United
States politics)   4. Political culture—United States—History—20th
century.   5. United States—Race relations.   6. Racism—United
States.   7. Afro-American civil rights workers—Attitudes.   8.
Political activists—United States—Attitudes.   I. Title.
    E839.5 .H67 1999
    305.8'00973—dc21   99-39676

Printed in the United States of America

To my stepson Jon J.

and my grandson Elvis Rishon,

and to April,

who has had the courage

to stand with me in these battles

Contents

IV

PROGRESSIVE EDUCATION

V

LOOKING BACKWARD

VI

FOREIGN AFFAIRS

Acknowledgments

MANY OF THE ESSAYS in this book appeared originally in the Internet magazine *Salon*, for which I have written a column every other Monday for more than two years. I am grateful to *Salon*'s editor, David Talbot, who probably disagrees with most of the contents of this volume, for the opportunity he has provided me to reach an audience outside the conservative ghetto to which the rest of the liberal media has consigned my writing since I had second thoughts nearly twenty years ago. When I was still on the political left, David showed similar courage in defending Peter Collier and me when we came under attack in 1980 in the professional association Media Alliance for writing the truth about the prison radical George Jackson and his attorney, Fay Stender.* David's integrity and courage were again manifest in 1993 when, as editor of the "Ideas and Opinions" section of the *San Francisco Chronicle*, he reprinted the story, "Black Murder, Inc.," which appears in this volume. It was first published in *Heterodoxy*, the magazine Peter Collier and I edit. David was (and is to this day) the only member of the national media to show interest in this story,

---

* See "Requiem" in David Horowitz, *Radical Son* (New York: Free Press, 1998), 309ff., where the story of this article is told and the attacks on it described.

which concerns the most celebrated political organization of the New Left and its involvement in the murder of innocents.

My hands-on editors at *Salon*, Andrew Ross and David Weir, who also disagree with my current views, could not have been more supportive personally and professionally if they had been political soulmates. If more people were capable of an ecumenical spirit like theirs, our political discourse would be far more civilized and our civic order, more humane.

Finally, I wish to thank Benjamin Kepple and Cris Rapp of *Heterodoxy*, who provided me with editorial and research assistance. Their dedication and care has made this manuscript better and more accurate that it would otherwise have been.

HATING WHITEY

Memories in Memphis

O N A RECENT TRIP TO THE SOUTH I found myself in Memphis, the city where Martin Luther King Jr. was struck down by an assassin's bullet just over thirty years ago. Memphis, I discovered, is home to a "National Civil Rights Museum," established by a local trust of African-Americans active in civil rights causes. Tucked out of the way on a side street, the museum is housed in the building that was once the Lorraine Motel, the very site where Dr. King was murdered. I decided to go.

Except for two white 1960s Cadillac convertibles parked under the motel balcony, the lot outside was empty when I arrived. It is part of the museum's plan to preserve the memories of that somber day in April three decades ago. The cars belonged to King and his entourage, and have been left as they were the morning he was killed. Above them, a wreath hangs from a balcony railing to mark the spot where Dr. King fell. Beyond is the room where he had slept the night before. It, too, has been preserved exactly as it was, the covers pulled back, the bed unmade, the breakfast tray laid out as though someone would be coming to pick it up.

Inside the building, the first floor of the motel has vanished completely, hollowed out for the museum's exhibits. The cavernous room has become a silent stage for the dramas of the movement King once led. These narratives are recounted in documents and photographs, some the length of wall frescoes, bearing images as inspirational today as then. In the center of the hall, the burned shell of a school bus recalls the freedom rides and the perils their passengers once endured. Scattered about are small television screens whose tapes recapture the moments and acts that once moved a nation. On one screen a crowd of well-dressed young men and women braves police dogs and water hoses vainly attempting to turn them back. It is a powerful tribute to a movement and leader able to win battles against overwhelming odds by exerting moral force over an entire nation.

As a visitor reaches the end of the hall, however, he turns a corner to a jarring, discordant sight. Two familiar faces stare out from a wall-size monument that seems strangely out of place—the faces of Malcolm X and Elijah Muhammad, leaders of the Nation of Islam. Aside from a portrait of King himself, there are no others of similar dimension in the museum. It is clear that its creators intended to establish these men along with King as spiritual avatars of the civil rights cause.

For one old enough to have supported King, such a view seems incomprehensible, even bizarre. At the time of these struggles, Malcolm X was King's great antagonist in the black community, leading the resistance to the civil rights hope. The black Muslim publicly scorned King's March on Washington as "ridiculous" and predicted the failure of the civil rights movement King led because the white man would never willingly give black Americans such rights. He rejected King's call for non-violence and his goal of an integrated society, and in so doing earned the disapproval of the American majority that King had wooed and was about to win. Malcolm X even denied King's racial authenticity, redefining the term "Negro," which King and his movement used to describe themselves, to mean "Uncle Tom."

King was unyielding before these attacks. To clarify his opposition to Malcolm X's separatist vision, King refused to appear on any platform with him, effectively banning Malcolm from the community of respect. The other heads of the principal civil rights organizations, the NAACP's Roy Wilkins and the Urban League's Whitney Young joined King in enforcing this ban. It was only in the last year of Malcolm's life, when the civil rights cause was all but won, and when Malcolm had left the Nation of Islam and rejected its racism, that King finally relented and agreed to appear in the now famous photograph of the two that became iconic after their deaths.

Yet this very reconciliation—more a concession on Malcolm's part than King's—could argue for the appropriateness of Malcolm's place in a "civil rights" museum. Malcolm certainly earned an important place in any historical tribute to the struggle of the descendants of Africans to secure dignity, equality, and respect in a society that had brought them to its shores as slaves. Malcolm's understanding of the psychology of oppression, his courage in asserting the self-confidence and pride of black Americans might even make him worthy of inclusion in the temple of a man who was never a racist and whose movement he scorned.

But what of Elijah Muhammad? What is a racist and religious cultist doing in a monument to Martin Luther King? This is a truly perverse intrusion. The teachings of Elijah Muhammad mirror the white supremacist doctrines of the Southern racists whose rule King fought. According to Muhammad's teachings, white people were invented six thousand years ago by a mad scientist named Yacub in a failed experiment to dilute the blood of the original human beings, who were black. The result was a morally tainted strain of humanity, "white devils," who went on to devastate the world and oppress all other human beings, and whom God would one day destroy in a liberating Armageddon. Why is the image of this bizarre fringe racist blown up several times life-size to form the iconography of a National Civil Rights Museum? It is as though someone had placed a portrait of the leader of the Hale-Bopp Comet cult in the Jefferson Memorial.

After I left the museum, it occurred to me that this image reflected a truth about the afterlife of the movement King created, the moral legacy of which was in large part squandered by those who inherited it after his death. The moral decline of the civil rights leadership is reflected in many episodes of the last quarter century: the embrace of racist demagogues like Louis Farrakhan and Al Sharpton, as well as indefensible causes like those of Tawana Brawley, O. J. Simpson, the Los Angeles riot, and the Million Man March on Washington, organized by the Nation of Islam and cynically designed to appropriate the moral mantle of King's historic event.

The impact of such episodes was compounded by the silence of black civil rights leaders over racial outrages committed by African-Americans—the anti-Korean incitements of black activists in New York, the mob attacks by black gangs on Asian and white storeowners during the Los Angeles race riot, the lynching of a Hasidic Jew by a black mob in Crown Heights, and a black jury's acquittal of his murderer. The failure of current civil rights leaders like Jesse Jackson, Kwesi Mfume, and Julian Bond to condemn black racists and black outrages committed against other ethnic communities has been striking in its contrast to the demands these same leaders make on the consciences of whites, not to mention the moral example set by King when he dissociated his movement from the racist preachings of Malcolm X.

This moral abdication of black civil rights leaders is integrally related to, if not fully explained by, their close association with a radical left whose anti-white hatred is a by-product of its anti-Americanism. The attitudes of this left toward blacks are so patronizing that one disillusioned activist was inspired to write a book about them entitled *Liberal Racism*.[*] As a result of this alliance,

---

[*] Jim Sleeper, *Liberal Racism* (New York: Penguin, 1997); see also Shelby Steele, *A Dream Deferred* (New York: HarperCollins, 1998).

ideological hatred of whites is now an expanding industry not only in the African-American community, but among white "liberals" in elite educational institutions as well. Harvard's prestigious W.E.B. DuBois African-American Studies Institute, for example, provided an academic platform for lecturer Noel Ignatiev to launch "Whiteness Studies," an academic field promoting the idea that "whiteness" is a "social construct" that is oppressive and must be "abolished."

The magazine *Race Traitor* is the theoretical organ of this academic cult, emblazoned with the motto: "Treason to Whiteness is Loyalty to Humanity." This is hardly a new theme on the left, echoing, as it does, Susan Sontag's perverse claim that "the white race is the cancer of history." (Sontag eventually expressed regrets about her remark, not because it was a racial smear, but out of deference to cancer patients who might feel unjustly slurred.) According to *Race Traitor* intellectuals, "whiteness" is the principal scourge of mankind, an idea that Louis Farrakhan promoted at the Million Man March when he declared that the world's "number one problem . . . is white supremacy." "Whiteness," in this view, is a category imposed on American society by its ruling class to organize the social order into a system of marxist-type oppression.* Consequently, "the key to solving the social problems of our age is to abolish the white race." This new racism expresses itself in slogans lifted right out of the radical 1960s. According to the Whiteness Studies revolutionaries, "the abolition of whiteness" must be accomplished "by any means necessary." To underscore that this slogan means exactly what it says, the editors of *Race Traitor* have explicitly embraced the military strategy of American neo-Nazis and the militia movement in calling for a John Brown-style insurrection that would trigger a second American civil war and destroy the symbolic (and oppressive) order of whiteness.

Such language is incendiary and fuels a widespread denigration of Americans—including Jews, Arabs, Central Europeans, Medi-

---

* See Noel Ignatiev and John Garvey, "Abolish the White Race By Any Means Necessary," in *Race Traitor* (New York: Routledge, 1996), 90-114.

terranean Europeans, East Indians, Armenians—who are multi-ethnic and often dark-skinned, but who for official purposes (and under pressure from civil rights groups like the NAACP) are designated "white." Unlike anti-black attitudes, which are universally decried and would trigger the expulsion of their purveyors from any liberal institution in America, this racism is not only permitted but encouraged, especially in the academic culture responsible for the moral and intellectual education of tomorrow's elites.

An anthology of the first five years of *Race Traitor*, for example, has been published by a prestigious, academic-oriented publishing house (Routledge) and was the winner of the 1997 American Book Award. Its jacket features praise by a prestigious Harvard professor, Cornel West, who writes: "*Race Traitor* is the most visionary, courageous journal in America." West's coziness with the racist Louis Farrakhan (he was a speaker at the Million Man March) has done nothing to tarnish his own academic reputation, his popularity with students, or his standing in the "civil rights" community. Afrocentrist racists like Leonard Jeffries, the late John Henrik Clarke, Derrick Bell, and Tony Martin—to name just a few—have also been integral parts of the academic culture for decades, often running entire academic departments. By contrast, a distinguished Harvard scholar, Stephan Thernstrom, who is white, was driven out of his classroom by black student leftists who decided that his lectures on slavery were politically incorrect because they did not reflect prevailing leftist views.

In recent decades, anti-white racism has, in fact, become a common currency of the "progressive" intelligentsia. Examples range from communist Professor Angela Davis, whose ideological rants are routinely laced with racial animosity (and who recently told an audience of undergraduates at Michigan State that the number one problem in the world was white people), to Nobel laureate Toni Morrison, whose boundless suspicions of white America amount to a demonization almost as intense as Elijah Muhammad's. In her introduction to an anthology about the O. J. Simpson case, *Birth of A Nation 'Hood*, for example, Morrison compared the symbolic meanings of the O. J. Simpson case to D.W. Griffith's epic celebration of the Ku Klux Klan, in order to imply that white America acted as the KKK in pursuing Simpson for the murder of Ron Goldman and Simpson's ex-wife.

With university support, *Race Traitor* intellectuals in the field of Whiteness Studies have produced an entire library of "scholarship" whose sole purpose is to incite hatred against white America, against "Euro-American" culture, and against American institutions in general. According to the editors of *Race Traitor*, "just as the capitalist system is not a capitalist plot, race is not the work of racists. On the contrary, it is reproduced by the principal institutions of society, among which are the schools (which define 'excellence'), the labor market (which defines 'employment'), the law (which defines 'crime'), the welfare system (which defines 'poverty'), and the family (which defines 'kinship')."* The editors of *Race Traitor* characterize the presence of whites on this continent as an unmitigated catastrophe for "peoples of color" and an offense to everything that is decent and humane. In the perspective of these race radicals, white America is the "Great Satan." In academic cant, they replicate the poisonous message of the black racists of the Nation of Islam.

Some of the manifestations of this anti-white racism are explored in this volume, the purpose of which is to open a frank discussion of a subject that is almost never directly discussed. Almost all the chapters first appeared as columns in the Internet magazine *Salon*, a left-of-center publication with sufficient editorial independence to include a dissident writer like myself. This, in itself, may be a hopeful sign of what may be possible if a dialogue is encouraged. The tolerance of *Salon*'s editors for the views in this book

---

* Ibid., 80.

should not be surprising, since they are the same views once advanced by the civil rights movement King led. Unfortunately, if experience is any judge, that will not make their author immune from charges of racism.

As those familiar with my autobiography, *Radical Son*, know, I once occupied the other side of the political divide. My views on race, however, have remained entirely consistent with my previous commitments and beliefs. I opposed racial preferences in the 1960s, and I oppose them now. Then, I believed that only government neutrality towards racial groups was compatible with the survival of a multi-ethnic society that is also democratic. I still believe that today.

What has changed is my appreciation for America's constitutional framework and the commitment of the American people to those ideals. America's unique political culture was indeed created by white European males, primarily English and Christian. It should be obvious to anyone with even a modest historical understanding that these antecedents are not incidental to the fact that America and England are the nations that led the world in abolishing slavery and establishing the principles of ethnic and racial inclusion—or that we are a nation besieged by peoples "of color" trying to immigrate to our shores to take advantage of the unparalleled opportunities and rights our society offers them.

The establishment of America by Protestant Christians within the framework of the British Empire was historically essential to the development of institutions that today afford greater privileges and protections to all minorities than those of any society extant. White European-American culture is a culture in which the citizens of this nation can take enormous pride, precisely because its principles—revolutionary in their conception and unique in their provenance—provide for the inclusion of cultures that are non-white and non-Christian (and which are not so tolerant in their lands of origin). That is why America's democratic and pluralistic framework remains an inspiring beacon to people of all colors all over the world, from Tiananmen Square to Haiti and Havana, who have not yet won their freedom, but who aspire to do so. This was once the common self-understanding of all Americans and is still the understanding of those who have been able to resist the discredited and oppressive worldview of the "progressive" left.

The left's war against "whiteness" and against America's democratic culture is integrally connected to the Cold War that America fought against the marxist empire after World War 11. It is in many respects the Cold War come home. The agendas of contemporary leftists are merely updated versions of the ideas and agendas of the marxist left that once supported the communist empire. The same radicals who caused the social and political eruptions of the 1960s have now become the politically correct administrators and faculty of American universities. With suitable cosmetic adjustments, the theories, texts, and even leaders of this left display a striking continuity with the radicalism of thirty and sixty years ago. Their goal remains the destruction of America's national identity and, in particular, of the moral, political, and economic institutions that form its social foundation.

The left's response to the observations contained in this volume is not difficult to predict. Impugning the motives of opponents remains the left's most durable weapon, and there is no reason to suppose that it will be mothballed soon. In the heyday of Stalinism, the accusation of "class bias" was used by communists to undermine and attack individuals and institutions with whom they were at war. This accusation magically turned well-meaning citizens into "enemies of the people," a phrase handed down through radical generations from the Jacobin Terror through the Stalinist purges and the blood-soaked cultural revolutions of Chairman Mao. The identical strategy is alive and well today in the left's self-righteous imputation of sexism, racism, and homophobia to anyone who dissents from its party line. Always weak in intellectual argument, the left habitually relies on intimidation and smear to enforce its increasingly incoherent point of view.

It is not that no one else in politics uses such tactics; it is just that the left uses them so reflexively, so recklessly, and so well. In the battle over California's Civil Rights Initiative (CCRI) to outlaw racial preferences, for example, the left's opposition took the form of a scorched-earth strategy, whose purpose was to strip its proponents of any shred of respectability. The chief spokesman for the anti-discrimination initiative, Ward Connerly, though he himself is black, was accused of anti-black racism, of wanting to be white, and of being a bedfellow of the Ku Klux Klan. (The left invited former Klan member David Duke to California to forge the non-existent connection, even paying his expenses for the trip.)

During the campaign, NAACP and ACLU lawyers who debated the Initiative with its proponents relied almost exclusively on charges of racism and alarmist visions of a future in which African-Americans and women would be deprived of their rights should the dreaded legislation pass. To make their case, the anti-CCRI groups sponsored television spots that actually featured hooded Klan figures burning crosses. A fearful voice-over by actress Candace Bergen explicitly linked Ward Connerly, California Governor Pete Wilson, and Speaker Newt Gingrich with the KKK, claiming that, if CCRI's proponents succeeded, women would lose all the rights they had won, and blacks would be thrown back to a time before the Civil Rights Acts.

In the years since the passage of the California Civil Rights Initiative, not a single one of the left's dire predictions has been realized. Women have not lost their rights and segregation has not returned. Even the enrollment of blacks in California's system of higher education has not significantly dropped,* although dema-

---

* The *Chronicle of Higher Education*, April 5, 1999, reported that enrollment of blacks on all the University of California campuses was only twenty-seven fewer students than in 1997.

gogues of the left—including the president of the United States—have used a shortfall in admissions *at the very highest levels* of the system (Berkeley and UCLA) to lead the public to believe that an *overall* decline has taken place. One year after the Initiative passed, enrollment had significantly fallen only at six elite graduate, law, and medical school programs in a higher-education system that consists of more than seventy-four programs. Yet there has been no apology (or acknowledgment of these facts) from Candace Bergen, the NAACP, the ACLU, People for the American Way, or the other leftist groups responsible for the anti-Civil Rights Initiative campaign and for the inflammatory rhetoric and public fear-mongering that accompanied it.

When an earlier version of a chapter in this book, "Why Democrats Need Blacks," was published in *Salon* magazine, the editors printed several long responses from black readers, including the award-winning Berkeley novelist Ishmael Reed. Reed suggested that I did not really care what happens to blacks and that I am insensitive to injustice when it is inflicted on blacks—a not-so-subtle imputation of racism. In a futile attempt to forestall such attacks, I had cited the opinions of black conservatives in the article itself. The critics' response was to dismiss these conservatives as "inauthentically black," "Sambos," "Neo-Cons," and "black comedians." From the point of view of leftists, the only good black is one who parrots their party line.

There is no real answer to such patronizing attitudes and nasty attacks. Nonetheless, in closing this introduction, I will repeat the response I made to Ishmael Reed in the pages of *Salon*:

> I have three black granddaughters for whom I want the absolute best that this life and this society have to offer. My extended black family, which is large and from humble origins in the Deep South, contains members who agree and who disagree with my views on these matters. But all of them understand that whatever I write on the subject of race derives

from a profound desire for justice and opportunity for everyone in this country, including my extended black family. It springs from the hope that we can move towards a society where individuals are what matters and race is not a factor at all.

I

GET WHITEY

I

Racial Paranoia

WHEN BILL AND CAMILLE COSBY'S SON, Ennis, was brutally murdered in 1997 during a robbery in Beverly Hills, the entire nation grieved with them. But a year later Camille Cosby unburdened herself in print with a diatribe against white Americans in a *USA Today* column entitled "America Taught My Son's Killer To Hate Blacks." The feelings expressed in this column could not be regarded simply as grief over her terrible loss. For such pain a mother could be forgiven almost any emotional excess. Written a year after the fact, however, the sentiments expressed in her *USA Today* column reflected long-held, carefully scrutinized, patiently-edited sentiments of hostility and rage against her native country and its white citizenry that could not be so easily excused. It was a form of race hatred that has become all too common among educated and successful African Americans.

Unlike the mothers of Nicole Brown Simpson and Ronald Goldman, who were destined to be disappointed by racially motivated "jury nullification," Camille Cosby saw swift justice rendered by the American system to the murderer of her son. The mainly white jury was not swayed to acquit the killer of Ennis Cosby because of his skin color, nor was there a racial constituency outside the courtroom hoping that he would "beat the system" and go free. Instead, the white prosecutor, judge and jurors worked to bring in a verdict of guilty with all deliberate speed. This was better justice than most Americans receive, white or black. Nonetheless, Camille Cosby was not satisfied; she believed that true justice had not been served. In her eyes, the killer himself was a victim—of America itself.

By then, most of the sailent facts in the case had come to light. It was questionable that race had played any role at all in the killing of Ennis Cosby. The gunman, a Ukranian immigrant, was high on drugs at the time of the shooting and told police shortly after his capture that he regretted what he had done and that he had pulled the trigger because the young man "took too long" to remove his wallet. But none of these facts impressed Camille Cosby: "Presumably [the killer] did not learn to hate black people in his native country, the Ukraine, where the black population was near zero," she wrote. "Nor was he likely to see America's intolerable, stereotypical movies and television programs about blacks, which were not shown in the Soviet Union before the killer and his family moved to America in the late 1980s." In Cosby's fevered view, America's "intolerable, stereotypical movies and television programs" were responsible for the death of her son.

It is a logic that is as familiar as it is paranoid. The charge that white Hollywood portrays blacks in a stereotypically negative fashion is a standard protest heard from black spokesmen ranging from Louis Farrakhan to Jesse Jackson. But it has little basis in fact. Going back to the 1940s, white Hollywood has produced and directed an entire library of features about black Americans and their struggle for equality (*Home of the Brave*, *Pinky*, *Sergeant Rutledge*, *To Kill A Mockingbird*, *The Defiant Ones*), not to mention many of the principal epics of black liberation and pride, *Roots* and *Malcolm X* (both produced by whites) and *Amistad* (written and directed by whites) to name three, and television sitcoms and series focusing on admirable black families (*Julia, The Jeffersons, Good Times, Sister Sister, I'll Fly Away*). At the same time, black artists have themselves produced many of the negative stereotypes, from "blaxploitation" films like *Super Fly* to gangsta rap videos, which are the targets of many of the complaints.

But it is the name Cosby that almost by itself represents a refutation of the paranoid claims that white America and Hollywood are hostile to blacks. Camille Cosby enjoys a fortune estimated in the hundreds of millions because of the success of a television show featuring her husband as the head of a model black family. For ten years, the *Cosby Show* was the top-rated television program in America (and Bill Cosby the top-earning entertainer) thanks to the loyalty of tens of millions of viewers who happened to be white. If America was the country of Camille Cosby's paranoid imagination, the success of both the real and fictional Cosbys would be inexplicable.

As if to demonstrate the irrationality of these complaints, the *Cosby Show* was actually attacked quite regularly in the years of its popularity, often by the same people. They accused the show of being "unrepresentative" and "unrealistic," in other words of being an attempt by white network executives to portray African Americans as *better* than they actually were, while hiding the poverty, oppression and other injuries of race that white America had inflicted on them.

Nor does the illogic stop there. On what basis does Camille Cosby make the claim that because there were no blacks in the Ukraine, the killer of her son must have learned racism by watching American television? Is she suggesting that the presence of a persecuted group is *necessary* to provoke the irrationality of bigots? Do racists need evidence to substantiate their racism? There are no Jews to speak of in countries like Poland and Japan, but Jew-hatred is rife in both places. Has Cosby forgotten (or as a leftist has she merely blanked out the memory of) Russia's racist culture that led to the mass expulsion of African students from Moscow's Lumumba University and Moscow's official protest at the Olympics that the American team's inclusion of black athletes was an unfair advantage because of blacks' innately superior abilities?

Early press reports of the Cosby murder indicated that, as a youth, Ennis Cosby's killer was raped by blacks in prison. What would Camille Cosby's reaction be to the claim that black rapists were responsible for her son's death? Yet that is exactly the logic she employs in attacking America for the drug-induced act of one immigrant sociopath. "Yes," she writes, "racism and prejudice are omnipresent and eternalized in America's institutions, media and myriad entities." *Eternalized*? Are white Americans born racists and destined to die as such? This is indeed the accusation made by black racists like law professor Derrick Bell, who in several popular books has claimed that America is irretrievably hostile to blacks. How are Cosby's and Bell's views that white Americans are inherently morally depraved different from the attitudes of southern crackers and KKK racists towards blacks?

Like Cosby, Bell is culturally a product of the communist left, which fifty years ago brought a petition to the United Nations, at the behest of the Kremlin, charging the United States with "genocide" in its treatment of blacks. Perhaps it is also appropriate to recall that the Cosbys were vocal supporters of the notorious Tawana Brawley, who falsely accused a group of whites of raping her. (Brawley, incidentally, has made an after-the-fact career out of touring campuses to repeat her lies at the invitation of black student associations who reward her with handsome fees for her testimony.) At the time, the Cosbys put up reward money for anyone who could prove Brawley's lies were true and appeared at rallies organized by Al Sharpton to incite hatred and violence against the innocent whites she smeared.

In her *USA Today* column, Cosby began her "proof" of what she believed to be America's ineluctable racism with the meaningless fact that the Voting Rights Act would technically expire in ten years. From this she concluded, preposterously, that "Congress once again will decide whether African-Americans will be allowed to vote" and commented "no other Americans are subjected to this oppressive nonsense." On what planet is Camille Cosby living? What could possibly have inspired the idea that whites are plotting to take away the voting rights of American blacks? What majority in this country would deny African-Americans the right to vote, a right guaranteed by the Fifteenth Amendment? To be sure, this right was once denied in the American South, but black Americans led by King and supported by the overwhelming majority of white Americans— including the government, the courts, and law enforcement agencies—restored it. The Voting Rights Act was passed by 90 percent majorities in Congress. The once segregated South is today a region whose major cities are run by African-American elected officials, while black legislators like congresswoman Cynthia McKinney are now regularly elected in majority white districts.

Camille Cosby is a woman whose country has showered her with privilege, making her family wealthy and famous beyond the wildest dreams of almost anyone alive, including all but a handful of the white targets of her wrath. Yet Camille Cosby's hatred of her country is so deep as to provoke the following preposterous observation: "African-Americans, as well as all Americans, are brainwashed every day to respect and revere slave-owners and people who clearly waffled about race . . . Several slave-owners' images are on America's paper currencies: George Washington ($1), Thomas Jefferson ($2), Alexander Hamilton ($10), Andrew Jackson ($20), Ulysses Grant ($50) and Benjamin Franklin ($100)." Forget that the characterizations of Hamilton, Grant and Franklin (whose last act was to file an anti-slavery petition to Congress) are probably libelous. What American is taught to praise these men for having owned (or possibly having owned) slaves? America is probably unique among the nations of the world in teaching every one of its children from kindergarten on that slavery was wrong, that all people are created equal, and that tolerance of differences is a cardinal virtue. Perhaps Cosby should direct her concerns to black leaders like Jesse Jackson and Louis Farrakhan who *are* still waffling about slavery in Africa more than a hundred years after the spiritual heirs of Washington and Jefferson abolished the institution in the United States.

Camille Cosby's column is, in fact, a cornucopia of common but unfounded complaints about "institutional racism" in American life made by the political left. She refers, for example, to the fact that "America's educational institutions' dictionaries define 'black' [as] harmful; hostile; disgrace; unpleasant aspects of life." She describes this as evidence that white people, who control language, apply the term "black" to African-Americans in order to denigrate them. But the responsibility for the term "black" is properly assigned to Malcolm X and his militant followers, who *demanded* that African-Americans be called "black" at a time when whites and their dictionaries universally referred to African-Americans as "Negro" and "colored." Subsequently, Jesse Jackson demanded that blacks be called "African-American," and white Americans again acquiesced.

The irrational hatred of America in general, and of white America in particular, manifested in Cosby's screed, is unfortunately the expression of more than an individual paranoia exacerbated by a perfectly understandable grief. Suppose, for example, that the mothers of Nicole Simpson and Ronald Goldman had authored a parallel column titled "Black America Taught Our Children's Killer to Hate Whites?" Is there a (white-owned) newspaper in America that would even print such a claim?

In contrast to Camille Cosby's perverse view of America as a nation of racists, it is worth repeating that this is the only country in the world where children are instructed from pre-school days that racism is morally wrong, that American blacks have been the victims of egregious crimes, and that expressing prejudice is socially unacceptable. In fact the only group that is allowed to vent racist venom publicly in America today are African-Americans themselves, as the deplorable outburst by Camille Cosby attests.

In her malicious column, Cosby also quoted the most celebrated and honored African-American writer of his generation, James Baldwin, to this embarrassing effect: "The will of the people, or the State, is revealed by the State's institutions. There was not, then, nor is there now, a single American institution which is not a racist institution." Can Baldwin be referring to the Supreme Court that ended segregated schools? The White House that sent federal troops to integrate schools in the South? The schools themselves that teach youngsters that racial prejudice is wrong? The Congress that enacted all the civil rights laws? The Equal Employment Opportunity Commission and the Justice Department that enforce these laws? Yet how many African American leaders are ready to step forward to dissociate themselves from such slanders, or from the vicious hate-America, hate-whitey sentiments expressed by such prominent and publicly acclaimed figures in the African American community as Camille Cosby, James Baldwin and Derrick Bell?

Ironically, a kind of answer was provided the day prior to the appearance of Cosby's *USA Today* column. On that day the chairman of the president's specially convened panel on race, and its most distinguished African-American member, John Hope Franklin, urged President Clinton to abandon the idea of creating a "color-blind" society. This should have been a warning to all Americans that the future of America's pluralistic, multi-ethnic social contract is in danger.

2

Hate Crimes

WHEN A YOUNG MAN named Matthew Shepard was tortured and left to die on the high plains of Wyoming simply because he was gay, the nation was outraged. Earlier that year, an even more brutal attack was made on the person of James Byrd Jr., a black man in Texas. Like Shepard's murder, Byrd's was followed by outpourings of anger and grief from editorial pages and political pulpits across the country.

These were appropriate, if extraordinary, responses to horrible crimes against ordinary citizens, whose untimely deaths would otherwise have been unremarkable because, gruesome as they were, they are all too common. It was the fact that the perpetrators and victims were set apart by communal bigotries, for which the crimes served as violent individual expressions, that made the acts seem so important. The enhanced sense of human depravity that colored the public reactions to these incidents lay in our shared conviction that their nature as hate crimes made them an outrage to the nation's sense of self, as well as a threat to its communal future.

Well and good enough. These responses are signs of health in the body politic, the presence of a will to summon the better angels of our nature, and to keep the savagery that lurks beneath the surface of any civilized society safely at bay. But these expressions did not exhaust the public response to the two crimes. While libertarians and conservatives looked on in dismay, a coalition of left-wing activists, led by Congressman Barney Frank and other gay spokesmen, mounted the Capitol steps in Washington to pressure Congress into passing a bill that would extend existing federal hate crimes legislation to cover the categories of gender, sexual orientation, and handicapped status, and to make all such crimes easier to prosecute. They were joined in the call by the president himself.

Conservatives immediately raised civil liberties concerns about the proposed legislation, arguing that probing the intentions of any perpetrator, and especially one involved in crimes against victims who are already the targets of community prejudice, poses troubling problems. One such issue was the temptation offered to aggressive prosecutors to impute such intentions where none might exist. In a sobering column, George Will recalled a recent example of perverse legal reasoning in applying the hate crime standard. In 1989, a white female jogger was raped and beaten into a coma by a gang of black and Hispanic youths on a "wilding" rampage in Central Park. The act was not deemed a "hate crime" by prosecutors, and the perpetrators did not suffer enhanced penalties under the law "because they also assaulted Hispanics that evening. They got more lenient treatment because of the catholicity of their barbarism." Of course, the act they committed—rape—could be characterized as a hate crime itself.

In the emotional melodrama of the Matthew Shepard killing, the left once again found political oxygen. Temporarily thrown by the feminist hypocrisies surrounding the impeachment of President Clinton, the left viewed the Shepard case as a way to recover its balance and to once again rally behind society's victims against its victimizers. The absence of conservatives and libertarians among the Capitol protesters only served to confirm the enduring sense of righteousness that fuels the progressive agenda.

This politics of the left is what George Will calls "a sentiment competition," which is "less about changing society than striking poses." The proposed multiplication of hate crime categories which stipulate that some crime victims are more important than others would be what Will calls "an imprudent extension of identity politics." It would work *against,* not for, the principle of social tolerance.

A little more than a year before the attack on James Byrd in Texas, three white Michigan youngsters hitched a train-ride as a teenage lark. When they got off the train, they found themselves in the wrong urban neighborhood, surrounded by a gang of armed black youths. One of the white teenagers, Michael Carter, aged fourteen, was killed. Dustin Kaiser, aged fifteen, who was brutally beaten and shot in the head, eventually recovered. The fourteen-year-old girl (whose name has been withheld) was pistol-whipped and shot in the face after being forced to perform oral sex on her attackers.

Though the six African-Americans responsible for the deed were arrested and convicted, their attack was not prosecuted as a hate crime. More to the point, most of the nation never knew that the crime had taken place. It was not reported on page one of the national press, and there was no public outrage expressed in the nation's editorials or in the halls of Congress. Indeed, the few papers that reported the incident nationally did so on their inside pages. Beyond the Great Lakes region, the stories often failed to mention the races of the participants at all. The crime took place on July 21, 1997, but among the readers of this book, there will not be one in a hundred who has even heard of it, because, as a hate crime, it was in a perverse sense politically incorrect. To notice that black people, as well as whites, can be responsible for vicious crimes of hate, is improper. Hate crimes can only be committed by an oppressor caste; therefore, what happened in Michigan was not a hate crime at all.

Two years ago, the most celebrated trial of the century focused on a black man accused of murdering two whites in what was apparently an act of blind rage. The idea that O. J. Simpson might have murdered his wife and a stranger *because* they were white was never even hinted by the prosecution, although the defense managed to turn the proceedings into a circus of racial accusations *against* whites.

The fact is that it is not tolerable in America to hate blacks, but it *is* okay in our politically correct culture to hate white people. Hollywood understands this rule of progressive etiquette. A recent film, *American History X*, features (for the umpteenth time) white neo-Nazis as the villains of a homily about racial bigotry. The idea is that race hatred is synonymous with "skin-heads" who are white. But a few years ago a sensational mass murder trial in Miami spotlighted a black cult leader named Yahweh Ben Yahweh, who required his cult members to kill whites and bring back their ears as proof of the deed. One of his recruits was a star football player. Seven people were murdered. But there was no Hollywood scramble for the rights to the Yahweh cult story, as there would have been if the colors were reversed or everyone had been white. As a result, few Americans are even aware that these murders ever took place.

In the fall of 1998, a German tourist was shot to death in Santa Monica, California, in front of his wife and children. The catalyst for the killing seems to have been his failure to understand the English commands of his attackers. The crime was committed by two African-American men and one African-American woman, though one would never know this from reading the *Los Angeles Times* or Associated Press accounts. (I had to verify their racial identities by calling the Santa Monica police department directly.) The word "hate crime" never surfaced in connection with the deed, either in the press accounts or in editorial commentaries that followed. But suppose that three whites had gone to a Hispanic neighborhood to rob inhabitants and had murdered an Hispanic immigrant because he could not speak English. Does anyone imagine that the press accounts would hide the identity of the attackers or that the question of whether it might be a hate crime would never come up?

According to Department of Justice figures, 85 percent of the crimes of interracial violence nationwide are committed by blacks against whites. Not surprisingly, the first hate-crime conviction to be appealed to the Supreme Court involved a black perpetrator and a white victim. Of course, the social redeemers who are in favor of hate-crime legislation rarely reflect on the practical consequences of the reforms they enact. It is enough if the thought behind the legislation feels moral and right.

How many of the interracial crimes of violence committed by blacks and other minorities are actually the result of black racism, and therefore hate crimes? There is no real way to tell. There is, however, plenty of anecdotal evidence that suggests the problem is not negligible. A recent spate of brutal and random murders in a single Los Angeles district, for example, was explained by one black inhabitant to a *Los Angeles Times* reporter as retaliation for the "fact" that "whites had taken all the black jobs."

Of course, the leftist academy has a ready answer for every question about black racism: *Only whites can be racist.* The alleged reasoning behind this assertion is that in our society only whites have power. This is the kind of absurdity that only an intellectual could think up. Forget the thousands of public officials great and small, police chiefs, judges, administrators, and members of congress, petty bureaucrats, corporate executives, and military officers now drawn from the ranks of minorities, who wield social power in a variety of forms. At the most elemental level, a black outlaw with a gun—and there are many—has the power of life and death over an unarmed law-abiding citizen of any race or color.

The doctrine that only whites can be racist is, in fact, itself an instigation to hate crimes. It is a doctrine that has already spread to the secondary schools. The week after the Shepard killing, a Seattle father called a national radio talk show on which I was a guest and told the audience that his son's class in junior high school had been discussing the hate crime concept because of the killing. During the discussion, the teacher informed the class that only heterosexual whites could be racists. The caller's son was unconvinced and brought up the savage beating of Reginald Denny by a group of black gang members during the Los Angeles riots. Surely, he suggested, this was a hate crime. But his teacher corrected him. Even though Denny was pulled from his truck solely because he was white, and then beaten within an inch of his life, he could not be the victim of racial attitudes. The attempted murder of Reginald Denny was actually an act of rebellion by people who were themselves the victims of a white racist system, and the act they committed, therefore, could not be considered a hate crime. This is the perspective of academics who teach Whiteness Studies, of law professors who teach "critical race studies," and no doubt of education professors busily transmitting the progressive worldview to the next generation of junior high school instructors.

This is one reason why conservatives and libertarians did not join Barney Frank and the left in promoting politically correct hate-crime legislation that would create a few more specially protected categories among us, as a kind of human Endangered Species Act. Sorting Americans into distinctive racial, ethnic, and gender groups, while designating whites and heterosexuals to be their "oppressors," makes the latter into legitimate targets of hate themselves. It thus becomes a way of exacerbating, rather than correcting, social disorder.

It is time to go back to the wisdom of the Founders, who wrote a constitution without reference to ethnic or gender groups. They did so in order to render us equal before the nation's system of law. It was an imperfectly realized ideal then, but that should be no excuse for abandoning the ideal now. We need to end the vicious libels of political correctness that have percolated their message of anti-white racism into our mainstream culture. The vast majority of white people do not hate or oppress black people, just as the vast majority of heterosexuals do not hate or oppress gays. We need to single out those individuals who do—whatever their race or gender—for condemnation and social ostracism. And we need to do the same to individuals who belong to minorities and are haters themselves. Most of all, we need to go back to the task of treating all Americans as individuals first, and as members of groups only secondarily, if at all.

3

A Rage to Kill

*I am writing this essay
sitting beside an anonymous
white male that I long to murder.*

bell hooks, *A Killing Rage*

WHEN I READ THIS SENTENCE, I found myself looking around the room nervously. For these are not the opening words of a new novel by Brett Easton Ellis, but a nonfiction essay by bell hooks,* an intellectual icon of the tenured left. Though only in her forties, hooks is a Distinguished Professor of English at the City College of New York, a former faculty member at Yale, and a phenomenon of the politicized academy. An awkward writer of ideological formulas and agitprop prose she has a wide-ranging influence in the politically correct university culture. The collection for which "A Killing Rage" is the title essay is one of a shelf of similar tracts that hooks has published, earning

---

* The lower-case affectation is hers.

her a sobriquet from the *New York Review of Books* as "the most prominent exponent of black feminism" in America.

The occasion for professor hooks's homicidal urge turns out to be nothing more than a lost seat on a commercial airline flight. As hooks relates the episode, she had seated herself in the first class cabin alongside a female friend, who is also black and identified only as "K"—perhaps an allusion to Kafka, so cultivated is hooks's sense of victimization. No sooner are the two women settled in their first-class seats, however, then a voice on the plane's speaker system calls K to the front of the cabin where her ticket is inspected. The stewardess informs K that she does not have a claim to the seat because her upgrade has not been properly completed. It is too late, moreover, to correct the fault.

The stewardess also introduces K to the anonymous white male who is the putative target of hooks's murderous intent, and who is holding the appropriately designated ticket. The man tells K that he is sorry to see her inconvenienced and sits down. Resigning herself to the inevitable, K gathers her belongings and relocates herself in coach.

No such passivity governs the reaction of bell hooks. She is unwilling to give up her own first class accommodation to join her friend in coach, but is ready instead to launch her attack: "I stare him down with rage, tell him that I do not want to hear his liberal apologies, his repeated insistence that 'it was not his fault.' I am shouting at him that it is not a question of blame, that the mistake was understandable, but that the way K was treated was completely unacceptable, that it reflected both racism and sexism." Her target, however, is no liberal wimp and lets her know "in no uncertain terms" that in his view the apology was sufficient. The professor "should leave him be to sit back and enjoy his flight."

But Madame Defarge is not to be appeased. "In no uncertain terms I let him know that he had an opportunity to not be complicit with the racism and sexism that is so all-pervasive in this society, that he knew no white man would have been called on the loud-speaker to come to the front of the plane while another white male took his seat. . . . Yelling at him I said, 'It was not a question of your giving up the seat, it was an occasion for you to intervene in the harassment of a black woman.'"

Her invective temporarily exhausted, hooks takes out a pad and starts to pen the notes from which she will later compose her account. "I felt a 'killing rage,'" she recalls. "I wanted to stab him softly, to shoot him with the gun I wished I had in my purse. And as I watched his pain, I would say to him tenderly 'racism hurts.'"

While hooks is thinking these sensitive thoughts, her intended victim becomes aware of her hostility towards him. "The white man seated next to me watched suspiciously whenever I reached for my purse. As though I were the black nightmare that haunted his dreams, he seemed to be waiting for me to strike, to be the fulfill-ment of his racist imagination. I leaned towards him with my le-gal pad and made sure he saw the title written in bold print: 'Killing Rage.'"

Two pages after this bizarre account, which is by now, undoubt-edly, an assigned course text about racial oppression, hooks makes the following myopic comment: "Lecturing on race and racism all around this country, I am always amazed when I hear white folks speak about their fear of black people." Apparently hooks is un-able to connect the aggression she projects to the reaction it pro-vokes.

I searched through hooks's text to find a more substantial source for her "killing rage," one less. . .well. . . trivial. But I was destined to be disappointed. There was no litany of personal abuse or racial assault that might justify her murderous passion.

Still a relatively young woman of limited intelligence and mod-est talent, hooks has already achieved the kind of academic emi-nence once reserved for intellects of extraordinary reach. It is a position that any of her peers, white or black, would surely envy.

Her perks include an adoring following, a six-figure income, and a global itinerary. Her lectures on "white supremacy" and related battle themes take her across America and Europe, where she is able to advance her cause not in the coffee-house venues of political vanguards, but in the temples of high culture once reserved for the intellectual aristocracy.

All this success and the accompanying accolades conferred on so young (and pedestrian) a mind, however, inspires only further resentment. "My rage intensifies," she writes, 'because I am not a victim." Hers is a typical radical contradiction. She enjoys the material privileges of the comfortable, but wants the moral rewards of those who lack them; she wants to wear the mantle of the scholar while posturing as a warrior for the cause.

Of course if hooks were not both radical and black, her confession of homicidal malice might provoke public alarm. Race crimes contemplated *by* whites are a serious matter. But a black killing rage *against* whites can easily be excused. It is, after all, a comprehensible response to historic grievance or—as many blacks actually do seem to regard it—morally justified "payback." It can also be seen by progressives like hooks as a necessary path to "liberation." The development of a proper killing rage may even be praiseworthy in the oppressed who otherwise would submit supinely to their fate. Thus, the repression of black killing rage, as hooks informs us, is the agenda of white supremacists.

"To perpetuate and maintain white supremacy," hooks writes, "white folks have colonized black Americans, and a part of that colonizing process has been teaching us to repress our rage, to never make them the targets of any anger we feel about racism." Students in hooks' classroom who resist such claims and believe that civilized order requires everyone, regardless of race, to restrain such instincts, are directed to helpful texts: "When such conflicts arise, it is always useful to send students to read *Yours In Struggle*," Professor hooks advises. While recommending this activist manual to her students, she nonetheless quibbles over the term "struggle," which seems too temperate for her tastes. What is really happening in America, in hooks's view, is not merely political *struggle,* but an "ongoing Black genocide and the patriarchy's war against women." Black rage, in these circumstances, is not merely "healing," but self-defense. Blacks who lack a proper killing rage are merely victims of the genocidal campaign that white America is waging against them: "When we embrace victimization, we surrender our rage."

These thoughts provide a transition to the second essay in hooks's text, which is a companion meditation about an oppressed black man who did not surrender his rage. Colin Ferguson was in fact born into a prosperous Jamaican family and was a sometime college student (perhaps even one of professor hooks's fans) before he went on an armed rampage on a Long Island commuter train. Before spending his rage, he killed six people (Asian and white) to avenge what he called "racism by Caucasians and Uncle Toms."

The Ferguson tragedy would seem to provide material for a sermon on the perils of such race-directed rages. But, for hooks, the massacre is only an occasion to renew her own. In her reading, Ferguson's deed provides a text on how the white media has turned one desperate, oppressed man into a racially-charged public symbol, with the sole purpose of baiting other blacks: "Even though the gunman carried in his pocket a list containing the names of male black leaders, the white-dominated mass media turned his pathological expression of anger towards blacks and whites into a rage against white people."

Of course, the black leaders on Ferguson's list were there because in his demented imagination they were traitors to the race: they had collaborated with evil whites. In a perverse way hooks recognizes this. Ferguson, she writes, had a "complex understanding of the nature of neo-colonial racism," a fact that the white press was eager to obscure. "He held accountable all the groups who help perpetuate and maintain institutionalized racism, including black folks [that is, Uncle Toms]." By manipulating the facts, the white media was able to use the tragedy as "a way to stereotype black males as irrational, angry predators," rather than to use it as an occasion "to highlight white supremacy and its potential 'maddening impact.'"

In real life, this task was left to William Kunstler, the leftist lawyer, who offered to mount a "black rage theory" defense of Colin Ferguson. According to Kunstler, white society normally drives black people into homicidal rages for which they cannot be held responsible. Ferguson was "not responsible for his own conduct"; therefore "white racism is to blame." A *National Law Journal* survey taken at the time of Ferguson's rampage found that fully two-thirds of blacks interviewed agreed with the "black rage" theory. Professor hooks offers her own supportive anecdotal insight, explaining that while she herself did not take any pleasure in the racial murders, "I heard many wealthy and privileged black folks express pleasure. These revelations surprised me since so many of these folks spend their working and intimate lives in the company of white colleagues."

At the time, most blacks harboring such feelings kept them to themselves. But some did not. During a rally held at Howard University, the "Harvard" of black colleges, Nation of Islam spokesman Khalid Muhammad compared the psychopath Ferguson to rebel slave leader Nat Turner. Muhammad told a laughing, cheering audience of middle-class black college students: "God spoke to Colin Ferguson and said '*Catch the train, Colin, catch the train.*'"

Studies conducted at Farrakhan's Million Man March revealed that 40 percent of the participants had a college education and incomes exceeding fifty thousand dollars. More than 70 percent had incomes of more than twenty-five thousand dollars. Farrakhan is now the most popular black leader among blacks, and he and his former henchman Muhammad are easily the most coveted and well-paid speakers for black student associations across the country. Indeed, inviting black racists to college campuses to bait whites has become a rite of African-American authenticity for well-funded black student associations at American universities. This contrasts with the historical experience of all other ethnic groups, where racist attitudes diminish with education and income.

A parallel phenomenon is the tolerance by social elites of all colors for racist outrage when it is committed by blacks. In the wake of the Million Man March, blacks burned a white man alive in a Chicago neighborhood, with no accompanying press comment. In Illinois, three blacks murdered a pregnant white welfare mother and her two white children, while "rescuing" her black fetus by cutting it out of her womb. No one called the attack racial even though a second black child of the woman was spared. A black city worker in Fort Lauderdale gunned down five white co-workers, again without the press intimating a racial element might be involved, even though several survivors testified the killer had used anti-white epithets in the workplace before. In Harlem, seven white customers were burned alive in a store torched by a black racist after Al Sharpton and other racial demagogues had led protests against its presence in the neighborhood because the owner was white. This did elicit some editorial commentary, but without a single acknowledgment by any public figure of any color that the black community might have its own racial problem.

Actually both anomalies—the epidemic of black middle-class rage against whites and the absence of outrage at racism by blacks—are connected by the ideological perception that racism is a systemic problem, rather than the result of individual acts. It is generally acknowledged that white racists in America—though an ugly presence—are harder and harder to find in positions of responsibility and power. Legal discrimination has been eliminated, and a large government bureaucracy has been created to punish acts of discrimination that are now forbidden by law. To sustain the idea that anti-black racism is still the paramount social issue, it has become necessary to suggest that the problem is "institutional," therefore both "subtle" and "pervasive." But this perspective automatically renders every black a victim and therefore every outrageous act committed by blacks potentially "understandable."

The phrase "institutional racism" originated in the Kerner Commission Report on the inner city riots that erupted following the Civil Rights Acts of 1964 and 1965 that ended legal segregation in the South. It was an attempt to explain—and to justify—the paradox of "rebellions" against a body politic that had just achieved equality before the law for all Americans. (That these riots might just be criminal eruptions apparently was not a political option.) The commission's reaction to the 1960s riots served to define the "second civil rights era," the distinguishing feature of which has been the squandering of the moral legacy of the first and the restructuring of the civil rights agenda as a radical cause. Its legacy has been the system of racial preferences called "affirmative action."

While intellectually more respectable than Farrakhan's crackpot religious claims, the theory of institutional racism inspires no less sweeping indictments of whites. Developed into a full-blown ideology by the "multicultural" academy, institutional race theory regards any statistical disparity of black representation anywhere in the culture as proof of white malevolence and of the necessity of racial preference remedies. The unspoken assumption of every such policy is that institutions where whites predominate must be forced to be fair to black applicants, even where there is no actual evidence of unfairness. But does even the most fanatical advocate of affirmative action quotas believe that Harvard, Yale, and other institutions of the liberal elite contrive to bar qualified African-American students from entry, and would continue to do so in the *absence* of these affirmative action laws? Then why are such laws necessary? Because, their proponents argue, the influence of "institutional racism" is so subtle that Harvard and Yale would nonetheless exclude qualified African-Americans without the coercive intervention of the state.

It is precisely because the theory of institutional racism and the affirmative action policies it has spawned are a radical rejection of the American system—of individual rights, equal opportunity, and equality before the law—that the most dramatic anomaly of the second civil rights era has been produced. Whereas the civil rights movement under Martin Luther King's leadership achieved its aims with the support of 90 percent majorities in both houses of Congress, a majority of Americans—roughly 70 percent—oppose the current civil rights agenda that embraces racial preferences. This opposition reflects the inability of most Americans to understand or respect the persistence of "black rage" in the face of the enormous social, cultural, and economic gains made by African-Americans, as well as their own sense that they accept African-Americans as fellow citizens and full partners in America's civic contract. This self-understanding is corroborated by every major opinion survey on race relations taken in recent years.

It is this reality that has spawned the peculiar angst of bell hooks. "Why," writes hooks, "is it so difficult for many white folks to understand that racism is oppressive not because white folks have prejudicial feelings about blacks (they could have such feelings and leave us alone) but because it is a system that promotes domination and subjugation?" In other words, for radical ideologues like hooks, actual racism is not the issue. The issue is a marxist fantasy of domination and subjugation. In conceding that individual racists are not the problem, hooks is neither original nor alone. She is simply a camp follower of the political left. In an issue of the *New Yorker* devoted to race relations, Angela Davis laments the passing of the 1960s when "there was a great deal of discussion about . . . the importance of understanding the structural components of racism. There was an understanding that we couldn't assume that racism was just about prejudice—which, unfortunately, is what not only conservatives but liberals are arguing today."

For the radicals, racism is not about prejudice but about imaginary structures of domination, which are evidenced in *any* disparity in the status of blacks and whites that appears to them to be in blacks' disfavor. Just as marxists are convinced that there is class "oppression" when everyone is not economically equal, so race radicals claim that racial oppression exists when any disparity appears between racial groups. As long, that is, as the disparity works against the "oppressed." No one, for example, argues that the diminishing presence of whites in major athletics is the result of a racial conspiracy by blacks or requires a government remedy.

The racialist view of American social institutions propounded by hooks, Davis, and other leftists has even been incorporated into a school of jurisprudence. Not since the segregationist era has the buttressing of a racialist philosophy been the work of American law schools. But now, at Harvard, Stanford, and other founts of legal scholarship, "critical race theorists" argue that blacks can do no wrong and whites can do no right. These law professors defend the importance of a "race-conscious perspective," elaborate the theory that only whites can be racist (because "only whites have power"), and defend common criminals, if they are black, as rebels against an oppressive system.*

The theme of institutional racism dominated Jesse Jackson's semi-literate rant at the Million Man March: "We've come here today because there is a structural malfunction in America. It was structured in the Constitution and they referred to us as three-fifths of a human being, legally.† There's a structural malfunction. That's

---

* Among the self-styled critical race theorists (and "critical race feminists") are Derrick Bell, Kimberle Crenshaw, Patricia Williams, Regina Austin, and Anita Hill.

† Of course this is maliciously faulty history. It was the slaveholders at the constitutional convention whose representatives wanted to count each slave as a full human being so as to maximize the slave states' voting power. It was the anti-slavery faction that did not want the votes of slaves to be equated with free votes. Eventually a compromise was reached to count a slave's vote as three-fifths that of a free person's, whether white or black (there were more

why there's a crack in the Liberty Bell. There's a structural malfunction; they ignored the Kerner Report. Now we have the burden of two Americas: one half slave and one half free."

The utility of "structural" racism for demagogues like Jackson is that even while acknowledging that the vast majority of whites are no longer overtly racist, the concept makes all whites guilty nonetheless. No individual white has to be a racist in actual thought or deed to *participate* in the racist system or to reap its privileges. Since the system appears to benefit whites the most, only whites as a group can properly be called its beneficiaries, and therefore racist. By the same token, since the black "half" of the nation is "unfree," its members can hardly be held accountable for themselves.

In this, as in other aspects of contemporary racial cant, bell hooks is an unfailing guide. Like Farrakhan, she prefers the term "white supremacy" to "racist" when describing enemies of the people—because the latter term suggests a search for individual culprits, while sophisticates know that it is the system that is at fault. Professor hooks, in fact, tells us that her own moment of truth came when she encountered white women in the feminist movement who sought the comradeship of blacks but who "wished to exercise control over our bodies and thoughts as their racist ancestors had." Whatever specifics lie behind this paranoid image (hooks fails to provide details), the emotional bottom line is clear: insofar as hooks feels less powerful in any relationship she has with whites, *for whatever reason*, she will regard herself as a victim of racism. Thanks to the widespread acceptance of the politics of victimhood, there are many successful blacks who see racists under the bed, and for similar reasons respond positively to demagogues like Farrakhan.

The concept of institutional racism not only insulates blacks from the charge of racism, but actually exculpates them *in advance*

---

than three thousand black freemen who owned slaves in the United States). Nowhere in the Constitution are the words "black" or "white" to be found, and nowhere is race specified or mentioned.

for any racial crime they might commit. Thus hooks, in a kind of preemptive jury nullification, finds herself innocent of the airplane murder she wanted to commit: "Had I killed the white man whose behavior evoked that rage, I feel that it would have been caused by . . . the madness engendered by a pathological context." In other words, even if she had done it, she did not do it. In fact, white people did it.

When blacks commit crimes, the truly guilty party is the white devil who made them do it. Even when hooks does not fully identify with an odious act committed by an African-American, she still finds a way to mitigate it. She disavows Farrakhan and his anti-Semitic screeds, but nonetheless asks: "From whom do young black folks get the notion that Jews control Hollywood? This stereotype trickles down from mainstream white culture. . . . Indeed, if we were to investigate why masses of black youth all over the United States know who Louis Farrakhan is, or Leonard Jeffries, we would probably find that white-dominated mass media have been the educational source."

In other words, if blacks are anti-Semitic, it is the white devil who taught them to be so. Of course, hooks's reasoning is so circular, she could just as well praise the "white-dominated media" for imposing the leftist view on the public that America is *institutionally* racist, since the media have generally embraced this canard. A representative front page "news article" in the *Los Angeles Times*, for example, purported to show that the traditional ladder of upward mobility for America's minorities no longer exists for blacks and Hispanics, thanks to institutional racism:

WHITES EARN MORE AT ALL LEVELS,
CHALLENGING BELIEF THAT EDUCATION
IS THE KEY TO PARITY DATA SHOWS

Whether they have dropped out of high school or invested years in a graduate degree, whether they have struggled to master English or not, California's minorities earn substantially less than Anglos—a disparity that challenges the long-held tenet that education is a key to equality . . .

This *Times* report was probably more powerful in persuading middle-class blacks who read it that the system is stacked against them than all the speeches of Louis Farrakhan. But the *Times* study, which was conducted from census figures by the *Times*'s own analysts, showed nothing of the kind. The term "Anglo," its euphemism for "whites," included minorities—Jews, Armenians, Arabs—who are victims of ongoing prejudice and hate crimes and yet (for reasons unexplained in the study) are successful and thus provide the *Times*'s yardsticks of "privilege." The category "Hispanic"—though ideologically useful—is sociologically spurious, since it includes South American Indians, Portuguese-speaking Brazilians, low-earning Puerto Ricans and high-earning Cubans.

The *Times*'s analysts made no allowance for the kind of educational degrees, graduate or otherwise, that its target groups possessed. It is well known that more blacks and Hispanics seek college degrees in low-paying fields like education rather than in higher-paying professions like physics or engineering. The *Times*'s analysts also failed to take into account age or on-the-job experience, obviously critical to earning potential. Yet the editors of the *Times* chose to print essentially meaningless but racially inflammatory statistics and to weave them into an analysis that corroborated the existence of "institutional racism." The article appeared on January 10, 1993. After reading it, I called the reporters responsible. They sheepishly admitted that they did not have the data to make the claims they had, but defended the decision to print the story anyway.

The theory of institutional racism, devised by radical academics and promoted by an irresponsible media, has also led to a religious expression of racial rage called "black liberation theology." Its chief text, written by the Reverend James Cone, was published by the Maryknoll press, an imprint of liberation theologians, who in the 1980s found Christ among the Sandinista dictators and El Salvador's communist guerrillas: "This country was founded for whites and everything that has happened in it has emerged from the white perspective. . . . What we need is the destruction of whiteness, which is the source of human misery in the world."

This kind of Afro-Nazism would seem hard to swallow even for a bell hooks. But she manages with little difficulty: "Cone wanted to critically awaken and educate readers so that they would not only break through denial and acknowledge the evils of white supremacy, the grave injustices of racist domination, but be so moved that they would righteously and militantly engage in anti-racist struggle." Or simply take out their aggressions on the nearest white available.

According to hooks, of course, such aggression doesn't happen. "It is a mark of the way black Americans cope with white supremacy that there are few reported incidents of black rage against racism leading us to target white folks. . . . [Whites] claim to fear that black people will hurt them even though there is no evidence which suggests that black people routinely hurt white people in this or any other culture." Actually, there is. In 1993, for example, Justice Department statistics show there were 1.54 million violent crimes committed by blacks against whites. By contrast, there were only 187,000 violent crimes committed by whites against blacks. Taking population into account, a white was fifty times more likely to be the victim of a violent crime committed by a black than vice versa. (The fact that there are many more white targets in the population may account for some of the disparity.) The crime of rape—an act of anger and aggression—stands by itself as a statistic. In 1994, there were twenty thousand rapes of white women by black men, but only one hundred rapes of black women by white men.

Of course, radical professors have an institutional explanation even for this extreme statistic. In *Two Nations: Black and White, Separate, Hostile and Unequal*, a book that has already become a classic of anti-white scholarship, Andrew Hacker attempts to explain the fact that while blacks constitute only 12 percent of the population, they commit 43 percent of the rapes, including rapes of white women even though, as he observes, the risk to the black perpetrators is greater:

> Eldridge Cleaver once claimed that violating white women has political intentions. . . . Each such act brings further demoralization of the dominant race, exposing its inability to protect its own women from the worst kind of depradation. Certainly, the conditions black men face in the United States generate far more anger and rage than is ever experienced by white men. To be a man is made doubly difficult, since our age continues to associate 'manliness' with worldly success. *If black men vent their frustrations on women, it is partly because the women are more available as targets, compared with the real centers of power, which remain so inchoate and remote.*

For this white apologist for black rage, as for the 1960s radical, the act of rape is not a vicious act against a defenseless individual but an understandable attempt to strike at the real culprit: the white supremacist system.

In the last analysis, all this sophistry is of a piece with the Kerner Commission's original decision to use the concept of "institutional racism" to justify a criminal riot. It should come as no surprise that leftists would applaud the 1992 race riot in Los Angeles and similar outrages as "uprisings," as though they belonged in a pantheon with Lexington and Valley Forge. In the Los Angeles riot, individuals and establishments were targeted simply because they were not black. Inner city businessmen posted "black owned" signs wherever possible out of sheer self-protectiveness. Two thousand Korean businesses that could not post such signs were destroyed *because* of their Korean ownership. A typical leftist defense of this outrage was offered by Harvard Professor Cornel West, who called the race riot a "monumental upheaval [that] was a multi-racial, trans-class, and largely male display of justified social rage." If that is not an incitement to future racial pogroms, what is?

Racism, as bell hooks thoughtfully informs us, hurts. But racists also often hurt themselves. Indeed, in hooks's own case, a self-inflicted wound is revealed to be the trigger of her "killing rage."

The incident on the plane flight that inspired these meditations began, in fact, with a series of familiar urban frustrations, which the professor's politically sensitive antennae quickly converted into a racial casus belli: "From the moment K and I had hailed a cab on the New York City street that afternoon we were confronting racism. The cabby wanted us to leave his taxi and take another; he did not want to drive to the airport. When I said that I would willingly leave but also report him, he agreed to take us." There is hardly a white New Yorker, however, who has not had the same experience.

Hooks and her companion face "similar hostility" when they stand in the "first-class line" at the airport: "Ready with our coupon upgrades, we were greeted by two young white airline employees who continued their personal conversation and acted as though it were a great interruption to serve us."

She interrupts the employees' conversation and is rebuffed by one of them, who reacts with something like the following: "Excuse me, but I wasn't talking to you." Professor hooks's aggressive response then shifts into radical gear and becomes an actual racial confrontation: "When I suggested to K that I never see white males receiving such treatment in the first-class line, the white female insisted that 'race' had nothing to do with it, that she was just trying to serve us as quickly as possible."

Even the effort to smooth over the situation is taken racially by hooks. She looks over her shoulder and sees that a line of "white men" has formed in back of them, and concludes that now her tormentors "were indeed eager to complete our transaction even if it meant showing *no* courtesy." To spite them all, hooks makes everyone wait anyway, summoning a supervisor to whom she complains about the racism of the airline employees. The supervisor listens and apologizes, while the tickets are processed by the "white female." When the transaction is complete, hooks glances cursorily at the tickets she has been given. She raises her eyes just in time, however, to catch the hostility of the employee she has humiliated. "She looked at me with a gleam of hatred in her eye that startled, it was so intense."

Somewhere in these emotional minefields, hooks's friend, fails to get her ticket properly marked for upgrade, and both of them then fail to catch the error. It is this confluence of mistakes (wholly understandable in light of the ruckus hooks needlessly creates) that later causes K to be "ejected" from her first-class seat. Her upgrade has been given to the white male, who probably waited patiently in the same line behind them and had his ticket processed correctly.

The entire incident and commentary on it reveal bell hooks to be a woman driven by racial resentments she has not begun to come to terms with, and in over her head on a university faculty. But she is also typical of the tenured left that has come into its own in the last decade in the American academy, a perfect expression of the misery the "multicultural" university has inflicted on itself and on the nation as a whole. In the real world, the term "institutional racism" is properly applied only to race-specific policies such as affirmative action itself. Its current vogue is an expression of racial paranoia—and little else. It is true that even paranoids have enemies. But it is also true that by projecting their fear and aggression onto those around them, paranoids create enemies, too.

II

Black Caucus

4

Martin's Children

URING THE DARKEST DAYS OF THE COLD WAR, the Italian writer Ignazio Silone predicted that the final struggle of that great conflict would be between the communists and the ex-communists. And so it seems to be among civil rights activists in the war over affirmative action.*

Jesse Jackson and the opponents of California's Proposition 209, which outlawed government race preferences, claim for themselves the mantle of the civil rights movement. They even staged a protest march in San Francisco on the anniversary of Martin Luther King's famous Washington event to make the point. But, on the other side of the barricades, the architects and principal spokesmen for Proposition 209 are also veterans of King's movement. It is no accident that Proposition 209 was called "The California Civil Rights Initiative" by its proponents or that its text was carefully constructed to conform to the letter and spirit of the landmark Civil Rights Acts of 1964 and 1965.

---

* For an account of these battles, see Lydia Chavez, *The Color Bind: California's Battle to End Affirmative Action* (Berkeley, Calif.: University of California Press, 1998).

51

Obviously it is not the goal of ending racism that divides the former activists. It is their conflicting memories of the past and differing strategies for the future. How much racial progress has been made since the federal government embraced the civil rights agenda? What is the best way to overcome the racial inequalities that persist?

For those opposed to Proposition 209, the answer is simple: racism has not changed its substance, only its form. In their view, whatever gains blacks have made have been forced upon a recalcitrant white populace. If the government were to be race neutral, historic prejudice would reassert itself despite the existing anti-discrimination laws. Even without this resurgence of prejudice, existing inequalities themselves create injustice. The remedy, therefore, must be continued government intervention to ensure equality of results. For the nation to eliminate affirmative action policies, as both Jesse Jackson and President Clinton have warned, would be to invite the "re-segregation" of American life.

A scholarly study by two civil rights veterans has now been introduced into this debate. Stephan and Abigail Thernstrom's *America In Black and White* reconstructs the history of racial progress and conflict in the postwar era and examines the impact of affirmative action solutions. The authors cite a statement made in 1996 by Atlanta's black mayor articulating the view implicit in the position of Clinton and Jackson that every black person in America "has benefited from affirmative action. There's not been anybody who's gotten a job on their own, no one who's prospered as a businessman or businesswoman on their own."

Yet consider these unruly facts presented in the Thernstroms's book:

- In 1940, 87 percent of American blacks lived in poverty. By 1960—five years before the Civil Rights Acts and ten years before the first affirmative action policies—the figure was down to 47 percent. This twenty year drop was an even greater and more rapid decline in black poverty than the one that took place over the next thirty-five years, a period which saw the black poverty rate come down to 26 percent as of 1995.

• In 1940, only 5 percent of black men and 6.4 percent of black women had middle class occupations. By 1970, the figures were 22 percent for black men (a nearly four-fold increase) and 36 percent for black women (a more than five-fold increase)—larger again than the increase that took place in the twenty years after affirmative action was put in place (roughly 1970) when the figures reached 32 percent and 59 percent.

The cause of black poverty, as the Thernstroms show (and the dramatic expansion of the black middle class should make self-evident), has little to do with race. Consequently, its solution will not be affected by affirmative action set-asides. Currently, 85 percent of all poor black children live in fatherless families. In other words, the poverty rate for black children without fathers is nearly six times that for black children with two parents. A far more effective anti-poverty program would be to promote black marriages.

Even in higher education, affirmative action has not been the indispensable agent its advocates imply. The rate of gain for blacks in college enrollments was greater between 1960 and 1970, before affirmative action policies were instituted (enrollments for blacks increased from 4 percent to 7 percent of the total college population), than it was in the decades after, between 1970 and 1980, when black enrollment went from 7 percent to 9.9 percent and between 1980 and 1994, when it went from 9.9 percent to 10.7 percent.

Of course, before affirmative action, many of these students were attending all black colleges in the South. The really significant gain from affirmative action was greater "diversity." The proportion of black students enrolled in predominantly white schools quadrupled between 1960 and 1980. This made white liberals and—to be fair— whites generally, feel good. But was it as good for the blacks who were enrolled, particularly those who were accepted to schools because of affirmative action double standards?

In 1965—before these policies were put in place—blacks were only about half as likely to actually graduate from college as whites. In 1995—after affirmative action took effect—the figure was exactly the same. As of 1995, almost half of African-Americans in the twenty to twenty-five age bracket had been enrolled in college, but barely one in seven of them held a bachelor's degree.

In the economic sphere, affirmative action policies had the net effect not of employing greater numbers of blacks or raising their living standards, but of shifting black employment from small businesses to large corporations and to government. In higher education, the net effect of affirmative action has been more perverse. In a system organized as a hierarchy of merit, a good student who can get As at Boston University might flunk out at Harvard. In 1995, there were only 1,764 black students nationwide who scored as high as 600 on the verbal SATs (the math scores were even worse). But, under affirmative action guidelines, all those students were recruited to Berkeley, Harvard, and similar elite schools where the average white student (not to mention the average Asian) normally had scores at least 100 points (and more likely 200) higher.

In short, at every level of the university system, the net effect of affirmative action has been to place African-Americans in college programs that exceed their qualifications. As a result, affirmative action students have lower grade point averages and higher dropout rates (by fifty percent and more) than students who are admitted without benefit of racial preferences. At Berkeley, for example, the gap in SAT scores between blacks and whites is nearly three hundred points. As this disparity would predict, blacks drop out of Berkeley at nearly three times the rate of whites. This is the unspoken nightmare of affirmative action's impact on the very minorities it was designed to help.

It is a poignant irony that the college that comes closest to racial equality in actually *graduating* its students in the era of affirmative action is Ole Miss, once the last bastion of segregation in the South. Now integrated, Ole Miss has resisted the new racial duplicity in admissions standards. The result is that 49 percent of all whites who enter Ole Miss as freshman graduate, and so do 48 percent of all blacks.

On the basis of the actual results, it is clear that affirmative action based on racial preference is unnecessary to racial progress, damaging to its supposed beneficiaries, and ineffective in terms of closing the income and education gaps between blacks and whites. While it may create additional privilege for some members of an already privileged black elite—86 percent of the affirmative action students at elite schools are from upper middle-class or wealthy backgrounds—its more durable effect is to create failure that is unnecessary. In addition, it aggrieves those whose achievements are real, but who become suspect because of the circumvention of standards. Finally, racial preferences incite the resentment of other groups, not only whites but also Asians, who see themselves displaced on the basis of race from their hard-won places of merit. In his book, *Liberal Racism*, veteran civil rights activist Jim Sleeper addresses the toxic effect of these good intentions. "Liberalism no longer curbs discrimination," he writes. "It invites it. It does not expose racism; it recapitulates and, sometimes, reinvents it."

Thus does the Cold War between the children of Martin Luther King beget ironies without end.

5

Amen Corner

A REVEALING ASPECT of the White House crisis that engulfed President Clinton in 1998 was the racial gap in public opinion polls, which was almost as wide as after the verdict in the O. J. Simpson murder case. When the world discovered in January that the president was having sex with a twenty-two-year-old intern, a *New York Times* poll found that 81 percent of blacks (as compared to 58 percent of whites) nonetheless approved the way the president was doing his job. When asked whether the president shared the moral values of most Americans, fully 77 percent of blacks (in contrast to less than half that fraction of whites) said yes. Nine months later, after the discovery of the stained dress and the release of the Starr report, 63 percent of blacks still thought the president—now a proven liar and philanderer—shared the nation's morality. It was *three times* the number of whites (22 percent) who did.

These are striking statistics, reflecting a unique community support of the president (even feminists were more ambivalent), and prompting attempts to explain it. According to a widely quoted comment by comedian Chris Rock, Clinton's African-American support was inspired by the fact that he is "the first black president." Explained Rock: "It's very simple. Black people are used to being persecuted. Hence, they relate to Clinton." The comedian was not alone in these thoughts. In an article exploring African-American reactions to the Clinton investigation, *New York Times* reporter Kevin Sack quoted NAACP head Julian Bond saying "You just can't help but think that some of this [investigation of Clinton] is race based," while Harvard Professor Alvin Poussaint reported that rumors were circulating in the African-American community to the effect that "[Clinton] must have had black ancestry."

A full-blown expression of these attitudes was on display in the *New Yorker*, where Nobel laureate Toni Morrison wrote of the crisis: "African-American men seemed to understand it right away. Years ago, in the middle of the Whitewater investigation, one heard the first murmurs: white skin notwithstanding, this is our first black president. Blacker than any actual black person who could ever be elected in our children's lifetimes. After all, Clinton displays almost every trope of blackness: single-parent household, born poor, working-class, saxophone-playing, McDonald's-and-junk-food-loving boy from Arkansas."

Perhaps one has to be a lapsed leftist like myself to react to the loopy anti-white attitudes laced into these cadences from one of our most celebrated and rewarded national literary figures. *Blacker than any actual black person who could ever be elected in our children's lifetimes?* Apparently, Colin Powell, the most popular presidential prospect in polls taken only two years before is not all that black, having been born into a two-parent household and, though poor in origins and familiar with discrimination, not known for his unhealthy food addictions or stereotypical musical tastes.

On the other hand, perhaps the liberal identification of blackness with victimization and social dysfunction is not so wide of the mark in explaining the sympathy of political leftists like Morrison and Bond or the support of the Congressional Black Caucus for

the immoralist from Little Rock. Perhaps it reflects a resonance in
the black community to the White House's cynical strategy of defining presidential deviancy down: "They all do it." *Roosevelt, Kennedy,
Eisenhower, Reagan, Bush—they all lie and cheat. So why shouldn't
our guy?* This certainly seems to be the corrosive logic behind which
some blacks have rallied to the defense of other criminal politicians,
like the corrupt and crack-addicted former mayor of Washington,
D.C., Marion Barry. It could easily account for the undertones of
racial paranoia ("they're out to get our guys") that surfaced when
African-American members of the Clinton Administration, Ron
Brown, Mike Espy and Hazel O'Leary came under investigation
for irregularities in office.

Which is precisely the way Toni Morrison frames Clinton's
problem: "When virtually all the African-American Clinton appoin-
tees began, one by one, to disappear, when the President's body, his
privacy, his unpoliced sexuality became the focus of the persecution, when he was metaphorically seized and body-searched, who
could gainsay these black men who knew whereof they spoke?"
According to Morrison the message from white America is clear:
"No matter how smart you are, how hard you work, how much coin
you earn for us, we will put you in your place or put you out of the
place." Or, to paraphrase the mantra of the late Malcolm X, *No
matter how high you rise, you're always gonna be a nigger to the man.*

Putting aside the paranoid overtones of such attitudes in the
era of Oprah Winfrey and Michael Jordan—or Toni Morrison for
that matter—one might still ask why Bill Clinton should be "our
guy" from an African-American point of view. Isn't this the Bill
Clinton who established his New Democrat credentials by delivering a verbal slap to Sister Souljah on the eve of his election in 1992
and by losing the phone number of Jesse Jackson for the next five
years? Isn't this the Bill Clinton who betrayed old friend and political soul-mate Lani Guinier, and who, after nominating her as
his civil rights chief, left her to the mercies of her political enemies,

all the while pretending ignorance of who she was and what she believed? Isn't this the Bill Clinton whose vaunted "dialogue on race"—the centerpiece of his racial initiative—was immolated by his own sex scandal while the final report of his Race Commission ended up calling merely for . . . more dialogue? Reviewing the report, liberal columnist Frank Rich summed up the Clinton record on race as follows: "high ideals, beautiful show, one-night stand."

Indeed, isn't this the Bill Clinton who brought Jesse Jackson back into the fold and wrapped himself in the protective cloak of the black community and its historic symbols only when he himself was in terminal trouble? Only after Democrats had lost the Congress and he no longer had the power to seriously advance the black community's agendas? Surely there have been few more repellent demonstrations of Clinton's user-ethic than his pilgrimage of atonement to Africa, at the height of the Lewinsky scandal and after he had been trapped in his labyrinth of lies and become an international laughing-stock. With Jesse Jackson and Maxine Waters and a delegation of African-Americans in tow, the President set off to wave the bloody flag, apologizing for slavery (to the wrong African country) in an attempt to wrap the sins of America around his own. Continuing his bid to hide his tarnished self under the mantle of black suffering, he went on to Martha's Vineyard to debase the memory of Martin Luther King's march on Washington, choosing the anniversary of that historic occasion for another unconvincing act of contrition. These are the kinds of gestures that give tokenism a bad name.

But not this time—at least not among African-Americans. Instead, the most prominent voices of black leadership joined willingly in Clinton's charades and rallied to his tarnished cause. There was civil rights legend John Lewis at the Martin Luther King anniversary, solemnly, tearfully forgiving Clinton and urging the rest of the country to forgive him as well. It was terrible, apparently, to be so judgmental of another human being. This was the same John

Lewis who not so long before was denouncing Newt Gingrich and congressional Republicans as "nazis" for attempting to reform a welfare system that had become destructive to inner city minorities and poor people.

This is what the liberal melodramas of conspiracy and witch hunt are really about: not racial persecution, which thankfully has been driven undergound in America, but political loyalty to a bankrupt liberalism, and its system of bureaucratic exploitation of dependency and economic waste. The previously cited *New York Times* report on black attitudes noted that "many of those interviewed said they not only subscribed to Hillary Rodham Clinton's statement that a 'vast right-wing conspiracy' had targeted her husband, but also that they believed the conspirators were motivated by a desire to reverse the gains made by blacks during the Clinton administration." One paranoia is linked to another. Leftists like Maxine Waters and Toni Morrison and demagogues like Charles Rangel have persuaded the African-American community that Republicans are racists who want to reverse the gains of the civil rights era. This is the really Big Lie that locks African-Americans into Clinton's corner, blocks reform, and protects the one-party political systems of America's largest cities.

If liberals want instances of political persecution or persecution of blacks, they need look no farther than their own character assassination of Clarence Thomas in an episode of sexual McCarthyism (to use Alan Dershowitz's inflammatory phrase) whose allegations pale in comparison to the charges against Clinton. Where are the liberal apologies for *this* racial outrage?

Or consider a more unpalatable thought: the political persecution of Newt Gingrich. Liberal leaders of the House, hoping to reverse the results of the Republican victory in the 1994 election, leveled more than seventy-four phony ethics charges against Gingrich (sixty-five of which were "laughed out of committee") before they were able to make one ludicrous claim stick. Out of a hundred Gingrich-loathing liberals who might read this text, there is not one who could describe the specifics of even that charge. Yet Gingrich was censured, fined, and politically destroyed by a relentless liberal smear campaign that included 120,000 union-financed television commercials falsely portraying him as an enemy of older Americans dependent on Medicare. There is not a single liberal now defending Clinton or bemoaning the unfairness of *his* prosecution who has offered any second thoughts about *this* witch-hunt.

That is because Gingrich's lynching, like that of Clarence Thomas, serves a liberal purpose. Just as Thomas is the dangerous black who has left the plantation, Gingrich is the alleged organizer of the "right wing conspiracy" that is seeking to bring down the left's leader in order to "reverse" the civil rights gains of African-Americans. Cease to believe in this mythology and what happens to the president, or to the leftist demagogues in the Congressional Black Caucus? What if Republicans were no longer available to function as racial bogey-men? What if African-Americans were to see that Republican policies like educational choice and Republican values like personal responsibility might work to the benefit of their communities? What if they were no longer to vote 90 percent Democratic? What if they were to free themselves from the chains of a one-party system that feeds them tokens and shamelessly exploits their moral capital for its own agendas?

These are the real stakes that keep the liberal melodrama alive, and that prevent a taken-for-granted community from fully entering the American polity and exercising its rightful power.

6

Democrats and Blacks

W HAT IF 90 PERCENT of the white electorate had turned out in the last election to vote for Republican candidates in virtually every electoral district across the country?

What if Newt Gingrich and Trent Lott had spent the weeks before the 1998 election visiting all-white churches and making not so covert appeals to the congregations' alleged racial interest in expanding the Republican majority, as Bill Clinton and Al Gore did for the Democrats?

What if Senator Carol Moseley-Braun had been defeated because 93 percent of whites voted against her (instead of 93 percent of blacks voting for her as they did)?

What if a Republican representing a white suburban district had received 94 percent of the vote against his opponent the way Charles Rangel actually did in his Harlem district? (This, mind you, was only 1 percent less than the widow of a Tennessee candidate, murdered by his opponent, received in defeating her husband's killer.)

What if Colin Powell was President and Tom Wolfe had written a piece like Toni Morrison's fatuous *New Yorker* article, hailing him as the first *white* African-American president because he did not come from a dysfunctional family, spoke the King's English, played the violin, and favored cuisine like quiche lorraine?

The morning after the election I received the following phone message from a member of my family who is black: "Well, I just had to call to chuckle over the election results. Black people finally got heard. I guess O. J. and Bill Clinton do have something in common." (Well, she got that last point right, though hardly in the way she probably meant it.) I decided not to respond in kind. But suppose the circumstances had been reversed, and the Democrats had lost big time, and I had called my black relative and said: "I just had to chuckle because white people were finally heard."

Of course, the double standard by which we have come to judge the behaviors of white and black Americans has gone so far that a significant portion of the public has been persuaded that the lock-step political choices of the African-American community are quite natural and are motivated by a justifiable racial solidarity—in other words, that they have nothing remotely in common with the counter-examples I have proposed, which would rightly be regarded as expressions of deplorable racial prejudice.

But are these racial reflexes of the African-American community so obviously appropriate to African-American interests, as liberals claim? Larry Elder, a black libertarian talk-show host in Los Angeles thinks they are not. Recently, Elder published the following list of "15 Reasons Why Blacks Shouldn't Support Clinton":

1. *Tax hikes.* During the Reagan years black teenage and adult unemployment fell dramatically because lower taxes stimulated business formation and expansion, creating employment opportunities for unskilled labor.

2. *Affirmative action.* This promotes the fallacious idea of the "Big Bang Theory of the Black Middle Class"—that the black middle class owes its existence and success to govern-

ment preferences rather than its own achievement. In fact, the growth of the black middle class was more rapid before affirmative action programs were put in place.

3. *Minimum wage increases.* The Nobel Prize economist Milton Friedman has observed that the minimum wage is "one of the most ... anti-black laws on the statute books" because it destroys entry level jobs for second paycheck earners, teens, and other unskilled workers.

4. *Welfare.* Clinton vigorously opposed welfare reform until Republicans forced him to sign on to it, and he threatens to undo the reforms in place. Yet welfare reform has liberated thousands of black Americans from the prospect of lifetime dependence on government handouts, at minimal levels of existence.

5. *Gun control.* Clinton and the Democrats oppose concealed weapons permits, yet inner city blacks remain the most vulnerable to violent crime. Meanwhile, studies show that in states that allow concealed weapons, murder rates have fallen.

6. *Opposition to school choice.* Threats of Clinton vetoes and Democratic opposition to voucher programs deny poor blacks the same options Bill Clinton, Jesse Jackson, and other Democratic leaders take to rescue their own kids from the traps of dangerous and failing public schools by sending them to the private schools of their choice.

7. *Opposition to the privatization of Social Security.* Blacks have shorter life expectancies than whites and hence stand to gain less from the Social Security benefits they are now forced

to fund. They would gain enormously by being able to control their own retirement funds.

8. *Expansion of government in health care.* Government mandated health insurance programs have vastly increased the costs of health care and decreased the chance that small businesses can afford ample benefit programs for their employees. As usual, the least skilled and most vulnerable get whacked the most.

9. *The betrayal of black friends.* Clinton lured Vernon Jordan and Betty Currie into positions of legal jeopardy through his self-serving lies.

10. *Expansion of the war on drugs.* In this area, black leaders have employed a double standard, opposing drug laws that penalize urban blacks disproportionately while remaining silent over Clinton's responsibility for these measures.

11. *The Race Advisory Board.* This Board promoted the tired liberal red-herring that what ails black America is a "lack of understanding" on the part of whites instead of welfare dependency, bad public schools (that liberals and Democrats run), illegitimacy, and criminal behavior.

12. *The reopening of the inquiry into the assassination of Martin Luther King.* The original investigation headed by black liberal congressman Louis Stokes (D-Ohio) closed the case years ago, after proving that James Earl Ray was the assassin. Re-opening the case keeps the "blacks-are-victims" cottage industry pumping.

13. *The White House defense of lying under oath.* This puts blacks,

who are more likely to suffer from the perjuries of law enforcement officers, at greater risk.

14. *Expansion of hate-crime legislation.* This exaggerates the frequency of such crimes, while depreciating the significance of the same-race crimes from which blacks suffer most.

15. *The war on cigarettes.* The tax penalties on smoking will fall disproportionately on lower income people who smoke more and can afford the taxes less.

It is not necessary to agree with all or even most of these points to see that there is no particular reason why the black community should vote like the populations of communist countries who lacked the ability to exercise free choice. By contrast, the Asian community in California split 55-45 percent in the race pitting a Chinese American, Matt Fong, against incumbent Senator Barbara Boxer. (Fong actually received a lower percentage of Asian votes.)

But while black Americans do not live in a totalitarian country, those blacks who do dissent from the liberal party line experience a level of hostility and intimidation in their own community that is unusual for democracies. Larry Elder himself has been the target of constant vicious attacks from the principal black newspaper in Los Angeles, numerous death threats inspired by such attacks, and finally a boycott from a radical black group called Talking Drum. The boycott caused Elder's employer, radio station KABC in Los Angeles, to lose millions of dollars in advertising. A year ago, the station's management informed Elder that he would be removed from his four-hour drive-time air slot. A replacement was hired and Elder's hours were reduced. Meanwhile, there was not a single editorial in the *Los Angeles Times* about the political movement to silence his voice, or a single protest by the ACLU and other liberal organizations normally quick to oppose such moves for censorship.

It took a conservative organization (which I happen to head) to mount an effort to defend Elder in the form of a half-million dollar television advertising campaign. This resulted in a dramatic boost in Elder's ratings, the firing of the station manager and Elder's replacement, and the restoration of his hours. Today, Larry Elder is the number one drive-time radio talk show host in Los Angeles and is about to be syndicated nationally.

Was the attack on Elder, accompanied by the unusual silence of liberal elites, an aberration? Hardly. In fact, it was integrally connected to the 90 percent black vote for Democratic Party candidates like Los Angeles Congresswoman and Black Caucus head Maxine Waters in the 1998 election. Waters was one of Elder's antagonists.

Liberals and the Democratic Party need the economic dependence and monolithic political choices of the African-American community in order to secure their own political power. That is why liberals and Democrats constantly inflame the racial fears of black Americans while maliciously demonizing conservatives and Republicans as their racial enemies. That is why they are either collusive in, or silent about, the character assassination of black conservatives like Clarence Thomas, Gary Franks, Ken Hamble, Thomas Sowell, and Ward Connerly.

Where would liberalism and the Democratic Party be without the dependencies of black Americans on government programs and government offices, and the monolithic politics that follow naturally? (Government actually employs 24 percent of black Americans—in contrast to 14 percent of whites—while blacks make up only 10 percent of the workforce).

Where would liberalism and the Democratic Party be if poor urban black youth were not trapped by their policies in dangerous and failing public schools? This situation—tragically destructive for African-Americans—ensures that billions of education dollars will continue to flow into the pockets of the administrative bureaucracies and public sector unions—particularly the teachers unions—which form the heart of the Democratic Party's political machine.

It is that same self-interest that causes the Democratic Party to defend affirmative action programs whose true (and virtually sole) beneficiaries are the black elites who are the enforcers of this political monolith. In *The Shape of the River*, a book written to justify affirmative action policies in education, former university presidents Derek Bok and William Bowen focus their attention on racial preference in admissions at twenty-eight elite colleges. Their study shows that 86 percent of the African-American beneficiaries of these racial preferences already come from the upper-middle and upper classes of the black community, and that they go on to top leadership positions in government and society.

If I were still a leftist, I would describe this privileged caste of African-Americans as a "*comprador* class" or "neo-colonial bourgeoisie" granted privileges by the imperial power to maintain its control over the colonial masses, and to secure the profits that flow from the system. The bottom line here is the aggrandizement of liberals, the Democratic Party, and their favored elites at the expense of minorities and the poor. That is the significance of the knee-jerk black support for Democratic big-government candidates in the 1998 elections.

7

Dealing with Racism

A PARADOX of the current civil rights debate is the way in which the terms of the historic conflict have been reversed. Martin Luther King Jr.'s triumphant crusade to extend America's constitutional covenant to all citizens is today scorned by the very heirs to his legacy. More often than not, moreover, it is the younger generation of educated, middle-class African-Americans—the primary beneficiaries of an integrated culture—who now take up the other side of the argument over segregation and racial preferences of thirty years ago.

Then the civil rights movement proclaimed as its goal a "color-blind society" and declared that racial distinctions made by government were cancers on the body politic and barriers to social progress not only in the American south, but the nation as a whole. In the current battles over "multiculturalism" and "affirmative action," however, these one-time partisans of universal standards and social integration stand on the side of racial preferences and support a double standard for government-designated groups. It is the traditional civil rights movement that now steps forward as the partisan of racial consciousness and tolerance towards racial separation, and it is the traditional civil rights leadership that supports "affirmative action" policies that result in government-enforced quotas for racial groups. It is the traditional civil rights activists who now march to oppose civil rights initiatives that seek to defend the principles for which King stood, and it is their efforts, which if successful, would put that historical process in reverse.

Clarence Page is a moderate voice in the "civil rights" camp and a bell-weather for the post-civil rights generation. A well-known television commentator and Pulitzer prize-winning columnist for the *Chicago Tribune*, Page was an adolescent at the time of King's efforts to integrate American institutions. His achievement of national influence and personal success can be taken as a symbol of the success of that movement.

Page is not enthusiastic about racial "nationalism" or even black militancy and has forcefully dissociated himself from "separatists." Unlike his more radical peers, he is not ashamed of expressing hope in the American dream. Yet, in a book-length manifesto called *Showing My Color*, Page has written an argument in defense of these disturbing radical trends. The very fact that someone like Clarence Page could write an apologia for race conscious government policies and even racial separation, shows how pervasive these trends have become.

Page takes the title of his book from a parental admonition he heard frequently in his youth: "Don't be showin' yo' color." Showing your color, he explains, "could mean acting out or showing anger in a loud and uncivilized way." More particularly, it meant playing to stereotype. In other words, "showing your color" really meant showing your *culture*—an irony that escapes the author. The title, he explains, "emerged from my fuming discontent with the current fashions of *racial denial*, steadfast repudiations of the difference race continues to make in American life [emphasis his]." Page then attacks the "'color-blind' approach to civil rights law" and laments the way the words of Martin Luther King have been "perverted" to support this view.

The argument of *Showing My Color* begins inauspiciously with a personal anecdote through which Page intends to establish that racism is, indeed, a "rude factor" in his life and, by extension, the lives of all black Americans. A problem that this anecdote shares with others that are often adduced on these occasions is that the incident he invokes to demonstrate the persistence of racism actually took place nearly forty years ago, in the segregated South. For Page, it is the memory of a trip to Alabama in the 1950s, where he encountered water fountains marked "colored" and "white." But who does not deplore this reality now? If you have to invoke a distant past to justify a present grievance, the case for the grievance is already undermined. Page seems unaware of the incongruity of his position.

Confronted by the tolerant attitudes of contemporary Americans, it has become fashionable among black intellectuals like Page to argue that even though change may appear to have occurred, it really has not. While overt racism may be behind us, a subtle and invisible system of power relationships continues to produce the same results: "Social, historical, traditional and institutional habits of mind that are deeply imbedded in the national psyche . . . work as active agents to impede equal opportunity for blacks." The name for these factors is "institutional racism": "[Racism] is not just an internalized belief or attitude. It is also an externalized public practice, a power relationship that continually dominates, encourages, and reproduces the very conditions that make it so useful and profitable." Though old-style racism may have been conquered, and is no longer an acceptable part of America's mainstream, this form of racism allegedly lives on as the defining fact of American life.

While premising his attitudes towards racial issues on this radical bedrock, Page presents himself as a more complex figure, a "progressive" inside whom a conservative struggles to emerge. In this, too, he is typical: "Conservatism resonates familiarly with me, as I think it does with most black Americans. We vote liberal, for liberalism has helped us make our greatest gains. But in other areas, we swing conservative. We want to believe that hard work will be rewarded. . . . We want to believe in the promise of America."

Page is not without courage in defending his conservative instincts, especially in view of the intimidating pressures within the black community to make visible figures like him bow to racial solidarity. Page does not hesitate to deplore the sick, anti-Semitic ravings of Louis Farrakhan, or to point out that spokesmen for the Nation of Islam have created a climate of racial hostility in the black community that led to the lynching of a Jew in Crown Heights a few years ago. Even in defending radical attitudes his arguments can be subtle. Thus Page responds to critics of black race consciousness by pointing out that "a minority that never has been allowed the luxury to feel secure in its own home culture does not easily let go of it to adopt the customs and attitudes of the mainstream culture."

Politically, Page chooses to be a Democrat because of what he describes as Republicans' assumption that "racism is no longer a problem," and their view that "government programs and agencies must be trimmed, even when those programs and agencies offer the last slender thread of protection the children of America's black slaves have against further slides back into oppression." In particular, he singles out conservative opposition to minimum wage laws, affirmative action employment policies, and welfare aid to mothers with dependent children, as examples of such attitudes. But there is also a cultural dimension to Page's differences with Republicans: "Klan membership dropped sharply in the early 1980s, according to researchers for the Anti-Defamation League and other Klan-watching groups, as many found a new, satisfying voice and vehicle in Republican Party politics. Enter David Duke." Well, yes, enter David Duke. But Duke was instantly proscribed by the Republican Party leadership including three living Republican presidents (one sitting at the time) which is a lot more than could be said about Louis Farrakhan and the two living Democratic presidents who have had many chances to condemn him by name and have not. Unlike Farrakhan's influence, Duke's does not reach outside Louisiana or into the chambers of Congress, while much of Duke's current rhetoric and argument is lifted directly from the pages of the multi-cultural left.

This lapse into partisan race-baiting provokes me to show my own color. I happen to be a Jewish conservative and a Republican, who nearly fifty years ago marched in support of Harry Truman's Fair Employment Practices Act and has been active in civil rights struggles ever since. Moreover, I can share personal anecdotes of anti-Semitism that are more current than Page's encounter with "white" and "colored" water fountains in the 1950s. When my wife, who is not Jewish, and I became engaged, she was confronted by several friends with the comment: "How can you marry a *Jew*? It's like marrying a black."

Given this kinship between scorned minorities (and Jews and blacks have no monopoly on such anecdotes), a more candid dialogue seems in order. The level of Jew-hatred in America is higher today than it has been in my entire lifetime, thanks largely to its legitimation through the poisonous rantings of Farrakhan and his followers, and the tolerance of these views by large sections of the black intelligentsia. No conservative politician would be seen in the company of David Duke, but a wide spectrum of liberal black political leaders have embraced Farrakhan. And that is in no small part a consequence of the free ride patronizing liberals in the national media give to such attitudes.

Black anti-Semites and their tolerant peers have legitimized public anti-Semitism in a way that no other group in America could. Nor does it seem that Jews can afford to feel as protected today by the American mainstream as are blacks, despite the eyebrows such a claim is sure to raise. When Marlon Brando launched an attack on Hollywood Jews on the Larry King show and went on about "kikes," "chinks," and "niggers," it was only the "N-word" that got bleeped by the CNN censors. "Institutional racism" can cut more than one way. If Yankel Rosenbaum had been a black lynched by a Jewish mob in Crown Heights, does anyone think an all-Jewish jury would have been selected or that the Jewish assassin would have been acquitted, as Rosenbaum's killer was?

Anti-Semitism has real-world consequences for Jews, just as surely as racism does for blacks. A Jew knows not to attempt a career in the auto business in Detroit, for example, without taking into account the "institutional" bias of the industry and thus the hazards of such an effort. I have stood in the living rooms of Grosse Pointe mansions and been made to feel like an intruding bug by their occupants on the basis of (what seemed to me at least) my ethnicity. But this does not lead me or my fellow Jews to call for affirmative action programs that would amount to a preference system for people of Jewish origin.

America is a large marketplace of job and living opportunities, with communities that are extremely tolerant at one end of the spectrum and bigoted at the other. Part of the challenge for ethnic minorities is to find the openings and opportunities that are already there for them. One has only to observe the entrepreneurial explosion among inner-city Koreans and Vietnamese, and to contrast that to the absence of similar success in adjoining black neighborhoods, in order to realize opportunity does exist and no government program can solve the problems endemic to some communities—because the source of those problems lies within the family, the individual, and the community's attitudes as well.

For a voting liberal, Page's familiarity with conservative writers is unusually broad. Consequently, his defense of affirmative action policies is unusually thoughtful. As a conservative who does not fit the liberal caricature of the angry white male threatened by minority advances, however, I still find his arguments off the mark. Like other defenders of these policies, Page begins in denial: "Despite myths to the contrary, affirmative action is not intended to promote people who are not qualified. It is intended to widen the criteria for those who are chosen out of the pool of the qualified." Unfortunately, the facts say otherwise. To refer once again to *The Shape of the River*, Bok and Bowen inadvertently show that without racial preferences and unequal academic standards, black enrollment at the top tier of these elite schools would drop by 73 percent.

The Bok-Bowen study was not available when Page wrote *Showing My Color*. But there were numerous public examples of racial double standards available to him at the time. The prominent black journalist Roger Wilkins, for example, was made University Professor of History at George Mason University despite the fact that he had *no* qualifications as a historian, never even having written a scholarly monograph. In a C-SPAN talk, Wilkins said that he was actually offered the choice of teaching anything he wanted and decided on history "because I was totally ignorant of history and figured that by teaching it I would learn it."* Wilkins was selected for the post over (among others) Professor Ronald Radosh, who at the time had been an academic scholar for twenty years, had published in professional journals, and had written several highly respected books in his field. Nor was this an isolated case. Julian Bond's failed political career led for no apparent reason other than the politics of race to concurrent professorships in history at *two* universities (Virginia and Maryland). Cornel West and Angela Davis hold two of the highest paid and most prestigious university chairs in America, despite their widely recognized intellectual mediocrity (in Davis's case, compounded by her disreputable career as a Communist Party *apparatchik* and a lifelong apologist for marxist police states).

Indeed, the weakness of the affirmative action case is exposed by the fact that its most intensely contested battlefields are elite

---

* *Booknotes*, C-SPAN 2, 2 April 1999, "The Festival of the Book."

universities. Page defends the (now eliminated) affirmative action programs at the University of California with the argument that enrollment levels of blacks would drop if affirmative action were ended. Would Page have us believe that the admissions departments of liberal universities are infested with angry white males conspiring to keep black enrollment down? Or with built-in "institutional biases" excluding blacks? In fact, since 1957, when the California regents adopted the "Master Plan," every single California resident *regardless of race* who graduated high school was guaranteed a place in the higher education system. On the other hand, matriculation from various points in the system, starting with community and junior colleges to positions at Berkeley and UCLA (its academic pinnacles) were based—until the advent of racial preferences—on grade point averages and meritocratic tests. What is wrong with that?

In defending racial preference policies that trump grades and test scores, Page invokes the "geographical diversity" criteria of the Ivy League schools in the 1950s: "Americans have always had a wide array of exotic standards for determining 'merit.'" Page doesn't seem to realize that "geographical diversity" criteria were introduced to *restrict* the enrollment of Jews. Page even quotes, without irony, a "friend" who said he was convinced he got into Dartmouth because he was the only applicant from Albuquerque: "I'm sure some talented Jewish kid from New York was kept out so I could get in." What has the "civil rights" argument come to, when it cites discriminatory policies of the past to justify discriminatory policies in the present?

When I went to Columbia in the 1950s, Jewish enrollment *with* the geographical diversity program in place, was 48 percent. That was the Jewish quota. We Jews were well aware of the anti-Semitic subtext of the geographical diversity program, and talked about it openly. But we did not launch protests or seek government intervention to abolish the program. The opportunity that *was* offered to us was an improvement over the exclusionary policies of the prewar years. Once the principle of Jewish admission was accepted by the Ivy League, even residual (or "institutional") anti-Semitism could not keep Jews, who constituted only 3 percent of the population, from flooding the enrollment lists. It was the academic performance of Jewish students in an environment that emphasized merit that ensured their place. Supporters of affirmative action are in a state of massive denial. The problem of black enrollment at elite universities is not the result of racist admissions policies. It is the result of poor black academic performance.

This denial has costly social consequences that Page and others like him are willing to overlook. The emphasis on nonexistent racism diverts attention from the real problem, which is the poor preparation of black students and the poor performance of public schools. Rigging academic standards, on the other hand, has resulted in dropout rates for affirmative action students that are dramatically higher than for students who do not have the standards rigged for them. These dropout rates are more than 50 percent, and sometimes as high as 70 percent. As Thomas Sowell points out, these are unnecessary failures produced by liberals who would rather feel good about recruiting unqualified black students to make their elite institutions "diverse," than sending them to middle-range (but perfectly adequate) schools, where they would have a chance of success. Looked at another way, affirmative action supporters would rather recruit minority achievers to institutions where they will feel inferior, than place them in settings where they are appropriately skilled and where they would have a chance to feel academically adequate and possibly superior.

Page opens his chapter on affirmative action with an anecdote about being passed over in his first attempt to get hired as a journalist. As a high school graduate in 1965, he applied for a summer newsroom job but was beaten out by a girl less qualified and younger, but white. Then came the Watts riot, after which Page was hired. Page's comment: "You might say that my first job in newspapers came as a result of an affirmative action program called 'urban ri-ots.'"

This is a familiar cliche of the left. White people only respond fairly to blacks when they have a gun to their heads. Malcolm X scorned the civil rights movement, referring in a 1963 speech to "the recent ridiculous march on Washington" because he believed, wrongly, that Americans would never give blacks their rights. But in retrospect many black intellectuals see him as a force behind the civil rights movement, because his violent racism scared whites, who reasoned: "Better King than a 'crazy nigger' like Malcolm X." What is striking about Page's reflection on his experience is that he does not pause to consider that this was his first job application out of high school, or that it was only for a summer position. Perhaps the men doing the hiring, for example, merely wanted to have a girl around the office, an unprofessional but not implausible reason for the choice.

More importantly, Page gives no thought to the possibility that he would have been hired eventually, even without the riots. Rec-ognizing that changes like integration take time is not the same as saying that they require force. Was it the threat of riots or of affirmative action laws that eventually made black athletes domi-nant in sports leagues whose owners (Marge Schott comes to mind) hardly rank among the socially enlightened? Or was it affirmative action that allowed black cultural artists to achieve an equally domi-nant position in the popular music industry? How did Oprah Winfrey, a black sharecropper's daughter from Mississippi, become mother confessor to millions of lower middle-class white women (and worth 550 million dollars in the process) *without* affirmative action? Page has no answer.

The principal reason conservatives oppose affirmative action is one that is given almost no attention by progressives eager to at-tribute base motives to their opponents: racial preference is an offense *in principle* to the core value of American pluralism—the neutrality of American government towards all its diverse communities. Affirmative action is a threat to inclusiveness, since privilege (and therefore exclusion) is established under affirmative action policies, not by achievement, but by law. The principle of affirmative action, which is inevitably a principle of racial preference, is a threat to what Felix Frankfurter identified as "the ultimate foundation of a free society . . . the binding tie of cohesive sentiment." Affirmative action based on principles like geographical diversity constitutes no such threat, but policies based on race do.

Another reason for opposing affirmative action is its social corrosiveness. Every time a black leader refers to the paucity of blacks on academic faculties or in the upper reaches of corporate life, the automatic presumption is that white racism is responsible. The legal concept of "racial disparity" embodies the same assumption. The idea that government must *compel* its white citizens to be fair to its minority citizens presumes that white America is so racist it cannot be fair on its own account. But this involves supporters of affirmative action in illogic so insurmountable it cannot be addressed. If America's white majority needs to be forced by government to be fair, how is it possible that this same majority (led by a Republican president, Richard Nixon) created affirmative action policies in the first place?

There is no answer to the question because affirmative action was not created in response to white racism. It was created because of the widespread failure of blacks to take advantage of the opportunities that became available when legal segregation was ended. Since liberals believe that social institutions are responsible for what happens to people, this failure had to be the result of *institutional* rather than individual factors.

The corrosive effect of thirty years of affirmative action policies has been to convince black Americans that whites are indeed so racist that some external force must compel their respect and, secondarily, that blacks need affirmative action in order to gain equal access to the American dream. The further consequence of this misguided "remedy" has been to foster a racial paranoia in the black community that is so pervasive that even the thinking of blacks who have benefited from America's racial generosity has been significantly affected. How significantly is revealed in the almost casual way the paranoia surfaces: "'Black is beautiful' was the slogan which made many white people nervous, as any show of positive black racial identification tends to do." *Does it really?* The television mini-series *Roots*, after all, was one of the most significant milestones of positive black racial identification—an epic of black nobility and white evil purporting to represent the entire history of American race relations. It was not only produced and made possible by whites, but also voluntarily watched by more whites than any previous television show in history. Conversely, most of the negative stereotypes of blacks in today's popular culture are the work of black stars and directors like Martin Lawrence and Spike Lee, not to mention the infamous gangsta rap industry, which celebrates black sociopathic behavior, and whose most profitable labels are owned and operated by blacks.

In gauging the size of the chip ominously perched on black America's shoulders, few measures can be so choice or familiar as the following passage:

> Black people may read dictionaries, but many see them as instruments of white supremacy. They have a point. Dictionaries define what is acceptable and unacceptable in the language we use as defined by the ruling class (*sic*). . . . The dictionary's pleasant synonyms for 'white' ('free from moral impurity . . . *innocent* . . . *favorable, fortunate* . . .') and unpleasant synonyms for 'black' ('. . . thoroughly sinister or evil . . . *wicked* . . . condemnation or discredit . . . the devil . . . sad, gloomy or calamitous . . . *sullen* . . .') are alone enough to remind black people of their subordinate position to white people in Anglo-European traditions and fact.

This is the standard racial canard repeated by Camille Cosby and others. But white Americans (dictionary-makers included) had nothing to do with identifying Clarence Page and his racial kindred as "black" in modern times. When Page and I were young, blacks were called "Negroes" or "coloreds." The words "Negro" and "colored" have no such negative connotations, moral or otherwise. It was Malcolm X who first embraced "black" as a term of pride, interpreting "Negro" as a term to connote a pliant black or "Uncle Tom." After Malcolm X's death, Stokely Carmichael and the new radical civil rights leadership aggressively promoted the new label with the slogan "Black Power" and demanded that the identification "black" be employed as a sign of respect. The white liberal cultural establishment—including the nation's principal press institutions, the universities and other legitimating agencies—swiftly obliged. It was then acquiesced in by the majority of white Americans who, for more than a generation now, have ardently *wished* that black America would finally get what it wanted from them and be satisfied.

When the layers are peeled from Page's discussion of "racism," what we are left with is a disappointing marxist residue: "Modern capitalist society puts racism to work, wittingly or unwittingly. It populates a surplus labor pool of last-hired, first-fired workers whose easy employability when economic times are good and easy disposability when times go bad helps keep all workers' wages low and owners' profits high. . . . Racism is one of many non-class issues, such as busing, affirmative action, or flag burning, that diverts attention from pocketbook issues that might unite voters across racial lines."

This is simple-minded, sorry stuff, but not unusual for liberals, black and white. The problem with the black underclass is not that it is underemployed, but that it is unemployable. Blacks who have fallen through society's cracks do not even get to the point of being "last-hired." The flood of illegal Hispanic immigrants into areas like south central Los Angeles, where they are rapidly displacing the indigenous blacks, shows that the jobs exist but that the resident black population either will not or cannot take advantage of these opportunities. The fact that one in three young black males in America is a convicted felon—a reality that Page does not begin to confront—does not help their employability. Once again, the specter of racism provides a convenient shield for the massive denial of problems that actually have very little to do with race.

In fact, the racial conflict in America is not driven by economics or even white prejudice. Rather, it is driven by radical political agendas—by Clarence Page's friends on the left like Manning Marable, Ronald Takaki, and Michael Lerner (names lifted from the back jacket blurbs for his book)—who keep up the drum beat of complaint about American racism and "oppression."

The very phrase "institutional racism" is, of course, of leftist provenance. Like "ruling class" it refers to an abstraction. It is a totalitarian term. It does not specify particular, accountable individuals. You are a class enemy (or, in this case, a race enemy) not because of anything you actually think or do, but "objectively"—because you are situated in a structure of power that provides you (white skin) privilege. Page is astute enough to see that if racism is defined as an *institutional* flaw, "it does not matter what you think as an individual" and therefore such a definition offers "instant innocence" to the oppressor. But he is not candid enough to acknowledge that the definition imputes instant culpability as well. While absolving individual whites of guilt, it makes all whites guilty.

The belief in the power of "institutional racism" allows black civil rights leaders to denounce America as a "racist" society, when it is the only society on earth—black, white, brown, or yellow—whose defining public creed is *anti*-racist, a society to which black refugees from black-ruled nations regularly flee in search of refuge and freedom. The phantom of institutional racism allows black leaders to avoid the encounter with real problems *within* their own communities, which are neither caused by whites nor soluble by the actions of whites, but which cry out for attention.

The problem with the discontent now smoldering inside America's privileged black intellectuals, so well expressed in *Showing My Color*, is that it can never be satisfied: "Nothing annoys black people more than the hearty perennial of black life in America, the persistent reality of having one's fate in America decided inevitably by white people. It is an annoyance that underlies all racial grievances in America, beginning with slavery, evolving through the eras of mass lynchings and segregated water fountains, and continuing through the age of 'white flight,' mortgage discrimination, police brutality, and the 'race card' in politics."

In Page's view, the unifying and ultimate goal of all black reformers, whether radicals like bell hooks or conservatives like Clarence Thomas, is "black self-determination." What Clarence Page and blacks like him want is "to free the destiny of blacks from the power of whites."

Within a single national framework, in which blacks are inevitably a minority, this is obviously an impossible goal. Those who advocate it are destined to frustration and anger, and thus to consider themselves perpetually "oppressed." The irony, of course, is that America's multi-ethnic society and color-blind ideal provides the most favorable setting for individuals of all origins to enjoy the freedom to determine their destinies, even if they happen to be members of a minority. Ask the Jews. For two thousand years Jews of the diaspora have not been able to free their destiny from the power of gentiles. But in America, they have done very well, thank you, and do not feel oppressed.

8

The Politics of Race

THE *Communist Manifesto* is probably the only marxist text that the millions of activists who responded to his message actually read. Inspired by its vision of a social redemption, Marxists went on to kill a hundred million people in the twentieth century and create the most oppressive tyrannies ever known. It is almost a decade since the empire that marxism built collapsed in ruins, but it is already evident that the lessons of this tragedy have not been learned. The progressive left and its political faith have survived even the catastrophe of their socialist dreams.

Of course, few people outside the universities today think of themselves as marxists, or will publicly admit to socialist aspirations. But behind protective labels like "populist" and "progressive," the old left is resurrected among us and with its destructive agendas fully intact. This makes the ideas of the *Manifesto*, discredited as they are, worth attending to again.

In fact, three destructive ideas advanced in Marx's tract form the core of the contemporary leftist faith. The first and most important is that the modern, secular, democratic world is ruled by alien powers. According to Marx, the democratic revolutions of the eighteenth century did not establish true democracies. Even though the citizens of industrial nations had dethroned their hereditary rulers and vested sovereignty in themselves, this did not mean they were free. Though liberated from serfdom, workers were now "wage-slaves," captives to capital, the alien power alleged by Marx to rule the modern world in a fashion analogous to the aristocracies and oligarchies of the past. Behind the façade of political democracy, governments are controlled by "ruling classes," the owners of capital who just as effectively keep the citizenry in chains.

The second idea of the *Manifesto* flows naturally from this analysis: Politics is *war* conducted by other means. It is this attitude that inspires the viciousness of left-wing politics, the desire to destroy the opposition entirely, to eliminate adversaries from the field of battle. It is also the perspective that creates the reckless disregard radicals have for institutions and traditions, for what has been created by the generations that went before. In order to create true freedom, the civil orders and binding faiths of democratic systems must be subverted and then destroyed. Treachery and lies are justifiable means to achieve such fiercely desired ends.

The third Marxist idea is the hope that inspires the destruction itself. The extinction of the existing order can lead without much forethought or preparation to a liberated future—a break with the entire history of humanity's enthrallment to these alien forces. It is a mystical creed: the very state which is to be destroyed as the instrument of class oppression, *in the very act of destruction* will be transformed into a means of human liberation. Animating the leftist faith is the idea that the left itself is the redeeming power, the social messiah through whom a world of social justice will be born.

Today the alien power thought by the left to control our destinies is only rarely described as a "ruling class," although it is still perceived as that. Refuted by the history of communist empires, the left has turned to new vocabularies and concepts to rescue it from its defeats. Today the ruling class is identified as the "patriarchy" or the "white male oligarchy," or in disembodied form as the force of "institutional racism" or "white supremacy." The result is a kitsch marxism that follows the basic marxist scheme but results in true intellectual incoherence. Marx's idea of a classless society may make a certain sense in theory even if it is unworkable in practice, whereas the idea of a race-less society or a gender-free society makes no sense at all.

The leftist agenda can be clearly seen in the heart of present conflicts over race, which pose a fundamental challenge to America's multi-ethnic social order. Thus, the proclaimed goal of affirmative action advocates is to "level the playing field." It is defined this way to highlight the left's claim that traditional civil rights solutions have failed to achieve "real" equality, by which is meant equality of results. Traditional civil rights solutions were focused on the fairness of the institutional process, the elimination of legal barriers to political power and individual opportunity. For Martin Luther King Jr. and the traditional civil rights movement, leveling the playing field simply meant extending to black southerners, the constitutional protections accorded to all Americans. It meant making all citizens, regardless of color, equal before the law. Leveling the playing field meant creating neutral rules that did not encompass color or ethnicity but made both irrelevant to the contests of civic and economic life. This was the idea of a "color-neutral" society. It was not that color would be unseen or denied, but that color would not affect individual outcomes, certainly not through the agency of the state. By these standards, the playing field became level once government ceased to play racial favorites, a goal achieved through the Civil Rights Acts of the 1960s.

But though the civil rights battles of the 1960s eliminated racial barriers, the results did not become equal. In the left's perspective, this could only be explained by a hidden racism. According to the left, procedural fairness merely masked an institutional bias that effectively preserves the status quo. Just as traditional marxists deride "bourgeois" democracy as a political sham to preserve the power of a ruling class, so the civil rights left dismisses equality of opportunity as a sham to preserve the superior position of a dominant race. In the old model, an institutionalized class system subverts the democratic form of free elections to preserve a hierarchy of social power. It does not matter that the political process is formally democratic, because the economic class system creates institutionalized inequality. (Of course, this marxist idea is refuted by the fluidity of the American class structure. Currently, 70 percent of American millionaires are first generation; in short, they earned their fortunes. Individual opportunity does exist, and thus individual freedom to succeed or fail.) The contemporary left and its liberal allies merely transpose this analysis (fatuously, it must be said) to the issue of race.

According to the civil rights left, it is the force of "institutional racism" that makes equal opportunity a myth. Educational admissions tests, so it is argued, are culturally rigged to appear neutral, while actually favoring applicants of the dominant color. But this claim is easily refuted. Asian immigrants, who struggle with both a foreign language and an alien culture, consistently score in the highest ranges of standardized tests, surpassing whites and gaining admission to the best schools. Affirmative action measures in education are in fact often designed by the left to *limit* opportunities for Asian minorities, while favoring low-scoring Hispanics and blacks.

The case of Asian-Americans shows that the leftist idea is impervious to factual evidence, and that when the left demands a level playing field, it is not really interested in neutral rules and equitable standards. Instead, the racial left wants to redistribute social goods according to its own plan and its own standards of "justice," which exclude persecuted minorities like Asians, Armenians, and Jews. The left is not interested in an equal process, and only rhetorically in an equal result. What interests the left is accumulating power, which it justifies as the power to arbitrate what is socially "just."

This power is necessarily a totalitarian power in the sense that to realize its agenda the left must invade and dominate the sphere of private life. Consider what it would mean to take the left's demand for equal results in racial competitions at face value. It is true, for example, that 40 percent of America's black children are poor. This condition obviously puts them at a disadvantage in any educational competition, just as the left contends. The left argues that to make up for this handicap, it is necessary to rig educational standards. But 85 percent of those poor black children come from single parent homes. It is *that* circumstance—and not any alien power like "institutional racism"—that actually handicaps them and leaves them unequal. This is the reality the left does not want to face.

A child born into a single parent family is *six times* more likely to be poor, regardless of race, than a child born into a family with two parents. By the time such children are ready to compete, they may suffer from dysfunctional behaviors, or have developed disabling habits, or have internalized cultural attitudes hostile to academic achievement, or simply lack the supportive environment a middle-class home provides. Excessive dropout rates among affirmative action students are the statistical indicators that these handicaps are real. No rigging of standards can make up for deficiencies like this.

In the face of such realities, what can leveling-the-playing-field mean? Making up for the mistakes of the biological parents? Forcing them to get married? Compelling them to be responsible to their children? Requiring them to teach their offspring to study hard and not be self-abusive? Should the state become a Big Brother for those who fall behind, taking over their lives and curtailing their freedoms?

The level playing field that would produce an equality of results is, in fact, a socialist utopia—and hence a totalitarian state. To achieve it would require a government both omniscient and wise, a state that would massively intrude into individual lives. Such a state would mandate comprehensive transfers of opportunity and wealth, and would have to conduct a relentless crusade against defenders of liberty and the rule of law. The call to level the playing field, pushed to its logical conclusion, is a call for the systematic subversion of American individualism and democracy. It is the kitsch marxism of our time.

In the aftermath of the communist collapse, the totalitarian danger is so remote that the normal tendency would be to discount it. But to do so would be to ignore the immediate threat inherent in the assault. It is very possible to destroy the foundations of social trust without establishing a social alternative, and it is the nihilistic ambitions of the radical assault that now present the most serious social threat. Underlying the idea of racial preferences, for example, is a corrosive premise that the white majority is fundamentally racist and cannot be fair. For those who embrace the idea, the institutions, traditions, and rules that white majorities have established merit no respect. The premise of affirmative action preferences is an assault on the very system of economic and legal neutrality that underpins our pluralistic democracy. By denigrating the rule of law as merely a mask for injustice and oppression, the left destroys faith in the very system that makes democracy possible.

In supporting racial preferences, the left appeals directly to the state to abandon its "color-blindness" and compel the white majority to open doors that would otherwise remain closed. It claims that minorities are "excluded" and "locked out" because statistics show disparities between minority representation in certain jobs, or at certain educational institutions, and their representation in the population at large. But discrimination against minorities is already outlawed, and there are no identifiable racists to blame for the alleged "exclusion" of some minorities, or some elements of minority communities from jobs or university admissions. The left's insinuation is that those minority elements who have fallen behind are locked out by invisible powers. "Institutional racism" is responsible.

But "institutional racism" is a radical myth. It is merely the discredited marxist idea that an alien power separates the citizens of democratic societies into rulers and ruled, the dominant race and the races that are oppressed. No one seriously contends, for example, that the admissions officers of America's elite colleges are racists. In fact, admissions officers are usually desperate to locate as many eligible minority applicants as they can, while offering large financial rewards to those they find. The University of California— one of the few institutions that has been compelled to eliminate its racial preferences—is still spending 160 million dollars, annually, on outreach programs designed to increase its minority enrollments. Since this is the case, it is hard not to conclude that any deficiency in minority admissions is the result of individual failures to meet universal standards.

Is America a country ruled by racist powers, as leftists claim? Are African-Americans oppressed? If so, what would explain the desire of so many black Haitians to come to American shores? Why were so many Haitians ready, a few years ago before their immigration was blocked, to risk life and limb to make the illegal passage across shark-infested waters? Was it their desire to be *oppressed*? Were they longing to be dominated by a master race? In fact, it is obvious why the Haitians wanted to come. It is because those who do come have more rights, more opportunity, more cultural privilege, and more social power in America than they had in their native Haiti, which has been independent and run by black governments for more than two hundred years. Indeed, as a result of America's pluralistic democracy, Haitian-Americans are freer and more privileged in America than they would be in any black-run country in the world. The simple truth that the rhetoric of bad faith is designed to obscure is that blacks are not oppressed in America; nor is anyone else. Yet kitsch marxism prompts powerful voices in our culture to talk as though they were.

The very presumption of the civil rights left that racial preferences are necessary because America is ruled by a racist majority is both logically contradictory and empirically false. In its hour of victory in the 1960s, the civil rights movement was supported by the vast majority of the American people, including federal law enforcement and the American military, and by ninety-percent pluralities in both congressional parties. Since those victories, public opinion surveys have shown a dramatic increase in the goodwill of whites generally towards the African-American minority and an equally precipitous decline in attitudes that could reasonably be called bigoted. Large increases in the number of black officials elected by majority white constituencies, and huge income transfers authorized by a predominantly white electorate to black inner-city communities establish beyond all reasonable doubt the solid empirical ground of these reports. Indeed, there would be no affirmative action preferences at all if not for the support of white officials elected by white constituencies.

The presumption that justifies racial preferences thus involves the left in an intellectual cul-de-sac. The white majority that allegedly cannot be fair in society at large is also a white majority in government itself. If whites must be compelled to be fair by government programs, how can they have designed and instituted those same programs? If the white majority is racist how can a government it dominates be counted on to redress racial grievances? The question is absurd because the premise is absurd. In fact it is America's white racial majority that ended slavery, outlawed discrimination, funded massive welfare programs for inner-city blacks, and created the very affirmative action policies that are allegedly necessary to force them to be fair.

Ironically, the move to subvert the state's neutrality—and with it the principle of "color-blindness" that lies at the heart of the rule of law—in the long run works against minorities and particularly African-Americans who have been seduced into promoting it. Groups that are numerically larger are bound to benefit more from political redistribution than numerically smaller ones. Over time, as the displacement of blacks by Latinos in urban centers like Los

Angeles already makes clear, the racial spoils system will transform itself into a system that truly locks blacks out.

Civil rights is just one battlefield in the real war of the left, which is the war against America itself. The big guns of this war are directed from the centers of intellect on the high ground of the university culture, where tenured radicals have created an anti-American ideology and forced it on the nation's youth through the curriculum. The thrust of this curriculum was summarized in a text by a constitutional law professor at one of America's elite universities a few years ago. In *Progressive Constitutionalism*, Robin West argues that "the political history of the United States . . . is in large measure a history of almost unthinkable brutality toward slaves, genocidal hatred of Native Americans, racist devaluation of non-whites and nonwhite cultures, sexist devaluation of women, and a less than admirable attitude of submissiveness to the authority of unworthy leaders in all spheres of government and public life." This is the credo of the progressive left.

Of course, the political history of the United States is exactly the reverse. It is in large measure the history of a nation that led the world in eliminating slavery, in accommodating peoples it had previously defeated, in elevating nonwhites to a position of dignity and respect, in promoting opportunities and rights to women, and in fostering a healthy skepticism towards unworthy leaders and towards the dangers inherent in government itself.

This is a vision that is now called "conservative," but only because leftists currently shape the political language of liberalism and have been able to define the terms of the political debate. There is nothing "liberal" about people who deny the American narrative as a narrative of freedom, or who promote class, race, and gender war in the name of social progress. But they have created a situation in which "conservative" describes those who cherish the constitutional and philosophical framework of American pluralism, and guard it against the advocates of a political bad faith.

III

PANTHER REFLECTIONS

9

Black Murder, Inc.
(1993)

A BOOK ARRIVED THIS MONTH that chilled my marrow. The author's face on the dust jacket was different than I remembered. Its hair was cropped in a severe feminist do, its skin pulled tight from an apparent lift, its eyes artificially lit to give off a benign sparkle. But underneath I could still see the menace I knew so well—an image from the darkest period in my life.

I first met her in June 1974, in a dorm room at Mills College, an elite private school for women in Oakland. The meeting had been arranged by Huey Newton, leader of the Black Panther Party and icon of the New Left. For almost a year before that I had been working with Newton, developing a school complex in the East Oakland ghetto. I had named it the Oakland Community Learning Center and was the head of its "Planning Committee."

The unusual venue of my first meeting with Elaine Brown was the result of the Panthers' odd disciplinary notions. They were actually Huey's notions because (as I came to understand later) the Party was absolutist and the leader's word was law. Huey had "sentenced" Elaine to Mills as a kind of exile and house arrest. "I sent her to Mills," he explained to me, "because she hates it there."

Elaine was a strikingly attractive woman, light-skinned like Huey, but with a more fluid verbal style that developed an edge when she was angry. I had been warned by my friends in the Party that she was also dangerous. A festering inner rage erupted constantly and without warning wherever she went. At such times, the edge in her voice would grow steel-hard and could slice through her target like a machete.

I will never forget standing next to Elaine, as I did months later in growing horror, as she threatened KQED-TV host Bill Schechner over the telephone. "I will *kill* you motherf———r," she promised him, if he went through with plans to interview the former Panther Chairman, Bobby Seale. Seale had gone into hiding after Huey expelled him from the Party that August. As I learned long afterwards, Seale had been whipped—literally—and then personally sodomized by Huey with such violence that he had to have his anus surgically repaired by a Pacific Heights doctor who was a political supporter of the Panthers. A Party member told me later, "You have to understand, it had nothing to do with sex. It was about power." But in the Panther world, as I also came to learn, nothing was about anything except power.

That day at Mills, however, Elaine used her verbal facility as an instrument of seduction, softening me with stories of her rough youth in the North Philly ghetto and her double life at the Philadelphia conservatory of music. Her narrative dramatized the wounding personal dilemmas imposed by racial and class injustice, inevitably winning my sympathy and support.

Elaine had the two characteristics necessary for Panther leadership. She could move easily in the elegant outer world of the Party's wealthy liberal supporters, but she could also function in the violent world of the street gang, which was the Party's internal milieu. Elaine was being punished in her Mills exile because even by Huey's standards her temper was explosive and therefore a liability. Within three months of our meeting, however, his own out-of-control behavior had forced him to make her supreme.

The summer of 1974 was disastrous for Newton. Reports had appeared in the press placing him at the scene of a drive-by shooting at an "after hours" club. He was indicted for pistol-whipping a middle-aged black tailor named Preston Callins with a .357 magnum, for brawling with two police officers in an Oakland bar, and for murdering a seventeen-year-old prostitute named Kathleen Smith. When the day arrived for his arraignment in this last matter, Huey failed to appear. Assisted by the Panthers' Hollywood supporters, he had fled to Cuba.

With Huey gone, Elaine took the reins of the Party. I was already shaken by Huey's flight and by the dark ambiguities that preceded it. As a "politically conscious" radical, however, I understood the racist character of the media and the repressive forces that wanted to see the Panthers destroyed. I did not believe, therefore, all the charges against Huey. Although disturbed by them, I was unable to draw the obvious conclusion and leave.

My involvement with the Black Panther Party had begun in early 1973. I had gone to Los Angeles with Peter Collier to raise money for *Ramparts*, the flagship magazine of the New Left, which he and I co-edited. One of our marks was Bert Schneider, the producer of *Easy Rider*, the breakthrough film of the Sixties which had brought the counter-cultural rebellion into the American mainstream. Schneider gave *Ramparts* five thousand dollars, and then turned around and asked us to meet his friend Huey Newton.

At the time, Newton was engaged in a life-and-death feud with Black Panther Eldridge Cleaver. Cleaver had fled to Algiers after a shoot-out with Bay Area police. (Eldridge later admitted that he ambushed them.) Schneider wanted us to take Eldridge's name off the *Ramparts* masthead, where he was still listed as "International Editor."

Huey's attraction to the Left had always been his persona as "Minister of Defense" of the Black Panther Party, his challenge to revolutionary wannabees to live up to their rhetoric and "pick up the gun." Huey had done just that in his own celebrated confrontation with the law that had left Officer John Frey dead with a bullet wound in his back. Everybody in the Left seemed to believe that Huey had killed Frey, but we also wanted to believe that Huey—as a victim of racism—was also innocent. Peter's and my engagement with the Panthers was more social than political, since *Ramparts* had helped the Party become a national franchise. Their military style left me cold, but now, a change in the times prompted the two of us, and especially me, to be interested in the meeting.

By the early 1970s, it was clear that the "Movement" had flamed out. As soon as Nixon signaled the end of the military draft, the "anti-war" demonstrations stopped and the protestors disappeared, marooning hardcore activists like myself. I felt a need to do something to fill the void. Huey Newton was really alone among Movement figures in recognizing the change in the *Zeitgeist* and making the most of it. In a dramatic announcement, he declared the time had come to "put away the gun" and, instead, to "serve the people," which seemed sensible enough to me.

Our meeting took place in Huey's penthouse eyrie, twenty-five floors above Lake Oakland. The Eldridge faction, which had condemned Huey for "selling out the armed struggle," had made much of Huey's lavish lifestyle in its intra-party polemics. But the apartment itself was sparely furnished, and I was ready to accept Schneider's explanation that it was necessary for "security." (A television screen allowed Huey to view entrants to the building.) Not only J. Edgar Hoover's infamous agents but also the disgruntled Cleaver elements might very well want to see Huey dead. There had been several killings already. One of Huey's East Coast loyalists, Sam Napier, had been shot, doused with gasoline, and set on fire.

Somehow, because of Huey's sober pronouncements and his apparent victory in the intra-party struggle, I regarded this reality as part of the past, and no longer threatening. Unlike Elaine, Huey was able to keep his street passions in check in the presence of the white intellectuals he intended to use. In all the time I worked with him, I never saw him abuse another individual, verbally or otherwise. I never saw him angry or heard him utter a threat. I never saw a gun drawn. When I opposed him on important political issues, as I did at our very first meeting, I found him respectful, a seduction I could not resist. (My partner, Peter, was more cautious and politically aloof and, as events were to prove, wiser than I.)

After the meeting, I offered to help Huey with the Party's community projects and to raise money for the Panther school. Huey wanted to buy a Baptist church facility in the East Oakland ghetto with an auditorium, cafeteria and thirty-five classrooms. In the next months, I raised more than one hundred thousand dollars to purchase the buildings on 61st Avenue and East 14th Street. The sixty-three-thousand-dollar down payment was the largest check I had ever seen, let alone signed. The new Oakland Community Learning Center was administered by the Planning Committee, which was composed of Panthers whom Huey had specially selected to work with me. Neither Bobby Seale, nor Elaine Brown, nor any other Panther leaders were among them.

The Learning Center began with more than one hundred Panther children. Its instruction was enriched by educationalists like Herbert Kohl whom I brought in to help. I took Kohl to see Huey in the penthouse, but the meeting went badly. Within days, Huey's spies had reported that Kohl (who was street smart in ways I was not) was telling people that Huey was using cocaine. When I confronted Herb, he said: "He's sniffing. He was sniffing when we were up there."

I had not been part of the 1960s drug culture and was so unfamiliar with cocaine that I had no idea whether Kohl was right. Huey's runny nose, his ability to stay alert despite the fifth of Courvoisier he daily consumed, the sleepless nights at Schneider's Beverly Hills home where (after Bert and his girlfriend Candice Bergen had gone to bed) Huey talked endlessly to me about politics and the millions of dollars the Party had squandered on bail—all these were telltale signs I could not read. I assumed the innocent possibility that Huey was "sniffing" because he had a cold, which is what I told Kohl, who probably thought I was shining him on. After the incident, Huey banished Kohl from the penthouse, but let him continue to help on the Learning Center.

The Center was operated by a front I had created called the Educational Opportunities Corporation, a California tax-exempt 501(c)(3). It was imperative—or so I thought—to keep the books of the school in order and to file appropriate tax reports so that hostile authorities would not be given a pretext to shut us down. This proved to be only another aspect of my politically induced innocence. Long after I had gone, too, I watched the Center operate illegally, without filing proper tax reports, while Huey and Elaine were diverting large sums of money (received as government grants) to themselves and their gunmen to keep them in fancy cars and clothes and, when necessary, out of jail. Unable to conceive such a possibility for the Black Panther Party, which everyone "knew" was targeted for destruction by J. Edgar Hoover, I engaged the services of our bookkeeper at *Ramparts*, Betty Van Patter, to keep the Learning Center accounts.

Virtually my entire relationship with Huey and the party was through the activities of the school. In the months following the purchase of the building on East 14th, it became apparent to me that things were not proceeding as planned. In particular, it was still exclusively a party operation.

I had never been enthusiastic about the party as such, which seemed to me merely an ideological sect whose time had passed. I had conveyed these views to Huey at the outset of our relationship and he had pretended to agree. He had even promised that if we purchased the facility and built an educational center, it would gradually be turned over to the East Oakland community and not become just another party institution.

Six months had gone by, however, and there were only Panthers in attendance. The impoverished black community around the school remained aloof, as did the black intellectuals (like Berkeley sociology Professor Troy Duster), whom I periodically approached to help out with the operation, and who would come up to the penthouse to see Huey, but afterwards never follow through or return. Adding to my dismay was the fact that the school head, Brenda Bay, had been replaced by Ericka Huggins, a prominent party figure and in my view a mentally unbalanced individual. (It did not improve my dim view of Ericka when I saw her punish a child by commanding the nine year old to write, one thousand times, "I am privileged to attend the Black Panther Party's Learning Center because . . .") My concerns about the school came to a head on May 19, 1974, which was Malcolm X's birthday.

A "Malcolm X Day" celebration was held in the school auditorium, which I attended. One after another, Bobby Seale, Elaine Brown, and other Panthers mounted the podium to proclaim the party as "the only true continuator of the legacy of Malcolm." Looking around at the familiar faces of the Panthers in the hall, I felt depressed and even betrayed. Huey had assured me that the Center would not become the power base for a sect, and had even excluded Bobby and Elaine from its operation to make me a believer. And yet now I could see that's all that it was.

At the next Planning Committee meeting in Huey's apartment, I braced myself and launched into a passionate complaint. On a day that all black Oakland should have been at the Center, I said, the occasion had been turned into a sectarian promotion for the Black Panther Party. My outburst was met by a tense silence from the others at the table. But Huey seemed unfazed and even to lend some support to what I had said. This duplicitous impression of yielding was almost a performance art with him.

Elaine had a similar talent for seduction when it fitted her agenda. In our first encounter at Mills, she had strategically brought the Malcolm X incident into our conversation. In her most disarming manner, she related how Ericka Huggins had reported to her and other members of the party, after the meeting, that "David Horowitz said that the Malcolm X Day celebration was too black."

It was a shrewd gambit, reminding me of my precarious position in the Panther environment, while at the same time making her appear as a friend and potential protector. She had her reasons to ingratiate herself with me then, because she knew that somehow I had Huey's ear, and she wanted desperately to end her exile. A month later, Huey kicked Bobby out of the party and her wish was granted. She became the new "Chairman." A month after that, Huey was gone to Cuba.

When Huey left, all the Panthers whom Huey had assigned to work with me—all the members of the Planning Committee except Ericka—fled as well. They left suddenly, without warning, in the middle of the night. A week earlier, which was the last time I saw them, they had worried about Elaine's new ascendance. When I asked why they were afraid of Elaine, they said "She's crazy." Now they had disappeared, and I had no way of contacting them to question them further.

Although I had been warned about Elaine's dark side, I had only seen benign aspects myself. Now, as she took charge of the party, she revealed another dimension of her personality that was even more attractive.

Where Huey had pretty much ignored the Learning Center after its creation, Elaine threw herself into its every detail, from curriculum to hygiene. She ordered it scrubbed from top to bottom, got proper supplies for the children, and made the Center's needs a visible priority. Soon, the first real community event was held on its premises. It was a teen dance attended by five hundred youths from the neighborhood. I could not have asked for a more concrete sign that things were going to be different. And these efforts were ongoing. Eventually Elaine would recruit Oakland dignitaries to the board of the Center, like Mayor Lionel Wilson and Robert Shetterly, the president and chairman of the Oakland Council for Economic Development. How could I not support her efforts in behalf of a project that had seemed so worthy and to which I had dedicated so much effort of my own?

There were other seductive aspects to her leadership as well. The Black Panther Party—the most male-dominated organization of the Left—was suddenly being led by an articulate, take-charge woman. And not just one woman. Elaine's right and left hands in the party organization—Joan Kelley and Phyllis Jackson—were also female, as was its treasurer Gwen Goodloe. With Huey gone under a dark cloud, Elaine and the Center were facing formidable odds. My social and racial privilege always afforded me a way out of these difficulties (as my leftist conscience was constantly reproving me). How could I face myself, if I abandoned their ship now?

I stayed. And when the party's treasurer, Gwen Goodloe, fled a week later, and Elaine became desperate over who would manage its finances, I suggested a solution. Betty Van Patter, who was already keeping the books for the Learning Center, might be of help in handling the general accounts.

This was to be my last act of assistance to the party. The crises of the fall had piled on one another in such swift succession, that I was unable to assess the toll they were taking. But in November, an event occurred that pushed me over the edge.

There had been a second teen dance, and this time there was a shooting. A Panther named Deacon was dead. His assailant, a black youth of sixteen, was in the county hospital. When I phoned Elaine to ask what had happened, she exploded in the kind of violent outpouring I had become used to by then, blaming the disaster on "the police and the CIA." This stock paranoia was really all I needed to hear. (Years later, I learned from other Panthers that the shooting had been over drugs, which the party was dealing from the school.)

When I walked into the school auditorium where Deacon lay in state (there is really no other term for the scene), I suddenly saw the real party, to which I had closed my eyes to for so long. Of course, the children were there, as were their parents and teachers, but dominating them and everything else physically and symbolically was the honor guard of Panther soldiers in black berets, shotguns alarmingly on display. And, added to this spectacle, mingling with the mourners, there were the unmistakable gangster types, whose presence had suddenly become apparent to me after Elaine took over the party: "Big Bob," Perkins, Aaron, Ricardo, Larry. They were fitted in shades and Bogarts and pinstripe suits, as though waiting for action on the set of a B crime movie. In their menacing faces there was no reflection of political complexity such as Huey was so adept at projecting, or of the benevolent community efforts like the breakfast for children programs that the Center provided.

Underneath all the political rhetoric and social uplift, I suddenly realized was the stark reality of the gang. I remember a voice silently beating my head, as I sat there during the service, tears streaming down my face: "What are you doing here, David?" it screamed at me. It was my turn to flee.

Betty did not attend the funeral, and if she had would not have been able to see what I saw. Moreover, she and I had never had the kind of relationship that inspired confidences between us. As my employee, she never really approved of the way Peter and I ran *Ramparts*. For whatever reasons—perhaps a streak of feminist militancy—she did not trust me.

As a precaution, I had warned Betty, even before Deacon's funeral, not to get involved in any part of the party or its functioning that she didn't feel comfortable with. But Betty kept her own counsel. In one of our few phone conversations, I mentioned the shooting at the dance. She did not take my remark further.

Later it became obvious that I had not really known Betty. I had counted to some extent on her middle class scruples to keep her from any danger zones she encountered in Panther territory. But this too was an illusion. She had passions that prompted her to want a deeper involvement in what she also perceived as their struggle against oppression.

There was another reason I did not express my growing fears to Betty. The more fear I had the more I realized that it would not be okay for me to voice such criticism, having been so close to the operation. To badmouth the party would be tantamount to treason. I had a wife and four children who lived in neighboring Berkeley, and I would not be able to protect them or myself from Elaine's wrath.

There were other considerations in my silence, too. What I had seen at the funeral, what I knew from hearsay and from the press were only blips on a radar screen that was highly personal, dependent on my own experience to read. I had begun to know the Panther reality, at least enough to have a healthy fear of Elaine. But how could I convey this knowledge to someone who had not been privy to the same things I had? How could I do it in such a way that they would believe me and not endanger me? Before fleeing, my Panther friends had tried to warn me about Huey through similar signs, and I had failed to understand. My ignorance was dangerous to them and to myself.

Finally, only the police had ever accused the Panthers of actual crimes. Everyone I knew and respected on the left—and beyond the left—regarded the police allegations against the Panthers as malicious libels by a racist power structure bent on holding down and eliminating militant black leadership. It was one of the most powerful liberal myths of the times.*

One Friday night, a month or so after Deacon's funeral, a black man walked into the Berkeley Square, a neighborhood bar that Betty

---

* In a lengthy investigative article for the *New Yorker*, which appeared in 1970, Edward Jay Epstein systematically punctured this myth and provided evidence for all to see that it was a hoax. But nobody paid any attention.

frequented, and handed her a note. Betty, who seemed to know the messenger, read the note and left shortly afterwards. She was never seen alive again.

On the following Monday, I received an anxious phone call from Tammy Van Patter, Betty's eighteen-year-old daughter, who had also worked for me at *Ramparts*. She told me her mother was missing and asked for my help. I phoned Elaine, but got Joan Kelley instead. Joan told me that Elaine had had a fight with Betty on Thursday and fired her. (Later, Elaine lied to investigating police, telling them she had fired Betty the previous Friday and hadn't seen her for a week before she disappeared.)

When Elaine returned my call, she immediately launched into a tirade against Betty, calling her an "idiot" who believed in astrology, and who "wanted to know too much." She said that Betty was employed by a bookkeeping firm with offices in the Philippines, and was probably working for the CIA. Then Elaine turned on me for recommending that Betty be hired in the first place. She noted that I was "bawling" at Deacon's funeral and had not "come around for a long time." Perhaps I was scared by the dangers the party faced. Why was I so concerned about this white woman who was crazy, when all those brothers had been gunned down by the police? White people did not seem to care that much when it was black people dying.

A week later, when Betty still had not turned up, I called Elaine one more time, and was subjected to another torrent of abuse culminating in a threat only thinly veiled: "If you were run over by a car or something, David, I would be very upset, because people would say I did it."

I was visited in my home by the Berkeley police. They told me they were convinced the Panthers had taken Betty hostage and had probably already killed her. From her daughter, Tammy, I learned that the very small circle of Betty's friends and acquaintances had all been questioned since her disappearance, and none had seen her for some time. She had left her credit cards and birth control pills at home, and thus could not have been going on an unexpected trip when she left Berkeley Square with the mysterious messenger for the rendezvous to which she had been summoned.

Betty was found on January 13, 1975, five weeks after she had disappeared, when her water-logged body washed up on the western shore of San Francisco Bay. Her head had been bashed in by a blunt instrument and police estimated that she had been in the water for seventeen days. She was forty-two years old.

By this time, everything I knew about Betty's disappearance had led me to the conclusion that the Panthers had killed her. Everything I knew about the party and the way it worked led me to believe that Elaine Brown had given the order to have her killed.

Betty's murder shattered my life and changed it forever. While I sank into a long period of depression and remorse, however, Elaine's star began to rise in Oakland's political firmament. A white woman who worked for the Black Panther Party had been murdered, but—despite our rhetoric about police conspiracies and racist oppression—there seemed to be no consequences for Elaine or her party.

The press made nothing of it. When Peter Collier approached Marilyn Baker, a Pulitzer Prize-winning reporter for Channel 5 with the story, she said she "wouldn't touch it unless a black reporter did it first." Betty's friends in the Bay Area progressive community, who generally were alert to every injustice, even in lands so remote they could not locate them on a map, kept their silence about this one in their own backyard. Peter also went to the police who told him: "You guys have been cutting our balls off for the last ten years. You destroy the police and then you expect them to solve the murders of your friends."

While the investigation of Betty's death continued, Elaine ran for the Oakland City Council and garnered 44 percent of the vote. The following year, under her leadership, the party provided the political machine that elected Oakland's first black mayor, Lionel Wilson. Elaine herself secured the endorsement of Governor Jerry Brown and was a Jerry Brown delegate to the Democratic Convention in 1976. (Before making his run, Brown phoned Elaine to find out what kind of support the party could provide him.) Tony Kline, a Panther lawyer and confidante of Elaine, was also a college roommate of the Governor and became a member of his cabinet. Using her leverage in Sacramento, Elaine was able to get approval for an extension of the Grove-Shafter Freeway, which had been blocked by environmentalists. On the basis of this achievement, she began negotiations with the head of Oakland's Council for Economic Development to control ten thousand new city jobs that the freeway would create.

In all these successes, the Learning Center was her showpiece. Capitalizing on liberal concerns for Oakland's inner city poor, she obtained contributions and grants for the school, and bought herself a red Mercedes. The party's political influence climbed to its zenith. It was an all-American nightmare.

While Elaine's power grew to alarming proportions, I intensified my private investigations into the Panther reality that had previously eluded me. I had to confront my blindness and understand the events that had led to such an irreversible crossroads in my life. I interrogated everyone I could trust who had been around the Panthers about the dark side of their operations, seeking answers to the questions of Betty's death.

I discovered the existence of the Panther "Squad"—an enforcer group that Huey had organized inside the party to maintain discipline and carry out criminal activities in the East Oakland community. I learned of beatings, arson, extortion and murders. The Learning Center itself had been used as the pretext for a shakedown operation of "after hours" clubs which were required to "donate" weekly sums and whose owners were gunned down when they refused.

I learned about the personalities in the Squad, and about their involvement in the killing. One of them, Robert Heard, was known as "Big Bob" in the party because he was six feet, eight inches tall and weighed four hundred pounds. Big Bob told friends, whom I talked to, that the Squad had killed Betty and more than a dozen other people, in the brief period between 1972 and 1976. The other victims were all black, and included the Vice President of the Black Student Union at Grove Street College, whose misfortune was to have inadvertently insulted a member of the Squad.

Betty's children commissioned Hal Lipset, a private investigator with connections to the Left (and to the Panthers themselves, who had employed him during Huey's trials) to investigate the case. Lipset confirmed the police conclusion that the Panthers had killed Betty. They also tried to get the case against the Panthers reopened, but with no success.

Then, in the summer of 1977, unable to stomach exile any longer, Huey suddenly returned from Cuba. He was given a welcome by the local left, culminating in a ceremony and "citizenship award" presented by Assemblyman Tom Bates, husband of Berkeley's radical mayor, Loni Hancock.

But not everyone would turn a blind eye to the Panther reality. The minute Huey stepped off the plane, Alameda County prosecutors began preparing to try him for the murder of Kathleen Smith, the eighteen-year-old prostitute he had killed three years earlier.

Huey made preparations too. One day before the preliminary trial hearings were to begin in Oakland, three Panther gunmen tried to break into a house in the nearby city of Richmond, where they expected to find the prosecution's chief eye-witness, Crystal Gray. It was the wrong house. (Gray lived in an apartment in the back.) The owner, a black bookkeeper, picked up her .38 and fired at the intruders. A gun battle ensued in which one Panther was killed and another, named Flores Forbes, was wounded.

Forbes fled the scene to seek the assistance of another Panther,

Nelson Malloy, who was not a Squad member and had only just joined the party. Fearing that the innocent Malloy might link him to the assassination attempt, Huey ordered a hit team to follow Malloy and Forbes to Las Vegas, where they had fled. The assassins found them and shot Malloy in the head and buried him in a shallow roadside grave in the Nevada desert. Miraculously he was discovered by tourists who heard his moans and rescued him, although he remained paralyzed from the neck down for the rest of his life.

Shortly after the Richmond incident, Elaine herself was gone. The Squad had never really accommodated itself to being ruled by a woman. When Huey returned, tensions between Elaine and the Squad reached a head, and Huey came down on the side of his gunmen. Elaine left for Los Angeles, never to return.

The botched assassination attempt on the prosecution witness, together with the headlines about Malloy's burial in the desert, destroyed the alliances that Elaine had so carefully built. Mayor Lionel Wilson, the head of Clorox, and the other Oakland dignitaries resigned from the Learning Center board. With its power diminished and its sinister reality in part revealed, the Panther Party had been de-clawed. I began to breathe more easily.

But I was still unable to write or make public what I had come to know about the party and its role in Betty's murder. I had given some of the information to reporter Kate Coleman who wrote a courageous story for the magazine *New Times*. It was called "The Party's Over" and helped speed the Panther decline. But I could not be a witness myself. I was no longer worried about being denounced as a racist or government agent by my friends on the Left if I accused the Panthers of murdering Betty. (Such a possibility would seem far more plausible after the Richmond events.) Nor would I have cared so much now about attacks from the Left. During the five years since Betty's death, my own politics had begun to change. But I retained a residue of physical fear.

Huey was alive in Oakland, armed and obviously crazy, and dangerous. I now realized how powerless the "law" in fact was. Huey seemed untouchable. He had managed to beat his murder rap with the help of testimony by friends ready to perjure themselves for the cause. The pistol-whipping case had been dropped as well. After being threatened and bribed, the tailor Preston Callins retracted his charges. For me, caution seemed to be the prudent course.

Then, in 1980, an event took place that provided me with an occasion to relieve myself of a portion of my burden. It provided a story that was parallel in many respects to what I had been through. It would afford me the opportunity to speak about things that had been unspeakable until now.

In May 1980, Fay Stender, an attorney who had defended Black Panther George Jackson, took her own life in Hong Kong. She had withdrawn to this remote city away from family and friends in order to kill herself after a member of Jackson's prison gang had shot and paralyzed her the year before. She had stayed alive just long enough to act as a witness for the prosecution in the trial of her assailant.

In writing "Requiem for A Radical," which recounted the details of her life and death, Peter Collier and I were able to lift a part of the veil that had obscured the criminal underside of the Black Panther Party. We described the army of thugs that had been trained in the Santa Cruz Mountains to free Jackson from his San Quentin cell. We described the "killing fields" in those same mountains where the Panthers had buried the corpses of Fred Bennett and others who had violated their party codes. We were also able to write honestly about Jackson himself, whom the Left had made into a romantic legend and who, like Huey, was a criminal psychopath. Obscured by the love letters Jackson had written in Soledad Brother, which Fay Stender had edited, was the murderer who had boasted of killing a dozen men in prison and whose revolutionary plan was to poison the water system of Chicago where he had grown up.

When our story appeared in *New West* Magazine, I learned through mutual friends that Bert Schneider, Huey's Hollywood patron, was unhappy with the account Peter and I had written. Although I sensed that Bert was aware of the party's criminal activities, including Betty's murder, I was not as afraid of him as I was of Huey, and I decided to go and see him. I did so on a principle I had learned from the *Godfather* movies, that you should get near to your enemies and find out what they have in mind for you. The Fay Stender story was not a direct hit on Huey or Bert and their reactions might tell me something I needed to know. Perhaps the past was not as alive for them as I imagined. Perhaps I did not have so much to fear.

Bert had an estate in the hills above Benedict Canyon. I called my name through the security gate and was admitted into the main house. Bert appeared, wearing a bathrobe, and in a quiet rage. He was angrier than I had ever seen him. "You endangered my life" he hissed at me.

I did not have the slightest idea what he was talking about. He directed me to a passage in our text about Jackson's attempted escape from San Quentin prison (an episode in which the Panther and his comrades slit the throats of three prison guards they had tied up, before Jackson himself was killed): "The abortive escape left a thicket of unanswered questions behind. . . . Had Jackson been set up? If so, was it by the Cleaver faction of the Black Panther Party? Or by Newton, fearful of Jackson's charismatic competition?"

A book about Jackson had described Bert as being in close contact with Huey during the escape attempt. But even with that in mind, I still could not understand why Bert was so agitated. I was already focusing, however, on something else Bert had said that had far greater significance for me. In defending his reaction to the article he had admitted "Huey isn't as angry as I am." It was the opening I was looking for. I told him I would like to see Huey, and a lunch was arranged.

When I arrived at Norman's, the North Berkeley restaurant that Huey had chosen, he was already there, sunk into one of the vinyl divans, his eyes liverish and his skin pallid, drunker than I had ever seen him. He was so drunk, in fact, that when the lunch was over he asked me to drive him back to the two-story house that Bert had bought for him in the Oakland Hills. When he invited me in, I was a little nervous but decided to go anyway. The decor—piled carpets, leather couches and glass-topped end tables—was familiar. Only the African decorative masks that had been mounted on the beige walls seemed a new touch.

As we sat down in Huey's living room, our lunch conversation continued. Huey told me about a project he had dreamed up to produce *Porgy and Bess* as a musical set in contemporary Harlem, starring Stevie Wonder and Mick Jagger. It was a bizarre idea but not out of character for Huey, whose final fight with Bobby Seale had begun with a quarrel over who should play the lead role in a film Huey wanted to make. Huey even showed me the treatment he had prepared in braille for Stevie Wonder, while complaining that the people around the singer had badmouthed him and killed the deal. When he said this his face contorted in a grimace that was truly demonic.

Then, just as suddenly, he relaxed and fell into a distant silence. After a minute, he looked directly at me and said: "Elaine killed Betty." And then, just as abruptly, he added a caveat whose cynical bravado was also typical, as though he was teaching me, once again, how the world really worked: "But if you write that, I'll deny it."

Until that moment I had thought Elaine was solely responsible for the order to kill Betty. But now I realized that Huey had collaborated with her and probably given the order himself. He might have said, "David, I'm sorry about Betty. It should never have happened, but I was in Cuba and couldn't stop it." But he did not. He

chose instead to point a finger at Elaine, as the one alone responsible. It had a false ring. It was uncharacteristically disloyal. Why
point the finger at anyone in particular, unless he could indeed have
prevented it and did not?

I went home and began contacting several ex-Panthers, who
were living on the East Coast. I asked them how Elaine, as a
woman, had been able to run the party and control the Squad. The
answer was the same in each case: Elaine had not really run the
party while Huey was in Cuba. Huey had run it. He was in daily
contact with Elaine by phone. The Squad stayed loyal to Elaine
out of fear of Huey.

Having gotten this far, I turned to the actual decision to kill
Betty. The same sources told me that Betty's fate had been debated
for a week. Elaine had provided Huey with the reasons for killing
Betty; Huey had made the final decision.

In 1989, fourteen years after Betty Van Patter disappeared, Huey
was gunned down by a drug dealer he had burned. It was a few
blocks away from where Huey had killed Kathleen Smith. It was
not justice. He should have died sooner; he should have suffered
more. But if I had learned anything through all this, it was not to
expect justice in this world, and to be grateful for that which did
occur, however belated and insufficient.

Huey's death allowed Peter and me to write his story and to
describe the Panther reality I had uncovered. (We called it "Baddest"
and published it as a new chapter in the paperback edition of our
book *Destructive Generation*.) By now, we had become identified
with the political Right (although "libertarian irregulars" might
better describe our second thoughts). What we wrote about the
Panthers' crimes, therefore, was either dismissed or simply ignored
by an intellectual culture that was still dominated by the political
Left. Even though Huey's final days had tainted the Panthers'
legacy, their glories were still fondly recalled in all the Sixties nostalgia that continued to appear on public television, in the histori-

cal monographs of politically correct academics and even in the pages of the popular press. The Panther crime wave was of no importance to anyone outside the small circle of their abandoned victims.

Then, in an irony of fate, Elaine Brown emerged from obscurity early this year to reopen the vexed questions of the Panther legacy. She had been living in a kind of semi-retirement with a wealthy French industrialist in Paris. Now she was back in America seeking to capitalize on the collective failure of memory with a self-promoting autobiography, *A Taste of Power*, published by a major New York publisher, with all the fanfare of a major New York offering.

With her usual adroitness, Elaine had managed to sugarcoat her career as a political gangster by presenting herself as a feminist heroine and victim. "What Elaine Brown writes is so astonishing," croons novelist Alice Walker from the dust jacket of the book, "at times it is even difficult to believe she survived it. And yet she did, bringing us that amazing light of the black woman's magical resilience, in the gloominess of our bitter despair." "A stunning picture of a black woman's coming of age in America," concurred *Kirkus Reviews*. "Put it on the shelf beside *The Autobiography of Malcolm X*." To the *Los Angeles Times*' Carolyn See, it is "beautiful, touching, astonishing. . . . Movie makers, where are you?" (In fact, Suzanne DePasse, producer of *Lonesome Dove*, who appears to have been the guiding spirit behind the book is planning a major motion picture of Elaine's life.) *Time*'s review invoked Che Guevara's claim that "the true revolutionary is guided by great feelings of love," and commented: "In the end, Brown discovers, love is the most demanding political act of all."

A *New York Times Magazine* profile of Elaine Brown, "A Black Panther's Long Journey", treated her as a new feminist heroine and prompted View and Style sections of newspapers in major cities across the nation to follow suit. Elaine, who reportedly received a

450,000 dollar advance from Pantheon Books, has been on the book circuit, doing radio and television shows from coast to coast, including a segment of the *MacNeil-Lehrer NewsHour*, where she appeared on a panel chaired by Charlayne Hunter Gault as an authority on black America. ("I hate this country," she later told the *Los Angeles Times*. "There's a point at which you're black in this country, poor, a woman, and you realize how powerless you are." In contrast, Elaine once told me privately: "The poorest black in Oakland is richer than 90 percent of the world's population.") At Cody's Books in Berkeley, two hundred radical nostalgists came to hear her, flanked by her "bodyguard," Huey's old gunman, Flores Forbes.

I read the book and, jaded though I was, still was amazed by this reception. The only accurate review seemed to come from the Bloods and Crips who flocked as fans to her Los Angeles appearance. *A Taste of Power* is, in its bloody prose, and despite the falsehoods designed to protect the guilty, the self-revelation of a sociopath, of the Elaine I knew.

"I felt justified in trying to slap the life out of her,"—this is the way Elaine introduces an incident in which she attempted to retrieve some poems from a radical lawyer named Elaine Wenders. The poems had been written by Johnny Spain, a Panther who participated in George Jackson's bloody attempt to escape from San Quentin. Elaine describes how she entered Wenders's office, flanked by Joan Kelley and another female lieutenant, slapped Wenders's face and proceeded to tear the room apart, emptying desk-drawers and files onto the floor, slapping the terrified and now weeping lawyer again, and finally issuing an ultimatum: "I gave her twenty-four hours to deliver the poems to me, lest her office be blown off the map."

Because Wenders worked in the office of Charles Garry, Huey's personal attorney, Elaine's thuggery produced some mild repercussions. She was called to the penthouse for a "reprimand" by Huey, who laughingly told her she was a "terrorist." The reprimand apparently still stings and Elaine even now feels compelled to justify the violence that others considered impolitic: "It is impossible to summarize the biological response to an act of will in a life of submission. It would be to capture the deliciousness of chocolate, the arousing aroma of a man or a perfume, the feel of water to the dry throat. What I had begun to experience was the sensation of personal freedom, like the tremor before orgasm. The Black Panther Party had awakened that thirst in me. And it had given me the power to satisfy it."

The thirst for violence is a prominent feature of this self-portrait: "It is a sensuous thing to know that at one's will an enemy can be struck down," Elaine continues. In another passage she gives one of many instances of the pleasure. Here, it is a revenge exacted, after she becomes head of the party, on a former Panther lover named Steve, who had beaten her years before.

Steve is lured to a meeting where he finds himself looking down the barrel of a shotgun. While Elaine's enforcer, Larry Henson, holds Steve at gunpoint, Elaine unleashes four members of the Squad, including the four hundred-pound Robert Heard, on her victim: "Four men were upon him now . . . Steve struggled for survival under the many feet stomping him. . . . Their punishment became unmerciful. When he tried to protect his body by taking the fetal position, his head became the object of their feet. The floor was rumbling, as though a platoon of pneumatic drills were breaking through its foundation. Blood was everywhere. Steve's face disappeared."

The taste for violence is as pervasive in Elaine's account as is the appetite to justify it in the name of the revolutionary cause. She describes the scene in Huey's apartment just after he had pistol-whipped the middle-aged black tailor Preston Callins with a .357 Magnum. (Callins required brain surgery to repair the damage): "Callins's blood now stained the penthouse ceilings and carpets and walls and plants, and [Huey's wife's] clothes, even the fluffy blue-and-white towels in the bathroom." This is Elaine's reaction to the scene: "While I noted Huey's irreverent attitude about the whole affair, it occurred to me how little I, too, actually cared about Callins. He was neither a man nor a victim to me. I had come to believe everything would balance out in the revolutionary end. I also knew that being concerned about Callins was too costly, particularly in terms of my position in the party. Yes, I thought, f— Callins."

Elaine deals with Betty's murder in these pages, too. "I had fired Betty Van Patter shortly after hiring her. She had come to work for the party at the behest of David Horowitz, who had been editor of *Ramparts* magazine and a onetime close friend of Eldridge Cleaver. He was also nominally on the board of our school. . . . She was having trouble finding work because of her arrest record." This is false on every significant count. Betty had no arrest record that Elaine or I knew about. I was one of three legal incorporators of the Learning Center and, as I have already described, the head of its Planning Committee. Finally, I had met Eldridge Cleaver only once, in my capacity as a fledgling editor at *Ramparts*. (Elaine's purpose in establishing this particular falsehood is clearly to link Betty to a possible plot: "I began wondering where Betty Van Patter might have really come from. . . . I began re-evaluating Horowitz and his old Eldridge alliance.") Elaine continues:

> Immediately Betty began asking Norma, and every other Panther with whom she had contact, about the sources of our cash, or the exact nature of this or that expenditure. Her job was to order and balance our books and records, not to investigate them. I ordered her to cease her interrogations. She continued. I knew that I had made a mistake in hiring her. . . . Moreover, I had learned after hiring her that Betty's arrest record was a prison record—on charges related to drug trafficking. Her prison record would weaken our position in any appearance we might have to make before a government body inquiring into our finances. Given her actions and her record,

she was not, to say the least, an asset. I fired Betty without notice.

Betty had no prison record for drug trafficking or anything else.
"While it was true that I had come to dislike Betty Van Patter," Elaine concludes, "I had fired her, not killed her."

Yet, the very structure of Elaine's defense is self-incriminating. The accurate recollections that Betty, who was indeed scrupulous, had made normal bookkeeping inquiries that Elaine found suspicious and dangerous, provides a plausible motive to silence her. The assertions that Betty was a criminal, possibly involved in a Cleaver plot, are false and can only be intended to indict the victim. Why deflect guilt to the victim or anyone else, unless one is guilty oneself?

Violence was not restricted to the Panthers's dealings with their enemies, but was an integral part of the party's internal life as well. In what must be one of the sickest aspects of the entire Panther story, this party of liberators enforced discipline on the black "brothers and sisters" inside the organization with bull-whips, the very symbol of the slave past. In a scene that combines both the absurdity and pathology of the party's daily routine, Elaine describes her own punishment under the Panther lash. She is ordered to strip to the waist by Chairman Bobby Seale and then subjected to ten strokes because she had missed an editorial deadline on the Black Panther newspaper.

A Taste of Power inadvertently provides another service by describing how the Panthers originally grew out of criminal street gangs and how the gang mentality remained the core of the party's sense of itself even during the heyday of its political glory. Elaine writes with authority, having come into the party through the Slausons, a forerunner of the Bloods and the Crips. The Slausons were enrolled en masse in the party in 1967 by their leader, gangster Al "Bunchy" Carter, the "Mayor of Watts." Carter's enforcer, Frank Diggs, is one of Elaine's first party heroes: "Frank Diggs,

Captain Franco, was reputedly leader of the Panther underground. He had spent twelve years in Sing Sing Prison in New York on robbery and murder charges." Captain Franco describes to Elaine and Ericka Huggins his revolutionary philosophy: "Other than making love to a Sister, downing a pig is the greatest feeling in the world. Have you ever seen a pig shot with a .45 automatic, Sister Elaine? . . . Well, it's a magnificent sight." To the newly initiated Panther, this is revolutionary truth: "In time, I began to see the dark reality of the revolution according to Franco, the revolution that was not some mystical battle of glory in some distant land of time. At the deepest level, there was blood, nothing but blood, unsanitized by political polemic. That was where Franco worked, in the vanguard of the vanguard."

The Panthers were—just as the police and other Panther detractors said at the time—a criminal army at war with society and with its thin blue line of civic protectors. When Elaine took over the party, even she was "stunned by the magnitude of the party's weaponry. . . . There were literally thousands of weapons. There were large numbers of AR-18 short automatic rifles, .308 scoped rifles, 30-30 Winchesters, .375 magnum and other big-game rifles, .30 caliber Garands, M-15s and M-16s and other assorted automatic and semi-automatic rifles, Thompson submachine guns, M-59 Santa Fe Troopers, Boys .55 caliber anti-tank guns, M-60 fully automatic machine guns, innumerable shotguns, and M-79 grenade launchers. . . . There were caches of crossbows and arrows, grenades and miscellaneous explosive materials and devices."

I remember vividly an episode in the mid-1970s, when one of the Panther arms caches, a house on 29th Street in East Oakland, was raided by the police and one thousand weapons, including machine guns, grenade launchers, and anti-tank guns were uncovered. Party attorney Charles Garry held a press conference at which he claimed that the weapons were planted by the police and that the 29th Street house was a dormitory for teachers at the Panther school (which it also, in fact, was). Then Garry denounced the police raid as just one more repressive act in the ongoing government conspiracy to discredit the Panthers and destroy militant black leadership. Of course, all right thinking progressives rallied to the Panthers' support.

And right thinking progressives are still rallying. How to explain the spectacle attending the reception of Elaine's book? After all, this is not pre-glasnost Russia, where crimes were made to disappear into a politically controlled void. The story of the Panthers' crimes is not unknown. But it is either uninteresting or unbelievable to a progressive culture that still regards white racism as the primary cause of all ills in black America, and militant thugs like the Panthers as mere victims of politically inspired repression.

The existence of a Murder Incorporated in the heart of the American Left is something the Left really doesn't want to know or think about. Such knowledge would refute its most cherished self-understandings and beliefs. It would undermine the sense of righteous indignation that is the crucial starting point of a progressive attitude. It would explode the myths on which the attitude depends.

In the last two decades, for example, a vast literature has been produced on the "repression of the Panthers" by the FBI. The "Cointelpro" program to destabilize militant organizations and J. Edgar Hoover's infamous memo about the dangers of a "black messiah" are more familiar to today's college students probably than the operations of the KGB or the text of the Magna Carta. In *A Taste of Power*, Elaine Brown constantly invokes the FBI specter (as she did while leader of the party) to justify Panther outrages and make them "understandable" as the hyper-reflexes of a necessary paranoia, produced by the pervasive government threat. A variation of this myth is the basic underpinning of the radical mind-set. Like Oliver Stone's fantasies of military-industrial conspiracy, it justifies the radical's limitless rage against America itself.

On the other hand, even in authoritative accounts, like William O'Reilly's *Racial Matters*, the actual "Cointelpro" program never amounted to much more than a series of inept attempts to discredit and divide the Panthers by writing forged letters in their leaders' names. (According to O'Reilly's documents, FBI agents even suspended their campaign when they realized how murderous the Panthers actually were, and that their own intelligence pranks might cause real deaths.)

Familiarity with the Panthers' reality, suggests a far different question from the only one that progressives have asked—Why so much surveillance of the Panthers?—namely: Why so little? Why had the FBI failed to apprehend the guilty not only in Betty's murder but in more than a dozen others? Why were the Panthers able to operate for so long as a criminal gang with a military arsenal, endangering the citizens of major American cities? How could they commit so many crimes—including extortion, arson and murder—without being brought to the bar of justice?

The best review of Elaine's book and the best epitaph for her party are provided ironically by Elaine herself. In the wake of the brutal and senseless whipping of Bobby Seale by a leader insane with drugs and political adulation, and a coterie too drugged with power themselves to resist, she reflects: "Faith was all there was. If I did not believe in the ultimate rightness of our goals and our party, then what we did, what Huey was doing, what he was, what I was, was horrible."

10

Johnnie's Other O. J.
(1997)

I FIRST HEARD THE NAME GERONIMO PRATT in the early 1970s, during a late night conversation with Huey Newton, the Minister of Defense of the Black Panther Party, now deceased. Pratt was the leader of the Los Angeles branch of the party and had been recently convicted of a robbery-murder in Santa Monica. The victim was a young elementary school teacher named Caroline Olsen, who was accosted with her husband by two gunmen on a Santa Monica tennis court on December 18, 1968. Caroline and Kenneth Olsen were ordered to lie down and give up their cash and jewelry, which they did. As the two predators left the scene, however, one of the gunmen emptied his .45-caliber weapon into their prone bodies, wounding Kenneth and killing his wife. Nearly two years later, Geronimo Pratt was charged with the murder and eventually convicted, despite the efforts of Johnnie Cochran, then a young, unknown attorney on the make, to present him as the victim of a police conspiracy.

It was not just the murder conviction that made Pratt a figure of interest to me at the time. Other Panthers had had run-ins with the law. But Pratt was a special case because Newton and the party, and their followers in the New Left, had hung him out to dry. Even though Pratt was a Deputy Minister of Defense and ran the Los Angeles party, there were no "Free Geronimo" rallies organized in his behalf, as there had been for Newton himself. Even more damningly, Newton and the other Panther leaders—Bobby Seale, David Hilliard, and Elaine Brown—flatly denied the alibi with which Pratt sought to save himself. He had claimed he was at a Panther meeting in Oakland at the time of the murder. The refusal of those who attended the meeting to confirm this story, as much as any other fact, sealed Pratt's fate.

There were "political" factors behind this decision to abandon Pratt to his legal fate. He had, in fact, been expelled from the Black Panther Party shortly after the murder of Caroline Olsen for his support of an anti-Newton Black Panther faction led by Eldridge Cleaver, the more violent wing of the party that had accused Newton of "selling out" the "armed struggle." To show their authenticity, Cleaver's followers had formed a Black Liberation Army, which had already launched a guerilla war in earnest in America's cities. Pratt was the party's "military expert" and had fortified the party's headquarters for a shootout with police, deploying machine guns and other automatic weapons in a firefight in which three officers and three Panther soldiers were wounded. At the beginning of August 1970, when Pratt was kicked out of the party, another member of the violent "Cleaver" faction, Jonathan Jackson, marched into a Marin County Courthouse with loaded shotguns to take hostages in an episode that cost the lives of a federal judge, Jackson himself, and two of his cohorts. Pratt had supported Jackson and his plan to use the hostages to liberate his brother George from San Quentin, where he was awaiting trial for murder.

The evening Huey and I talked about Geronimo, he explained to me that Pratt, a decorated Vietnam veteran, was psychotic, a "crazy man" who had not only committed the Santa Monica murder, but actually enjoyed violence for its own sake. Huey attributed Pratt's aberrant behavior to his war experience, although in fact he had not met Pratt prior to his military discharge.

And that was the way it remained for me for twenty-five years, during which time I discovered that Newton himself was a cold-blooded killer and the Panthers a political gang that had committed many robberies, arsons, and murders. By the time Johnnie Cochran brought the case of Geronimo Pratt before a national public, I was almost ready myself to give Newton's enemy the benefit of the doubt. Perhaps some other Panther had killed Caroline Olsen and used Pratt's car in committing the crime, as his supporters maintained. Perhaps the murder weapon, a distinctive .45 caliber model used in the military and identified by several witnesses as belonging to Pratt had actually belonged to someone else, as he claimed.

But there was a detail from that conversation with Newton that I could never forget and yet never quite believe either. Pratt was so crazy, Newton told me, that "he couldn't get an erection unless he was holding a knife in his hand." This detail would come up again in the aftermath of Pratt's release in the late spring of 1997, when an Orange County Superior Court Judge, Everett Dickey, agreed with Cochran, who was still on the case, that the prosecution had wrongfully concealed from the original jury the information that their key witness, a former Panther named Julius Butler, was a police and FBI "informant. It was Butler who had identified the .45 as Pratt's weapon and—even more damning—claimed that Pratt boasted to him that he had killed Caroline Olsen. It was Butler—and the adroit use Cochran made of him—that led to Pratt's being granted a new trial. Johnnie Cochran and a compliant press named him a "hero" and "victim of injustice."

In the tapestry of Johnnie Cochran's political career, the case of Geronimo Pratt has been a central thread. A young Johnnie Cochran, just setting out on his career in the law, was Pratt's counsel in the original trial. By his own account, it was the Pratt case that "radicalized" him, persuading him that America's criminal justice system was unfair to black men. It showed him, too, that his failure to play the "race card" had led to the conviction of his client. He resolved never to make this mistake again. When Cochran later took on the legal battle that made him famous, he told his client, O. J. Simpson, under indictment for the brutal murder of his wife and an innocent bystander, "I'm not going to let happen to you what happened to Geronimo Pratt." After getting Simpson acquitted, Cochran visited the imprisoned Pratt and reiterated the promise he had made that he would never rest "until you are free."

Johnnie Cochran's defense strategy made the two cases into the legal equivalent of Siamese twins. Cochran had rescued Simpson from almost certain conviction by focusing on officer Mark Fuhrman and alleging a racist police conspiracy to plant evidence that would frame a popular black hero. In the Pratt case, Cochran focused on chief prosecution witness Julius Butler and alleged an FBI-sponsored "cointelpro" conspiracy to frame a political hero who was black. As in the Simpson case, Cochran's indictment of the law as conspiratorial and racist was the heart of the appeal that freed Pratt. Indeed, the Simpson case was itself a factor in the Pratt appeal. The climate of public opinion had been so turned against law enforcement by Cochran and other racial demagogues that all the defense had to show was that Julius Butler, the prosecution's chief witness, had had contacts with the law prior to the trial (but well after the murder). That proved sufficient to taint the verdict. In playing the race card for Simpson, Cochran also put it on the table for Geronimo Pratt.

It was this use of the race card, along with that odd comment Huey had made to me over twenty years earlier, that led me to inquire into the decision to give Geronimo Pratt a "new trial" and inevitably—since the only eyewitness to the murder, Kenneth Olsen, was also now dead—to free him.

To understand the flimsy construction of the argument that

prompted this decision and eventually freed Pratt, one has to look at the court's original rejection of an almost identical appeal Pratt made in 1980 which reviewed in detail every significant point of the case. At that time, Pratt was supported in his petition by a blue ribbon list including Congresswoman Maxine Waters, Congressman Pete McCloskey, current San Francisco mayor Willie Brown, the ACLU, the president of the California Democratic Council, and the chair of the Coalition to Free Geronimo Pratt. The central claim made by Pratt's defenders then has not changed in nearly twenty years: "A totally innocent man has languished in [prison] since mid-1972. . . . He was sent there as the result of a case which was deliberately contrived by agents of our state and federal governments. . . . [His] conviction was the result of a joint effort by state and federal governments to neutralize and discredit him because of his membership in the militant Black Panther Party."

This time the nation's press bought the argument whole. But the facts, summarized in the earlier opinion from the court record, reveal the argument to be a political fiction. Though the information that follows was easily available to reporters, none of it made its way into the reams of newsprint that described and celebrated Pratt's release.

This time, in the appellate judge's opinion and in the reportage that followed, Julius Butler was defamed as a "police informer." But, as the 1980 appellate review of the trial shows, it was not until August 10, 1969, about seven months and three weeks *after* the murder of Caroline Olsen, and more than a month after Butler had been kicked out of the Black Panther Party, that Butler made his first voluntary contact with any law enforcement official. The law enforcement official he met with was a black LAPD officer, Sergeant Duwayne Rice, whom Butler had met when the Black Panther Party made him its official "liason" with the police department. Butler gave Rice a sealed envelope. The envelope was addressed to Rice and had the words "Only to be opened in the event of my death" printed on the outside. Butler did not reveal the contents of the envelope to Rice, who placed it in a locked safe.

As it happened, Butler was observed by FBI agents giving the envelope to Rice. Three days later, on August 13, the FBI approached Butler and questioned him for the first time. He refused to answer their questions about what was in the envelope and told them nothing about its incriminating contents.

The FBI then went to Rice and attempted to get him to give up the envelope that Butler had entrusted to him. But Rice also refused. Shortly afterwards, the FBI threatened him with prosecution for obstruction of justice and withholding evidence. But even in the face of these threats, Rice held firm. He would neither open the envelope nor turn it over to the agents. It took the FBI another fourteen months, until October 20, 1970, under circumstances which I will turn to in a moment, to get police to give up the letter so that they could open it themselves and read Butler's testimony that Geronimo Pratt had killed Caroline Olsen.

When Butler's envelope was finally opened, now twenty-two months after the murder, the letter inside was for the first time read by police. It described a factional struggle in the Black Panther Party and said that the writer was fearful because of threats on his life made by Geronimo Pratt and other Panther leaders, including Roger Lewis, whose nickname was "Blue." The letter offered "the following Reason I feel the Death threat may be carried out," namely that Geronimo and the other Panthers "were Responsible for Acts of murder they carelessly Bragged about": "No. 1: Geronimo for the Killing of a White School Teacher and the wounding of Her Husband on a Tennis Court in the City of Santa Monica some time during the year of 1968.

"No. 2: Geronimo and Blue being Responsible for the Killing of Capt. Franco [a Panther leader] in January 1969 and constantly stating as a threat to me that I was just like Franco and gave them No Alternative but to 'Wash me Away.'"

This was and remains the most irrefutable incriminating evidence linking Geronimo Pratt to the tennis court murder. Yet, it is not even addressed, as an issue, in Judge Dickey's decision to accept Johnnie Cochran's newest appeal. (Nor has Cochran raised it as an issue himself.) Roger "Blue" Lewis, in a recorded prison interview with attorneys for the state, has also testified that Geronimo Pratt killed Caroline Olsen and that the murder weapon was his. Eyewitnesses placed Pratt at the murder scene and at an attempted robbery committed moments before. Neither Pratt nor his attorneys have denied that the car driven by the murderer belonged to Pratt. Notwithstanding all these material facts, no other piece of evidence is as incontrovertible and unimpeachable as the letter from Julius Butler contained in the sealed envelope.

Although Butler was accused by Cochran of being a police and FBI informant, working with law enforcement to frame Pratt, Butler did not give this envelope to the FBI or the police. He had never had a single contact with the FBI up to this point in time. Nor did he give the envelope to the Los Angeles Police Department, "racist" or otherwise. He gave it to a friend, who was a policeman, whom he trusted, and who was black.

In addition to their accusations that Butler was an informer, the defenders of Geronimo Pratt speculate that the prosecution of Pratt was the result of a "Cointelpro" conspiracy by the FBI to "neutralize" leaders of the Black Panther Party. Their references, typically vague, are meant to insinuate incriminating possibilities without having to specify concrete evidence. But they are in fact irrelevant. By the time of Pratt's trial for the murder of Caroline Olsen, the FBI's famous "cointelpro" program had been terminated by J. Edgar Hoover. Moreover, Pratt was no longer a Panther. Three months earlier, in August 1970, he had been expelled from the party by Newton. The official "declaration" of his expulsion, complete with the charge that he had threatened to assassinate Newton, was not made public by the Panthers until Pratt's arrest.

On December 4, 1970, two months after the letter was opened, Pratt was indicted by a grand jury on one count of murder, one count of assault to commit murder, and two counts of robbery. He was arraigned in April 1971 and was convicted a year later on July 28, 1972. Throughout the trial, Pratt maintained that he was in Oakland at the time of the murder attending a meeting of Panther leaders. For nearly twenty years thereafter, the surviving Panther leaders—Bobby Seale, David Hilliard, and Elaine Brown—denied Pratt's story, and left him to his fate. It was their decision to change their stories that led to the new and successful appeal of which Elaine Brown was one of the organizers. The judge's decision was based on new evidence, obtained by Cochran, that Butler had talked to law enforcement before the trial, but well after the murder. As we have seen, this evidence is irrelevant, since Butler's original accusation that Pratt was guilty of murder had been sealed in an envelope and withheld both from the FBI and the police.

In the 1980 court opinion denying Pratt's original appeal, the conspiracy theory, which Cochran later refurbished, is succinctly refuted:

> First, it is noted that Julius Butler did not give the letter to the FBI but to a trusted friend (Sergeant Rice) for safekeeping only to be opened in the event of his death. . . . Second, logic dictates that if the FBI with the aid of local law enforcement officers had targeted Pratt and intended to "neutralize" him by "framing" him for the December 18, 1968, murder of Caroline Olsen they would not have waited over fourteen months after the letter was handed to Sergeant Rice to have the contents of the sealed letter disclosed.

The circumstances under which Butler's letter was finally opened are even more damning for the conspiracy claim. The FBI agents who had observed Butler transferring the sealed envelope, walked over to Sergeant Rice after Butler left and demanded that he turn over the envelope to them. Rice refused. Then, as a precaution, he gave the envelope to yet another black police officer, Captain Edward Henry, who put it in his safe deposit box, still sealed. Rice told no one in order that the FBI would not know its location. What next transpired is best told in Sergeant Rice's own words:

> Soon after this incident [the initial demand for the letter from the FBI], the FBI threatened to indict me for obstruction of justice for refusing to turn over the letter to them. Some time the next year I was involved in a fight with a white Los Angeles police officer. Due to this fight, and other allegations against me, I became the subject of an internal police investigation. During this investigation I was questioned by the Los Angeles Police Department regarding what Julius Butler had given me and ordered to turn it over to the police department. When I refused, I was threatened with being fired for refusing a direct order.

The FBI was also pressuring Butler about his involvement in the Black Panther Party and a possible firearms violation. (Butler had purchased an illegal submachine gun in October 1968, while still a Panther, and did not want to reveal the name of the person he had given it too—another puzzling posture for a "paid informant.") In fact, the questioning of Butler by the FBI after he was observed delivering the envelope to Sergeant Rice is the principal source of the false impression successfully promoted by the Cochran team that Pratt was on the payroll as an informant for the agency. Yet, in turning down Pratt's 1980 appeal, the court noted that "It would be unnatural for the FBI not to be inquisitive about the contents of the sealed envelope once aware of its existence." In the records of the seven FBI interviews with Butler, the only mention of Pratt is "that Pratt had a machine gun was common knowledge" and that "Pratt also had a caliber .45 pistol." There is no mention of the crucial fact, still hidden in the sealed envelope, that Pratt had boasted of killing a white school teacher and wounding her husband on a Santa Monica tennis court in 1968.

In fact, an exhaustive review of the FBI records by a Deputy Attorney General of California states categorically that "Prior to [Pratt's] indictment [for the crime] in December 1970, there are no FBI documents connecting [Pratt] with the tennis court murder." Pratt's indictment was based on the evidence in the envelope sealed by Julius Butler. It was opened at Butler's request in October 1970—twenty-two months after the murder took place—because, as he put it, the FBI was "jamming" him. At the same time, the Internal Affairs investigators were also jamming Rice, who appealed to Butler to release the document.

The Cochran appeal that eventually secured Pratt's release in May 1997 added only minor details to the original 1980 appeal that was rejected. Its new element was information voluntarily turned over by prosecutors that seemed to amplify the claim that Butler had some kind of involvement with law enforcement *after* the sealed envelope was delivered to Rice. The key new claim, for example, was the existence of an "informant" card that the District Attorney's office voluntarily turned over to Cochran's team. When I asked one of the original prosecutors about this, he maintained that the "informant card" was insignificant. "When you take someone to lunch you have to provide a chit for the lunch," he explained. "'Informant' is a convenient category, and that's all there is to it." The record indicates nothing else. In the notes of the interviews that were submitted to the Court, Butler's consistent response to agents' questions is that he is no longer with the party and is not able to give them an informed opinion on the issue.

But no matter how one parses the language of these reports, or interprets "informant cards," none of the evidence brought forward by Cochran in any way alters the picture of Julius Butler's relations to law enforcement outlined above. Butler did not take his charges against Pratt to the police, but strenuously withheld them for nearly two years, until forced by the Internal Affairs investigation of Rice to give them up.

In conducting his appeal, Johnnie Cochran called Julius Butler a "conniving snake" and "liar" and "police informant." As in the Simpson case, he had great success with this line of attack before the credulous public and willing press. Los Angeles Urban League president John Mack was only one of many who swallowed the slander whole. At the time of Pratt's release, Mack told the *Los Angeles Times*: "The Geronimo Pratt case is one of the most compelling and painful examples of a political assassination on an African-American activist."

Cochran's brief for Pratt religiously followed the pattern of the Simpson defense. It was an attack on law enforcement as a racist conspiracy to "get" his client. A principal problem for Cochran's theory is the fact that Butler is black and that, until Cochran's charges, he was a responsible member of the community, a lawyer, a law-abiding citizen, and a church elder. As part of Cochran's assault on Butler's character he alleged that Butler carried a grudge, which was the result of thwarted ambition. Cochran claimed that when "Bunchy" Carter, the leader of the Los Angeles Panthers was killed in January 1969 by a rival gang headed by Ron ("Malauna") Karenga in a shoot-out at UCLA, Butler became jealous of the fact Pratt rather than he was made head of the party.

Once the story of the sealed envelope is understood, however, the Cochran hypothesis falls apart. If jealousy was Butler's motive, why didn't he go to the police immediately? Why did he hand over a sealed letter to a friend and wait nearly two years to deliver it to authorities who would indict Pratt, and then did so only under duress?

In fact, Butler did not even deposit his "insurance" letter into the safekeeping of Sergeant Rice immediately after the murder, when he was passed over for Pratt. He did so only after he was relieved of his Panther duties and only after he had been physically threatened by Pratt and his lieutenants, who were conducting a purge in the party's ranks seeking the "agents" who might have set up Bunchy Carter's murder. (One prosecutor I interviewed suggested that it was Pratt who had set up Carter. Pratt was in charge of Panther security, yet was absent when the shooting took place.) The cause of Butler's conflict with Pratt was not envy, but a growing concern about the party's direction. In his letter, Butler wrote:

> During the year of 1969 I began to notice the party changing its direction from that set forth by Huey P. Newton, and dissented with some theorys [sic] and practices of the So. Calif. Leadership. During the months of June and July 1969 I more strongly critisized[sic] these Leaders, because I felt they were carelessly, and foolishly doing things that didn't have a direction benificial [sic] for the people. I also critisized [sic] the Physical Actions or threats to party members who were attempting to sincerly [sic] impliment [sic] programs that oppressed people could Respond to.

The incident that most depressed Butler was the pistol-whipping of a seventeen-year-old Panther named Ollie Taylor, who was suspected of working for Karenga's gang. The incident led to false imprisonment and assault-with-a-deadly-weapon charges against Butler, Geronimo Pratt, and Roger Lewis. Butler's feelings about this incident were so regretful that he pled guilty to the charges in the case. Pratt was also tried but the juries were hung 10-2 and 11-1 for conviction.

According to Butler, Pratt masterminded the torture-interrogation of Taylor, holding a cocked weapon at Butler's head while ordering him to beat the suspect. Under oath at his own trial, Pratt not only denied leading the interrogation but claimed that the beating had taken place before he arrived and that he had reprimanded Butler, telling him this was not the Panther way to deal with suspects. (We know, however, from other cases, like Alex Rackley's torture in New Haven, that it was.) Pratt then said he had relieved Butler of his position in the party's security force, and placed him under "house arrest." At Pratt's trial, the victim of the beating, Ollie

Taylor, confirmed Butler's version of the events and flatly contradicted Pratt's story.

Reading Butler's testimony about the Ollie Taylor incident, I had a jolt of recognition that resolved any remaining doubt I may have had as to the integrity of Butler's account, not only of these matters, but of those regarding Pratt's guilt. For it was in examining Butler's testimony that Newton's story about the eroticism of violence in Pratt's psyche resurfaced in my mind with riveting force:

Q. Was Ollie Taylor in the room at this time?
A. Yes.
Q. Okay?
A. Ollie Taylor was sitting in the middle of the room, and I was sitting next to Ollie Taylor, and I was trying to talk to Ollie Taylor on the basis of "Give as much information about yourself to clear yourself," and Geronimo stated to me that the shit he was talking was a bunch of bullshit... I looked over and he cocked the hammer on the pistol.
Q. Where was the pistol pointed, if at all?
A. It was actually right between me and Ollie Taylor, because I was sitting side-by-side with Ollie Taylor.

   Then I noticed that Geronimo had an erection, and he stated, "If you don't move, I'll blow your head off," and he said 'Furthermore, I think maybe you're siding with him,' so he told me to slap Ollie Taylor.

   He say, "You interrogate," so I did it in the pretense of trying to—at that time I was frightened of Geronimo's behavior, very seriously frightened. I had never seen a man with an erection.

Before Butler could complete the sentence, his attorney interrupted with an objection that the course of inquiry was irrelevant. But as far as I was concerned, the sentence did not need to be finished. Here were two different figures, both intimate with Pratt, but otherwise separated by distance, status, and motivation, who remarked on the erotic charge violence gave him.

Despite the persuasive evidence of Pratt's guilt and the persuasive testimony contained in the handling of the letter that Butler was not part of a police or FBI conspiracy to frame Pratt, Johnnie Cochran prevailed in court. In granting Pratt a new trial, Dickey concluded that "this was not a strong case for the prosecution without the testimony of [Julius] Butler," and that it was reasonably probable that Pratt could have obtained a different result "in the entire absence of Butler's testimony," or had the prosecution revealed Butler's contacts with law enforcement. His opinion did not go into any detail by way of explaining how these contacts would or should have affected the verdict, given the testimony of the sealed envelope.

Reading Dickey's opinion is a depressing experience for anyone concerned about American justice. The salient reason cited by Judge Dickey for overturning the original verdict is that the prosecution concealed the "fact" that "[Butler] had been, for at least three years before the trial, providing information about the Black Panther Party and individuals associated with it to law enforcement agencies on a confidential basis."

The statement, as we have seen and as court records show, is false and misleading. Julius Butler had no contact with the FBI or law enforcement prior to his delivery of the sealed letter to Sergeant Rice, seven months after the murder and less than two years before the trial. The letter's identification of Geronimo Pratt as the killer of Caroline Olsen was available to the jury and was a centerpiece of the court proceeding, a fact which is not even addressed in Dickey's opinion—nor is the whole history of Butler's withholding of the incriminating document despite efforts by the FBI and the police to pry it from him. These would seem to establish beyond any reasonable doubt that Julius Butler was not an informant and was not cooperating with the FBI, the police, or the prosecutors of Geronimo Pratt, prior to Pratt's arraignment for the murder. Moreover, Butler's testimony at the trial was entirely consistent with the information contained in the incriminating letter and with his behavior throughout the case.

Why hasn't justice prevailed in this matter? Why is a clearly guilty individual free? The answer lies in the climate of the times, in which the testimonies of officers of the law have become more readily impeachable than the testimony of criminals. As in the O. J. Simpson trial, the appeals process in the Pratt case has been turned by Johnnie Cochran into a class action libel against the FBI, the police, the prosecution, and its chief witness. And as in the Simpson case, Johnnie Cochran's fictional melodrama has defeated the politically incorrect truth.*

---

* This account of the case of Geronimo Pratt was written in 1997. Two years later, another appeal for a new trial, this time by prosecutors, was rejected by the court. Geronimo Pratt was set free.

IV

Progressive Education

I I

Academic Politics

GRADUATION CEREMONIES on America's college campuses have become occasions to reflect on the near total domination of the left over the institutions of higher learning, a politicization of academic life unprecedented in the history of our democracy. Typical of one recent graduation cycle was the ceremony at the University of Michigan, whose invited speaker was racial extremist Mamphela Ramphele, a leader of South Africa's far left "black consciousness" movement. The four previous graduations at Michigan featured First Lady Hillary Clinton, political ally and friend of Mrs. Clinton, Marian Wright Edelman, liberal cartoonist Cathy Guisewite, and former Spelman College president and veteran of the communist left Johnetta Cole. By contrast, notable conservatives like former Education Secretary William Bennett, Nobel Laureate Milton Friedman, authors Tom Clancy and William F. Buckley, and Supreme Court Justices Antonin Scalia and Clarence Thomas were passed over as potential orators not only by Michigan but by all three thousand-plus colleges and universities across the land.

Any political bias revealed in the selection of commencement speakers is overshadowed, however, by the political bias evident in university hiring practices during the school year itself. A *Wall Street Journal* article by Vincent Carroll recently described the situation at the University of Colorado, where the number of registered Democrats on the faculty exceeded the registered Republicans by thirty-one to one. There was not a single Republican or conservative in the English, psychology, journalism, philosophy, women's studies, ethnic studies, and lesbian and gay studies departments. This is in a state where registered Republicans outnumber Democrats by more than one hundred thousand and have elected six of eight members of the Colorado congressional delegation.

On the basis of personal experience I can attest that this situation is fairly typical of colleges across the United States. In the last few years, I have spoken on over one hundred college campuses in every corner of the country—north, south, east, and west. I have spoken before audiences at state schools and private schools, religious schools and state institutions, technical schools and liberal arts colleges—rural and urban, small and large. At every single one of them, without exception, I have found that professors who are conservative in their outlook constitute a mere handful on any given liberal arts campus. They are more isolated, more politically excluded, more intimidated, and more restricted in their opportunities for scholarly advancement and political expression than communist and pro-Soviet professors were in the McCarthy period, during the height of the Cold War.

Of the colleges where I have appeared, only four invited me officially. By contrast, communists like Angela Davis, and racial extremists like Khalid Muhammad and Kwame Ture, are regularly asked to speak by university administrators and student governments—and paid handsome sums to do so. In 1998, Ms. Davis, whose speaking fee is twenty thousand dollars, was the featured official speaker at the University of Chicago's Martin Luther King Day commemorations. Davis is fawned on by administrators and faculty alike at her appearances, which are more like regal visits. In 1998, she was also a featured speaker at Brandeis, a campus to which the conservative former United Nations Ambassador Jeane Kirkpatrick had been officially invited but then dis-invited after leftists protested her scheduled appearance. Conservative figures like myself, by contrast, have to rely on small conservative student groups for invitations and off-campus conservative organizations for expenses. Wherever I go, I make it a point to ask the students who invite me how many conservative professors are available to be their official campus advisors and sponsors. The answer invariably is: two or three. That is, two or three out of the entire faculty who are willing to identify themselves openly as conservatives.

This deplorable situation did not happen by accident. It is the result of a McCarthyism operating inside these academic institutions, fueled by the atmosphere of "political correctness" that has enveloped the academy since the ascension of the tenured left. The hegemony of this left has resulted in politicized hiring practices, systematic exclusion of dissenting voices, and an atmosphere of political intimidation to a degree seen only in countries ruled by communist or fascist or theocratic dictatorships. In America, however, the state is not the enforcer of political orthodoxy. It is leftist faculty members and pliant administrators who are responsible for this state of affairs.

Because intellectual censorship is exercised at the faculty level, it is carried out with an efficiency that an outsider like Senator McCarthy could never have achieved. The prevailing intellectual environment on American campuses resulting from this situation has been chillingly described by the literary critic Harold Bloom. In an interview recorded by Mark Edmundson in *Trotsky Without Orchids*, Bloom described faculty politics as "Stalinism without Stalin. . . . All of the traits of the Stalinists in the 1930s and 1940s are being repeated . . . in the universities in the 1990s."

Letters responding to the *Wall Street Journal* article on the situation at the University of Colorado put flesh on Bloom's observations. One letter writer was a professor who also served as a faculty advisor to College Republicans at Cal Poly in San Luis Obispo. "Republican faculty members operate on a 'don't ask, don't tell' basis to the best of our ability," she wrote. "At official faculty meetings, Democratic fund-raising requests, political buttons, bumper stickers and petitions are very publicly circulated, putting non-tenured faculty in a very difficult position." After this professor was "outed," a department colleague told her "we would never have hired you if we'd known you were a Republican."

This unconscionable situation has been challenged in a legal case against the University of California School of Journalism at Berkeley. The plaintiff in the case is Michael Savage, a political conservative who is also the premier radio talk show host in the San Francisco Bay Area. Savage is a former academic with a doctorate, two masters and eighteen published works to his credit. In 1997, the journalism school began a search for a new dean and printed an advertisement in the *New York Times* soliciting applications for the position. The school emphasized that it was interested in radio and television journalists particularly. Savage applied. Despite his impressive qualifications, however, he was swiftly informed by the chairman of the search committee, Professor Troy Duster, that he would not even be interviewed for the job. Troy Duster is an old acquaintance of mine, a Berkeley leftist who has not had significant second thoughts about his radical views.

The applicant who was eventually selected for the new deanship was Orville Schell, another Berkeley radical, who would have known Duster and the other leftists on the search committee for thirty years. Schell has no doctorate, and although he has written several books on China and authored some op-ed pieces, is not a working journalist. His main occupation is a pig farm he owns in Bolinas, an upscale community just north of San Francisco. Orville's real credential for the Berkeley deanship was that he had the same radical politics as Troy Duster and the faculty powers who control the journalism school.

Michael Savage was made aware of these connections when he was informed how Schell was chosen. The retiring dean of the school had called Schell, who was a friend, to ask his advice as to whom they might pick to be the new dean. Schell volunteered himself. In short, the placement of the *New York Times* ad was little more than a pro forma exercise to justify the decision—already made—to hire a political comrade for the position.

This is not a small matter. According to a recent poll conducted by the Freedom Forum, a liberal foundation in Tennessee, 89 percent of American political journalists covering Washington politics voted for Bill Clinton, and only 7 percent identified themselves as conservatives. The journalism profession in America has undergone a sea change in recent years. Previously, beat reporters were just that, reporters. They often did not have undergraduate college degrees, not to mention degrees from journalism schools. But now they do, and notoriously they write editorial content into their reporting. There is a direct connection between the leftist control of journalism schools like Berkeley and the leftward bias in the national media.

Michael Savage decided to fight the political octopus he encountered at Berkeley rather than meekly yield to its superior power. He turned to the Individual Rights Foundation (IRF), a public interest law group I created, for help. The legal director of the IRF, Patrick Manshardt, has filed suit against the Regents of the University of California and also against Professor Troy Duster, both as an individual and in his capacity as chairman of the search committee. In other words, the IRF intends to hold the radicals directly accountable for their assault on the very soul of the American university and the integrity of the Fourth Estate.

The IRF case is based on two contentions. The first is that this political selection of a University of California dean constitutes political patronage, which is illegal under the labor laws of the state of California. The second is that requiring a political litmus test for applicants for a deanship is a violation of Michael Savage's First Amendment rights, which hold that one may not be excluded from public employment based on political affiliation.

The Michael Savage case illuminates the ongoing political subversion of the institutions of higher learning in America. In today's poisoned academic atmosphere, Afrocentric racists can expound theories of blood destiny, queer theorists can promote the "revolutionary" idea of pursuing promiscuous sex in public places while an epidemic rages, and both can do so with the resources, imprimatur, and encouragement of the university itself. Intellectual charlatans and political extremists can control entire departments and liberal arts faculties. But conservative scholars are treated as intellectual pariahs and forced to seek refuge in "think tanks" outside the university, and generally are denied access to any but conservative audiences.

The politicization of the university and the debasement of scholarship are a national tragedy of incalculable dimensions. If the situation is to be remedied, it can only be by a restoration of the integrity of these institutions parallel in magnitude and scope.

12

Postmodern Professors

W HEN THE IMPEACHMENT OF BILL CLINTON ran out of
gas, there was consolation in the fact that for the nation much of the damage was reparable and many of the
scars would be readily healed. As a new election cycle rolled into
view, Bill Clinton, along with his seductions and prevarications,
would in due course be gone. As the impeachment ended, fresh
faces became the focus of public attention. There was renewed respect for the privacy rights of public figures, and new skepticism
about the Special Prosecutor Law that liberals contrived as a weapon
against conservatives and conservatives turned into a weapon against
liberals, and then against themselves.

But one institution, whose corruptions thrust it to the fore in
the presidential crisis, would not be so easy to mend. This was the
American university, which in the midst of the presidential battle
volunteered a contingent of scholars to serve a partisan cause.

As the House Judiciary Committee was gearing up for its impeachment inquiry in October 1998, a full-page political ad appeared
in the *New York Times*, entitled "Historians In Defense of the Constitution." The historians declared that in their professional judg-

ment there was no constitutional basis for impeaching the president, and to do so would undermine the constitutional order. The historians' statement was eagerly seized on by the president's congressional defenders and deployed as a weapon against his congressional accusers. In the none-too-meticulous hands of these political pols, the signers became four hundred "constitutional experts" who had weighed in with an authoritative constitutional judgment that exposed the Republicans' attempt at a "coup d'etat." One of the three organizers of the statement, Professor Sean Wilentz, even appeared before the House Judiciary Committee to warn the impeachers that "history will hunt you down" for betraying the nation. On the day his Senate trial began, the president himself referred reporters to the battalion of "constitutional experts" who had gone on record to assert that under the law of the land he should not have been impeached.

Those who signed the statement, however, are not constitutional experts at all. One of them, Julian Bond, is not even a historian, though two universities—Maryland and Virginia—have appointed him a "professor of history." Currently head of the NAACP, Bond is a veteran politician with a failed career whose university posts can only be understood as political appointments for past service. Another signer, Henry Louis Gates, is not a historian, but a talented essayist and professor of literature. A third, Orlando Patterson, is a first-rate sociologist, but not a historian. Perhaps the three constitute an affirmative-action cohort to increase the African-American presence and reassure everyone that the signers were suitably diverse. All three, of course, are men of the left.

Sean Wilentz is himself a *Dissent* socialist, whose expertise is social, not political, history, though his scholarship does cover the period of the American founding. A second organizer, C. Vann Woodward, is a distinguished historian of nineteenth- and twentieth-century America, but also not specifically a historian of the Constitution. The third, Arthur Schlesinger Jr., is a partisan Democrat who has written adoring books on Andrew Jackson, Franklin Roosevelt, and the Kennedy brothers, as well as a book on the presidency.

These three were, if anything, more qualified than almost all the other "historians in defense of the constitution." With a handful of exceptions like Pauline Maier, who had indeed studied and written about the American founding, and Clinton partisan Garry Wills, the others on the list had even fewer credentials than the organizers to pronounce on these matters. Todd Gitlin, for example, is a professor of sociology and cultural studies, whose only contribution to historical knowledge is a tendentious book justifying the 1960s from the perspective of a former president of Students for a Democratic Society. Jon Weiner is a writer for the *Nation* whose major publication is a book on John Lennon's FBI file. Michael Kazin is another *Nation* leftist whose work as a historian is on American populism. John Judis is a *New Republic* editor and man of the left who wrote a biography of William Buckley and a book on twentieth-century conservatives. Jeffrey Herf's expertise is modern German history; Robert Dallek and Bruce Kuklick are twentieth century diplomatic historians, who have also written books on Lyndon Johnson and the occupation of Germany. Maurice Isserman is also a *Nation* regular and a historian of the twentieth-century American left.

Another signer, Ellen Du Bois, can be taken as typical of a large cohort of what have become the thoroughly politicized humanities. She is a professor of women's history at UCLA and a militant feminist. She is joined as a signer by other zealots whose academic work has been the elaboration of feminist themes. These include Gerda Lerner, Linda Gordon, Ruth Rosen, Sara Evans, Christine Stansell (Wilentz's wife), and Alice Kessler-Harris. Two months after the *Times* ad appeared, while the House of Representatives was pursuing its impeachment vote, a notice was posted on the Internet announcing that Du Bois would be a speaker (along with two other well-known leftists) at a "Reed College Symposium on the Joy of Struggle." The symposium was a presentation of the Reed College Multiculturalism Center and was co-sponsored by the Feminist Union, the Queer Alliance, Earth First, Amnesty at Reed, the Latino/a Student Association, and the Reed student activities office.

To be sure, not all the signers were ideologues, but the statement they signed reflects the long-standing political corruption of the American academy, and was itself a political deception. By massing four hundred historians "in defense of the Constitution," the organizers implied that these well-known liberal and left-wing academics were scholarly experts defending the document's original intent. Since when, however, had liberals and leftists become defenders of the doctrine of original intent? Were any of the signers on record as opposing the loose constructionism of the Warren Court? Were any of the scholars exercised when the Brennan majority inserted a nonexistent "right of privacy" into the Constitution to justify its decision in *Roe v. Wade*? Were any of them outspoken defenders of Judge Robert Bork—the leading theorist of "original intent"—when a coalition of political vigilantes set out to destroy his nomination to the Supreme Court, even soliciting his video store purchases to see if he had rented x-rated films? Not only was the answer to all these questions negative, but dozens of the same historians, including organizers Arthur Schlesinger Jr. and Sean Wilentz, were "veterans of the politicized misuse of history" (as Ramesh Ponnuru put it in a *National Review* article on the episode), having previously signed a tendentious "historians brief" to the Supreme Court supporting abortion.

Concern for the original intent of the Constitution apparently enters these academic hearts only when it can be deployed against Republicans and conservatives. This probably explained why the office address listed at the bottom of the historians' statement was the Washington address of People for the American Way, a national lobby for the political left.

Partisan political pronouncements by groups invoking the authority of a profession are treacherous exercises. They misrepresent what scholarship can do, such as deciding questions that are inherently controversial. More importantly, they cast a chill on academic discourse by suggesting there is a party line for the historical profession. When Jesse Lemisch, a notable left-wing historian, tried to organize a counter-statement favoring impeachment (over Clinton's wag-the-dog policy in the Gulf), he received vicious e-mails from his colleagues.

The kind of politicization reflected in these episodes is, in fact, a fairly recent development in academic life. Its origin can be traced to a famous battle at the annual meeting of the American Historical Association (AHA) in 1969. At that meeting, a "radical caucus" led by Staughton Lynd and Arthur Waskow attempted to have the organization pass an official resolution calling for American withdrawal from the Vietnam War and an end to the "repression" of the Black Panther Party. Opposition to the resolution was led by radical historian Eugene Genovese and by liberal historian H. Stuart Hughes. Four years earlier, Genovese had become a national cause celebre when he publicly declared his support for the Communist Vietcong. He nonetheless opposed the radical call for such a resolution as a "totalitarian" threat to the profession and to the intellectual standards on which it is based. Hughes, who had been a peace candidate for Congress, joined in asserting that any anti-war resolution would "politicize" the AHA and urging the members to reject it.

Hughes and Genovese narrowly won the battle, but eventually lost the war. The AHA joined other professional academic associations in becoming organizations controlled by the political left. A recent memoir by a distinguished academic scholar and admistrator, Alvin Kernan, sums up the developments this way: "But while Marxism may have failed in Moscow, class conflict thrived on the American campus, where gender, race, and class politics increasingly drove academic debate. If the 1970s had been the time of radical theories, then the 1980s were the time when politics began increasingly to replace professionalism in the universities. Government lent powerful reinforcement to the new concept of university regulations and funding that favored social justice over knowledge or merit. Women and minorities could now openly use their subjects to argue for the purposes of their cause."*

The politicization has gone so far that a few years ago the philosopher Richard Rorty smugly applauded the fact that "The power base of the left in America is now in the universities since the trade unions have largely been killed off." As if to confirm this claim, a *Nation* editorial written by one of the signers of the historians' statement, boasted that "three members of the *Nation* family" have just been elected to head three powerful professional associations—the American Historical Association, the Organization of American Historians (OAH) and the Modern Language Association (MLA)—with a combined membership of fifty-four thousand academics.†

The president-elect of the AHA, Columbia professor Eric Foner, is indeed the scion of a family of well-known American communists, a die-hard proponent of the "innocence" of the Rosenberg spies, a sponsor of university events honoring Communist Party stalwarts Angela Davis and Herbert Aptheker, a lifelong member of the radical left and recently even an organizer of the secretaries' union at Columbia with an eye towards re-forging a 1930s-style Popular Front between radical intellectuals and organized labor. David Montgomery, the new president of the OAH, is described in the *Nation* as "a factory worker, union organizer and Communist militant in St. Paul in the Fifties. . . . Montgomery's ties to labor remain strong: He was active in the Yale clerical workers' strike and

---

* Alvin Kernan, *In Plato's Cave* (New Haven, Conn.: Yale University Press, 1999), 247.

† Jon Weiner, "Scholars on the Left, " *Nation*, February 1, 1999.

other campus and union struggles." Edward Said, the new president of the MLA, is a former member of the Palestine Liberation Organization (PLO) governing council and was the most prominent apologist in America for PLO terrorism until he fell out with Yassir Arafat over the Oslo peace accords, which Said regards as a "sellout" to Israeli imperialists.

That is the bad news. The good news is more modest. The historians' statement was not an official resolution of either the AHA or the OAH, and neither Montgomery nor Eric Foner signed it. When asked, Foner said he did not think it was appropriate for him to do so because of his position as head of an organization representing fifteen thousand members, many of whom might not agree with its sentiments. That was the right idea, but unfortunately he was unable to extend it to the issue at hand. Thus he did not think the volatile political statement by four hundred professors, invoking the authority of their profession, was itself inappropriate, even though almost all of them lacked competence in the subject.

The deeper problem revealed by this episode is the serious absence of intellectual diversity in university faculties. Such diversity would provide a check on the hubris of academic activists like Wilentz and his co-signers. The fact is that leftists in the university, through decades of political hiring and promotion, and through systematic intellectual intimidation, have virtually driven conservative thought from the halls of academe.

A call made to one of the handful of known conservatives allowed to teach a humanities subject at Princeton confirmed the following suspicion: in Sean Wilentz's history department not a single conservative can be found among its fifty-six faculty members. If Wilentz believes in the original intent of the Constitution to create a pluralistic society, that lack of diversity is something for Professor Wilentz to be more concerned about than the fact that House Republicans differ with his interpretation of constitutional issues.

As it happens, the hero of the lost battle for scholarly neutrality, Eugene Genovese, has formed a new organization, the American Historical Society, to take politics out of the profession. Already one thousand historians have joined. On the other hand, several signers of the historians' statement are already charter members, including Wilentz himself. If Genovese's organization is serious, it will eventually have to chasten politicians like Sean Wilentz and promote a scholarly distance from partisan line-ups. Even more importantly, it will have to press for the systematic hiring of professors with under-represented conservative viewpoints. This is a daunting task, but without such a commitment to intellectual diversity, the profession can hardly hope to restore its damaged credibility.

13

The Loafing Class

IGHER EDUCATION TODAY is a good news-bad news story. The good news is that a university degree can provide a pass to all to the prodigious bounties of the American economy. The bad news is that the price of the pass can be the equivalent of a Ferrari, putting the average student into hock for a good chunk of his or her working life. As the price tag of a degree has gone up, moreover, the quality of the educational product has declined in a parallel arc. At universities that charge more than one hundred thousand dollars for a Bachelor of Arts degree, professors of English have taken to teaching courses on racism and imperialism, instead of writing and literature. Meanwhile, sociologists now discourse on the "social construction" of scientific truths of which they are as ignorant as their students. In liberal arts and social science courses generally, the discredited doctrines of Marx and his communist disciples abound. Meanwhile, under the gale of real world economic forces, the university is everywhere in the process of restructuring and redefining itself. Credentialed professors are more and more inaccessible to students, as more and more teaching chores are being transferred to less qualified graduate assistants whose labor cost is smaller. New corporate colleges and technical schools have become an educational growth industry in response to the declining significance of the academic degree.

The source of these developments is obviously complex, but a recent article in the prestigious academic journal *Social Text* offers testimony worth pondering. Couched as a personal memoir and written by one of the magazine's principal editors, "The Last Good Job in America" is a self-portrait of today's liberal arts professor as slacker-in-residence. Its author, Stanley Aronowitz, is one of the leading figures of the academic left. Aronowitz was a labor organizer in the 1960s who received his doctorate from a college extension program and was recruited to the Graduate Center of City University of New York (CUNY) by one of his 1960s comrades already on the faculty.

City University is New York's publicly-funded higher-education opportunity for minorities and children of the working classes. Like other over-burdened educational institutions, it is in the process of academic "downsizing," replacing full professors like Aronowitz with less qualified and lower paid teaching assistants in an attempt to match revenues with costs. Twenty years ago, CUNY hired Aronowitz "because they believed I was a labor sociologist." In fact, as he admits in *Social Text*, this was just a scam: "First and foremost I'm a political intellectual. . . . [I] don't follow the . . . methodological rules of the discipline." After being hired as a sociologist, Aronowitz enrolled in the hottest new academic fad and created the Center for Cultural Studies to escape the rigors of his professional discipline. "Cultural Studies" provided him with a broad umbrella under which to pursue his marxist politics and pass them on to his unsuspecting students.

As an editor of the fashionable left-wing journal *Social Text* and head of the Center for Cultural Studies, Aronowitz is more than just a professor. He is an academic star with a six-figure salary and a publishing resume to match. In today's politicized university, it is thoroughly in keeping with Aronowitz's elevated academic status that his chef d'oeuvre is a book called *Science As Power*, whose core thesis is the Stalinist proposition that science is an instrument of the ruling class. Of Aronowitz's book, a reviewer for the *Times Literary Supplement* said: "If the author knows much about the content or enterprise of science, he keeps the knowledge well hidden."

Non-leftist readers of Aronowitz could hardly have been surprised last year when he and his fellow editors at *Social Text* were snookered by Alan Sokal. Sokal, a physicist, submitted a phony paper on quantum mechanics and postmodernism to demonstrate that the magazine would publish pure nonsense about science if the nonsense was politically correct. Although the Sokal article was an international scandal,* Aronowitz's own university seems not to have noticed that its professor had been exposed as an intellectual fraud or that, by his own admission, he has long since abandoned the discipline that he was hired to teach. Shortly after the publication of "The Last Good Job in America," Aronowitz was made "*Distinguished* Professor of Sociology" at CUNY.

The "last good job in America" turns out to be the job that Stanley Aronowitz has created for himself at the expense of New York taxpayers and the economically disadvantaged minorities who make up the CUNY student body: "What I enjoy most is the ability to procrastinate and control my own work-time, especially its pace: taking a walk in the middle of the day, reading between the writing, listening to a CD or tape anytime I want, calling up a friend for a chat." It turns out that Aronowitz teaches only one two-hour course a week. This is a seminar—no surprise here—in Marxism. On Mondays and Wednesdays, Aronowitz does not even leave his house.

During the week of non-activity that his *Social Text* article re-

---

* The article and subsequent controversy are reported in Alan Sokal and Jean Bricmont, *Fashionable Nonsense: Postmodern Intellectuals' Abuse of Science* (New York: St. Martin's Press, 1998).

views, Monday and Wednesday are the days devoted to writing a piece for the *Nation* on "the future of the left," and of course the article for *Social Text* on what a good job he has—and the pay is not too bad either. Of course, Aronowitz discloses this coyly, positioning himself as a social victim: "I earn more by some five thousand dollars a year than an auto worker who puts in a sixty-hour week." The last time I checked, an auto worker made forty dollars an hour, which factors out to twenty-four hundred dollars a week (not including overtime) or over 120,000 dollars a year—and one can be sure the auto worker does not make cars only two hours a week for only nine months out of the year.

For nearly three decades, Aronowitz and other academic leftists have been escaping the reality of their failed revolution in America's streets during the 1960s by colonizing the American university, subverting and debasing its curriculum. In the course of this self-absorbed intellectual destruction, they have abused the educational aspirations of unsuspecting students, poor and well-fed alike. And even while this equal opportunity exploitation goes on, they never lose the ability to see themselves as the victims of vast conspiracies of the political right: "We know that the charges against us—that university teaching is a scam, that much research is not 'useful,' that scholarship is hopelessly privileged—emanate from a Right that wants us to put our noses to the grindstone just like everybody else." And why not?

The Gucci marxists of the tenured left are certainly not lacking in chutzpah. The conclusion to Aronowitz's memoir is, naturally, a call to arms, but phrased in the form of a reproof to his comrades for not advancing their struggle militantly enough: "We have not celebrated the idea of *thinking* as a full-time activity and the importance of producing what the system terms 'useless' knowledge. Most of all, we have not conducted a struggle for universalizing the self-managed time some of us still enjoy." Loafers of the world unite!

14

Campus Brown Shirts

T HE LOUISIANA DEMAGOGUE HUEY LONG was once asked whether he thought fascism could ever come to America. His answer was "Yeah, but it'll come calling itself anti-fascism." America is not close to such a future, but it is hard not to recall Huey Long's observation in connection with an episode that occurred recently at Columbia University.

The occasion for this episode was a conference at Columbia organized by a conservative group called Accuracy in Academia. The title of the conference was "A Place at the Table: Conservative Ideas in Higher Education," and its purpose was to highlight the lack of intellectual diversity in the politicized academic environment. Among the announced speakers were two university trustees, Ward Connerly and Candace DeRussy, and the author Dinesh D'Souza, whose book *Illiberal Education* was one of the first to draw attention to political correctness in academic life.

The ceremonies were scheduled to begin with a Friday evening dinner, addressed by Connerly, who is currently heading a national civil rights campaign to end racial preferences. Connerly was coming off an electoral victory in Washington, which had become the second state after California to ban such preferences. According to Accuracy in Academia president Dan Flynn, who wrote a report on the event, a hundred and forty students and professors attended the dinner, which was held in the East Room of Columbia's Faculty House.

These were not the only people in attendance, however. The mere presence of someone like Ward Connerly, expressing ideas the campus left does not want to hear, was enough to rouse a hundred raucous radicals into action at the conference site. They threw up a picket line outside the dinner and hurled obscenities and racial epithets at those entering Faculty House. Bear in mind that these same students, like Columbia itself, had previously welcomed such rabid anti-Semites and racial demagogues as Nation of Islam spokesman Khalid Muhammad and rap star Professor Griff, and that Columbia's history department had honored unrepentant communists like Herbert Aptheker and Angela Davis.

Columbia not only welcomes such race-haters, but pays them handsomely out of student funds to propagate their bigotry. By contrast, the conservative conference organized by Accuracy in Academia featured no rabble rousers, no hate-agendas, and actually *paid* the university a fee of eleven thousand dollars to hold its event on campus and showcase Connerly speaking in behalf of a single standard for all Americans and against racism in all its manifestations.

In a healthy academic environment, a university administration might be expected to respond to the outrage that took place at Columbia by disciplining the students who abused the free speech privileges of others, who hurled racial epithets at those they disagreed with, and who posed a threat to public safety. But these days such thoughts are far from the minds of university administrators whose profiles, as Peter Collier once observed, are a cross between Saul Alinsky and Neville Chamberlain.

In fact, the decision Columbia president George Rupp made

the first night of the conference was exactly the opposite. Rupp is the chairman of the Association of American Universities, and his solution to the problem created by the demonstrators was to ban those students who had registered for the conference and whose only offense was their desire to hear the speakers, from attending the sessions the following day. As security guards were placed at the entrance to Columbia's Faculty House, its director, John Hogan, piously explained that the action was wholly consistent with free speech because only the audience and not the speakers were subject to the order. It was a nice distinction: you can speak, but nobody will be allowed to listen.

With their event effectively closed down by the university, the organizers decided to move the conference to neighboring Morningside Park. But the Ivy League mob followed them. The first speaker of the day, Dinesh D'Souza, was shouted down by chants of "Ha! Ha! You're Outside/We Don't Want Your Racist Lies." (It was a pure libel against D'Souza, an Indian immigrant.) Demonstrators held up signs that said ACCESS DENIED, WE WIN: RACISTS NOT ALLOWED AT COLUMBIA and THERE'S NO PLACE AT THE TABLE FOR HATE, which shows just how out of touch the protesters were with their own reality. But then, so was the Columbia administration. An official brochure tells visitors that "Columbia University prides itself on being a community committed to free and open discourse and to tolerance of differing views." Orwell could not have constructed it better.

A distressing aspect of the Columbia incident was the absence of almost any public commentary on the event from civil libertarians, from public officials, or from the nation's press. Imagine the uproar if Randall Terry and his Operation Rescue squads had surrounded a campus abortion clinic, blocked its entrance, and attempted to harass and intimidate those who entered, and the President of an Ivy League school had ordered his security forces to block the entrance to the clinic, while a college official explained that no one was interfering with anyone's right to perform an abortion, just barring those who wanted one from entering.

Judging by the results of their actions, the demonstrators knew what they were doing. The attack was intended to strike fear into the hearts of the student community, and to further marginalize the ideas of conservatives in the academic world. These goals were effectively accomplished. One student who registered for the event, but decided not to attend, explained to the organizers that "I did not attend the conference for a number of reasons, the most important being that I did not feel it would be good for my academic future and safety."

Elsewhere, similar intimidations have produced similar results. Among the public at large, those who support the civil rights initiatives that Ward Connerly has promoted are in the overwhelming majority, but support for Connerly's initiatives on college campuses has been muffled. While 55 percent of Californians voted to end racial preferences in the state two years ago, the faculty Senate of the University of California at Berkeley lined up 152-2 in support of such discrimination. Does anyone imagine that fear of collegial ostracism did not play a large role in this otherwise unfathomable ratio?

The incipient fascism that erupted at Columbia did not spring *de novo* from the heads of a few campus idiots. It is a logical consequence of decades of university pandering to intellectual terrorists and campus criminals who regularly assault property, persons, and reputations, and almost always get what they want. In the last thirty years, under the pressures of the left, campuses have moved a long way down the road of ends justifying means. If the cause is perceived to be just, it is all right to ruin reputations with loose charges of racism or sexual harassment or even rape to achieve it. If the goal is racial equality, it is all right to discriminate. If "progressive" ideas are the wave of the future, it's okay to silence anyone who disagrees.

This brown-shirt activism is supported intellectually by the spread of anti-liberal ideas in university curricula. The most powerful intellectual influences in the academy derive from the intellectual traditions of marxism and European fascism. Identity politics, coupled with fashionable Nietzschean clichés about the will to power, form the core of current ideological fashions among campus radicals. But what are these postmodernist and multicultural trends but the fascist politics of the *Volk* that swept German and Italian universities in the 1930s? The intellectual left of the 1990s owes more to Mussolini than to Marx.

A schism has even developed within the left over these issues—between the identity racialists and "postmodern" irrationalists on the one hand, and an older generation of "neo-Enlightenment" leftists who have been bravely defending class analysis and—mirable dictu—reason itself. The most prominent of these critics are Alan Sokal, Todd Gitlin, Eric Hobsbawm, and Michael Tomasky. They are a beleaguered force, balding Cassandras crying in the wilderness amidst the fiercer and more numerous passions of the radical young. In the ideological war zone, as the Columbia outrage shows, the new identity politics rules. And identity politics, based on racial and gender categories, and on nihilistic assumptions that power is all, culminate in a posture in which the rules of civility and democratic process, not to mention the principles of academic freedom, are dismissed as so much social mystification. Objectivity, reason, color-neutrality, and truth are illusions that obstruct the coming social redemption. This is the stuff that totalitarian dreams are made of.

In an ironic way, and despite the continental provenance of much of its worldview, identity radicalism also incorporates a profound element of American mischief. At its heart is an American individualism—solipsistic, arrogant, community-be-damned, *le monde c'est moi*—run amok. The intellectual currents of identity politics began to blossom during the "Me Decade" of the 1970s, so it should hardly be surprising if they give expression to the desires of a con-

quering, devouring American Ego unrestrained by any social contract. Me, me, my, my—*my* rights, *my* pain, *my* rage *uber alles*.

So blinded are these campus bands of the self-righteous and the
self-absorbed, they do not even notice the cognitive dissonance
when a bunch of over-privileged, under-disciplined white guys hurl
racial epithets at a Ward Connerly—in origin a poor black from
the segregated South. And all in the name of promoting social
justice for people of color. Huey Long would have approved;
George Orwell would have understood.

15

I, Rigoberta Menchu, Liar

THE STORY OF RIGOBERTA MENCHU, a Quiche Mayan from Guatemala, whose autobiography catapulted her to international fame, won her the Nobel peace prize, and made her an international emblem of the dispossessed indigenous peoples of the western hemisphere and their oppression by European conquerors, has now been exposed as a political fraud, a tissue of lies, one of the greatest academic hoaxes of the twentieth century.

During the last decade, Rigoberta Menchu had become a leading icon of university culture. In one of the more celebrated "breakthroughs" of the multicultural left, a demonstration of left-wing faculty and students at Stanford University led by the Reverend Jesse Jackson had chanted "Hey, hey, ho, ho, western culture's got to go!" The target of the chant was Stanford's required curriculum in Western Civilization. University officials quickly caved before the demonstrators, and the course title was changed simply to "CIV," removing the offensive identification with the West. Works by "Third World" (mainly marxist) authors previously "excluded" were now introduced into the canon of great books as required reading. Chief among these was an autobiography by an indigenous Guatemalan and sometime revolutionary, *I, Rigoberta Menchu*, which now took its place beside Aristotle, Dante, and Shakespeare as the Stanford student's introduction to the world.

Published in 1982, *I, Rigoberta Menchu*, was actually written by a French leftist, Elisabeth Burgos-Debray, wife of the Marxist, Regis Debray, who provided the *foco* strategy for Che Guevara's failed effort to foment a guerilla war in Bolivia in the 1960s. The idea of the *foco* was that urban intellectuals could insert a military front inside a system of social oppression and provide the catalyst for revolutionary change. Debray's misguided theory got Guevara and an undetermined number of Bolivian peasants killed, and is at the root of the tragedies that overwhelmed Rigoberta Menchu and her family which are (falsely) chronicled in *I, Rigoberta Menchu*.

As recounted in this autobiography, the story of Rigoberta Menchu is the stuff of classic marxist myth. The Menchus were a poor Mayan family living on the margins of a country from which they had been dispossessed by Spanish conquistadors whose descendants, known as *ladinos*, tried to drive the Menchus and other Indian peasants off unclaimed land they cultivated. As she tells her story, Rigoberta was illiterate and was denied an education by her peasant father, Vicente. He refused to send her to school because he needed her to work in the fields and because he was afraid that the school would turn his daughter against him. So poor was the Menchu family because of their lack of land that Rigoberta had to watch her younger brother die of starvation. Meanwhile, her father was engaged in a heroic but frustrating battle with the *ladino* masters of the land for a plot to cultivate. Finally, Vicente organized a resistance movement called the Committee for Campesino Unity to advance the land claims of the *indigenas* against the *ladino* masters. Rigoberta became a political organizer, too.

Enter the Guevara-Debrayist guerrilla *foco*. The indigenous resistance movement organized by Rigoberta's peasant father linked up with an armed revolutionary force—the Guerrilla Army of the

Poor (ERG). Now the peasants had a fighting chance. But the *ladino* descendants of the conquistadors called on the brutal Guatemalan security forces to crush the rebellion and preserve the status quo of social injustice. Vicente Menchu was killed, and the surviving family was forced to watch Rigoberta's brother burned alive. Rigoberta's mother was raped and also killed.

As told by Rigoberta, the tragedy of the Menchus is "the story of all Guatemala's poor." The author of *I, Rigoberta Menchu* makes this linkage explicit: "My personal experience is the reality of a whole people." It is a call to people of good will all over the world to help the noble but powerless indigenous peoples of Guatemala and other Third World countries to gain their rightful inheritance. Made internationally famous by the success of her book and by the Nobel Prize she was awarded in 1992, Rigoberta is now head of the Rigoberta Menchu Foundation for Human Rights and a spokesperson for the cause of "social justice and peace."

Unfortunately for this political fantasy, virtually every important claim that Rigoberta makes is a lie. These lies concern the central events and facts of her story and have been deliberately concocted to shape its political content and to create a specific political myth. This myth begins on the very first page of Rigoberta's text: "When I was older, my father regretted my not going to school, as I was a girl able to learn many things. But he always said: 'Unfortunately, if I put you in school, they'll make you forget your class; they'll turn you into a *ladino*. I don't want that for you and that's why I don't send you.' He might have had the chance to put me in school when I was about fourteen or fifteen but he couldn't do it because he knew what the consequences would be: the ideas that they would give me."

To the trusting reader, this looks like a perfect realization of the marxist paradigm, in which the ruling ideas become the ideas of the ruling class that controls the means of education. But, contrary to her assertions, Rigoberta was not uneducated. Nor did her father oppose her education because he feared the schools would indoctrinate her in the values of the *ladino* ruling class. According to classmates, teachers, and family members, Vicente Menchu did send his daughter, Rigoberta, to school. In fact, he sent her to two prestigious private boarding schools operated by Catholic nuns, where she received the equivalent of a middle-school education. (In a telling irony, it is most likely that she was recruited there to the marxist faith and became a spokesperson for the communist guerrillas.) Because Rigoberta was indeed away at boarding school for most of her youth, moreover, her detailed accounts of herself laboring eight months a year on coffee and cotton plantations and organizing a political underground are also false.

These and other pertinent details have now been established by anthropologist David Stoll, one of the leading academic experts on Guatemala. Stoll interviewed more than 120 Guatemalans, including relatives, friends, neighbors, and former teachers and classmates over a ten-year period as the basis of his new biography, *Rigoberta Menchu and the Story of All Poor Guatemalans*. To coincide with the publication of Stoll's book, the *New York Times* sent reporter Larry Rohter to Guatemala to attempt to verify Stoll's findings, which he was readily able to do.

Perhaps the most salient of Stoll's findings is the way in which Rigoberta has distorted the sociology of her family situation, and that of the Mayans in the region of Uspantan, to conform to marxist precepts. The Menchus were not landless poor, and Rigoberta had no brother who starved to death, at least none that her own family could remember. The *ladinos* were not a ruling caste in Rigoberta's town or district, in which there were no large estates or *fincas* as she claims. Far from being a dispossessed peasant, Vicente Menchu had title to 2,753 hectares of land or about seven thousand acres. The twenty–two-year land dispute described by Rigoberta, which is the central event in her book leading to the rebellion and the tragedies that followed was, in fact, over a tiny, but significant, 151 hectare parcel or less than 400 acres. Most importantly, Vicente

Menchu's "heroic struggle against the landowners who wanted to take our land" was in fact not a dispute with representatives of a European-descended conquistador class but with his own Mayan relatives, the Tum family, headed by his wife's uncle.

Vicente Menchu did not organize a peasant resistance called the Committee for Campesino Unity. He was a conservative peasant insofar as he was political at all. Even more importantly, his consuming passion was not any social concern, but the family feud with his in-laws, who were small landowning peasants like himself. It was his involvement in this family feud that caused him to be caught up in the larger political drama enacted by students and professional revolutionaries, that was really irrelevant to his concerns and that ultimately killed him.

At the end of the 1970s, coincident with a global Soviet offensive, Cuba's Communist dictator, Fidel Castro, launched a new phase in Cuba's foreign policy, sponsoring and arming a series of guerrilla uprisings in Central America. The most significant of these were in Nicaragua, El Salvador, and Guatemala, and followed lines that had been laid down by Regis Debray and Che Guevara a decade before. The leaders of these movements were generally not Indian peasants but urban Hispanics, principally the disaffected scions of the middle and upper classes. They were often the graduates of cadre training centers in Moscow and Havana and of terrorist training camps in Lebanon and East Germany. (The leaders of the Salvadorean guerillas even included a Lebanese communist and Shi'ite muslim named Shafik Handal.)

One of these forces, Guatemala's Guerrilla Army of the Poor showed up in Uspantan, the largest township near Rigoberta's village of Chimel, on April 29, 1979. According to eyewitnesses, the guerrillas painted everything within reach red, grabbed the tax collector's money and threw it in the streets, tore down the jail, released the prisoners, and chanted in the town square "We're defenders of the poor" for fifteen or twenty minutes.

None of the guerilla intruders was masked, because none of

them was local. As strangers, they had no understanding of the Uspantan situation in which (as Stoll verified) virtually all the land disputes were between the Mayan inhabitants themselves. Instead, they perceived the social problem according to the marxist textbook version, which has now been perpetuated by Rigoberta and the Nobel prize committee through Rigoberta's book. In their first revolutionary act, the guerrillas executed two local *ladino* landholders.

Thinking that this successful violence had established the guerrillas as the power in his region, Vicente Menchu cast his fate with them, providing them with a meeting place, and accompanying them on a protest. But Guatemala's security forces, which had been primed for Castro's Soviet-backed hemispheric offensive, responded by descending on the region with characteristic brutality. The killings that ensued were abetted by enraged relatives of the murdered *ladino* peasants seeking revenge on the leftist assassins. The trail of violence left many innocents slaughtered in its wake, including Rigoberta's parents and a second brother (whose death Rigoberta sensationalizes by falsely claiming that he was burned alive and that she and her parents were forced to witness the act).

The most famous incident in Rigoberta's book is the occupation of the Spanish embassy in Guatemala City in January 1980 by a group of guerrillas and protesting peasants. Vicente Menchu was the peasant spokesman. The occupation itself was led by the Robin Garcia Revolutionary Student Front. A witness described to David Stoll how Vicente Menchu was primed for his role: "They would tell Don Vicente, 'Say, "The people united will never be defeated,"' and Don Vicente would say, 'The people united will never be defeated.' They would tell Don Vicente, 'Raise your left hand when you say it,' and he would raise his left hand."

When they had set out on the trip that brought them to the Spanish Embassy, the Uspantan peasants who accompanied the student revolutionaries had no idea where they were going or what the purpose of the trip actually was. Later, David Stoll interviewed a survivor whose husband had died in the incident. She told him that the journey originated in a wedding party at the Catholic church in Uspantan. Two days after the ceremony, the wedding party moved on. "The señores said they were going to the coast, but they arrived at the capital." Once there, the student revolutionaries proceeded with their plan to occupy the embassy and take hostages, with the unsuspecting Mayans ensnared. Although the cause of the tragedy that ensued is in dispute, David Stoll presents persuasive evidence that a Molotov cocktail brought by the revolutionaries ignited and set the embassy on fire. At least thirty-nine people, including Vicente Menchu, were killed.

As a result of Stoll's research, Nobel laureate Rigoberta Menchu has been exposed as a political agent working for terrorists who were ultimately responsible for the death of her own family. So rigid is Rigoberta's party loyalty to the Castroist cause, that after her book was published and she became an international spokesperson for indigenous peoples, she refused to denounce the Sandinista dictatorship's genocidal attempt to eliminate its Miskito Indians. She even broke with her own translator, Elisabeth Burgos-Debray, over the issue of the Miskitos. (Burgos-Debray, along with other prominent French leftists had protested the Sandinista attacks.)

Rigoberta's first response to Stoll's exposure of her lies was, on the one hand, "no comment" and, on the other, to add another lie— the denial that she had anything to do with the book that made her famous. But David Stoll listened to two hours of the tapes she made for Burgos-Debray (which provided the text for the book) and concluded that the narrative they recorded was identical to the (false) version of the facts in the book itself. Of course, Rigoberta did not disclaim authorship of the book when she accepted her Nobel Prize.

Under the pressure of Stoll's scrutiny, Rigoberta erected a second line of defense—that her self-portrait was really a composite reality based on many Guatemalan lives. But, if the source pool is large enough, a composite portrait becomes a license to select any data that will "prove" any particular case. If Rigoberta's own story had to be falsified so extensively to make it conform to her political "truth," why is there any reason to believe that it is in fact true?

The fictional life of Rigoberta Menchu is a piece of communist propaganda designed to incite hatred of Europeans, and the societies they have built, and to organize support for communist and terrorist organizations at war with the democracies of the West. It has become the single most influential social treatise read by American college students. At the behest of leftist professors, over fifteen thousand theses have been written on Rigoberta Menchu the world over—all accepting her lies as gospel. Rigoberta herself has been the recipient of fourteen honorary doctorates from prestigious institutions of higher learning, and the Nobel Prize committee has made Rigoberta an international figure and spokesperson for "social justice and peace."

Almost as remarkable as the hoax itself, and indicative of the enormous cultural power of its perpetrators, is the fact that the revelation of Rigoberta's mendacity has changed almost nothing. The Nobel committee has already refused to take back her prize, many of the thousands of college courses that make her book a required text for American college students will continue to do so, and the editorial writers of the major press institutions have already defended her falsehoods on the same grounds that supporters of Tawana Brawley's parallel hoax made famous: even if she's lying, she's telling the truth.

In an editorial responding to these revelations and typical of press reactions, the *Los Angeles Times*, glossed over the enormity of what Rigoberta, the Guatemalan terrorists, the French left, the international community of "human rights" leftists, the Nobel Prize committee fellow-travelers, and the tenured radicals who dominate the American academic community have wrought. While recognizing that something has gone amiss, the *Times* concludes that it would be wrong to tarnish the entire cause because of the excesses of Rigoberta's book: "After the initial lies, the international apparatus of human rights activism, journalism and academia pitched in to exaggerate the dire condition of the peasants when a simple recounting of the truth would have been enough."

But would it? If a simple recounting of the truth would have been enough, then Rigoberta's lies would be unnecessary. So why tell them? If there was any truth in the myth itself, the Guatemalan guerillas would have had more support among the indigenous people and would not have been wiped out in two or three years. The fact is that there was insufficient social ground for the armed insurrection that these Castroists tried to force, as there was insufficient ground for Guevara's suicidal effort in Bolivia years before. Ultimately, the source of the violence and ensuing misery that Rigoberta Menchu describes in her destructive little book is the leftist intelligentsia itself. Too bad leftists in United States universities haven't the decency to acknowledge this, and to leave the Third World alone.

16

Visit to a Small College

I T IS THE SEASON when high school juniors, parents in tow, set out on their tours of ivied campuses, in search of the right investment for their education dollar. This spring I made a similar tour. Speaking at colleges in Chicago, Boston, Lewiston (Maine), New Haven, Quinnipiac (Connecticut), Houston, Dallas, and College Station (Texas), I conducted my own hands-on survey to see how American colleges have changed since I was an undergraduate in the 1950s. Or, to be more precise, to check conclusions I had already drawn about these matters on the basis of previous trips I had made in the last decade.

When I was an undergraduate, the censors attacked the university from without. Now, they are entrenched in the faculties and administrations themselves. Then, the university defined itself as an institution "dedicated to the disinterested pursuit of knowledge." Now, every term of that definition is under siege by postmodernists and deconstructionists who have become the new academic establishment and have redefined the university as "an institution dedicated to social change." That is one reason why the academy, once perceived as a redoubt of intellectual freedom and cutting-edge discourse, has become the butt of snickering jokes about political correctness and the font of Kafkaesque tales about bureaucratic censorship and administrative obtuseness.

In Chicago, I encountered a very bright second-year graduate student in the famous Committee on Social Thought program who had previously completed four years of undergraduate work at Harvard where he had never heard the name Friedrich von Hayek. In a way, it was the most shocking anecdotal evidence I retrieved in my forays into the halls of learning. It is not just that Hayek won a Nobel Prize for economics in 1973, or that he is the author of a classic text of the modem era, *The Road to Serfdom*, which was already required reading for students at Columbia when I went there in the 1950s, or that he is one of the three or four greatest social thinkers of the twentieth century—the Karl Marx of the libertarian-conservative worldview. Any of these would have been reason enough to make this student's ignorance dismaying. But Hayek is also one of the handful of social scientists who (along with his teacher Ludwig von Mises) demonstrated more than sixty years ago why the socialist system could not work and, thus, why it would eventually collapse, as it did in 1989. The implosion of the Soviet empire was a dramatic vindication of the analysis Hayek and his colleagues had made.

It was not the first time I had encountered on university campuses ignorance of Hayek and other conservative intellectuals, nor was it accidental. Such ignorance is a direct consequence of the tenured left's dominance of liberal arts institutions and its politicization of the curriculum and the faculty hiring process since the 1960s. This, in fact, was the subject of the lectures I gave at the campuses I visited.

At Bates College in Maine, for example, I spoke in defense of the following proposition: "The Intellectual Tradition of the Left is Bankrupt and Its Hegemony at Bates Is An Abuse of Academic Freedom." To anticipate the situation I encountered at this pricey

liberal arts college, let me quote an e-mail I received from a professor at Smith, a comparable institution, when I challenged the
faculty there about these academic abuses: "I would gladly crush you
in a debate on students' so-called 'right not to be ideologically in-
doctrinated in the classroom,'" wrote Professor E. C. Graf. "Your
phrase 'students' academic freedom' is already a laughable oxymo-
ron, as if students ever head such a thing or ever should. . . . As for
admitting that I 'indoctrinate' my students instead of teaching them,
tell me, my friend, when has there ever been a difference?"

In a rare departure from the norm, I received an invitation to
Bates from the Dean of the College, who informed me shortly after introducing himself that he was a "leftist." Out of one hundred or so colleges I have spoken at in the last several years, as I
have mentioned, I have been officially invited only to four. The
college administrations will roll out no red carpets, provide no hono-
raria or airfares for a conservative like me, as they will for my former
political comrades on the left, nor will faculty members offer credit
to students for attending my lectures (a common practice as well).
Even on this visit to Bates, where the dean himself invited me, my
reception proved to be a little unusual.

I arrived at the airport in Portland the night before my scheduled evening lecture, where a university-provided driver picked me
up and deposited me at the door of an apartment that the university had also made available. But there the hospitality stopped.
Until my evening lecture the next day, I was left to my own devices, wondering whether the dean who invited me would like to
have a lunch or even coffee in his offices to get acquainted. In fact,
as noon approached the day after my arrival, I decided to drop in
on the dean to thank him for my invitation and inquire if he would
like to have lunch. When I got there, a secretary informed me he
was unavailable. Instead, a student escort was provided to take me
to the school cafeteria, where I ate by myself. The cafeteria meal
was complimentary, and the dean, perhaps feeling guilty about my

unannounced appearance, eventually showed up to take me back to his office. In manner he was entirely cordial, while explaining that he had taken some criticism from members of his faculty merely for inviting me. When I returned to California, I received a somewhat testy letter from him because of a full-page advertisement I had run in the school paper on the day of my lecture, which he had not seen at the time. The advertisement announced that the dean was inviting students to attend my evening talk. It then continued with the following headline: "Marxism Is A Resurgent Doctrine in the Former Soviet Empire and Apparently on American Campuses Too."

Below this headline was a reminder to students that the false doctrines of marxism had led to the deaths of one hundred million people. Below that was a selection of book titles written by authors like Thomas Sowell, David Gress, and myself, offered as "antidotes" to what students were being taught by their professors at Bates.

In all fairness, the dean had a point, which I readily conceded. I had undoubtedly made his life more difficult. Still, his anguish was just another indication of the pressure he was under from his leftist faculty because of my visit. How left? Well, in the Bates catalogue, one course listed was called "The Cuban Revolution: Problems and Prospects" which included a two-week on-site visit to Cuba. Aviva Chomsky, daughter of the MIT grouser, had taught the course until she left Bates for a more "working-class" school (as the dean regretfully informed me). At my talk that evening, I could not resist making the observation that the Cuban revolution had no prospects.

Since I had a whole day to kill before my scheduled talk, I decided to sit in on one of Bates's political-science courses to check my impressions of academic life. I asked students for directions to the building in which political science courses were taught, and went to the department office on the ground floor. None of the administrators seemed to have a problem with my desire to audit a class. Accordingly, I approached a professor as she was entering her classroom and asked permission to attend.

She was an Indian woman in her thirties and spoke with an English accent. She seemed pleased at the prospect of having an adult in her audience and had no hesitation inviting me in. All through the class she smiled at me and talked in my direction—and even encouraged me to answer a question when the rest of the class could not. She taught from a single text, and it was obvious from her remarks that the class consisted in reading through the text a chapter at a time. In the college courses I had attended at Columbia some forty years ago, there was rarely an "official" text for the course, and if there was one, my professors seldom referred to it. Any text included was more an aid to students. The real "text" for the course was the professor's lecture, and students were expected to read several books by leading scholars in the field whose views usually differed strongly from the professor's. A political science course devoted to modem industrial societies, as this one was, might have had required readings by Weber, Marx, Durkheim, Tonnies, and Hayek.

In this course, however, there was a single six hundred-page text entitled *Modernity*, edited by the well-known English New Leftist Stuart Hall. Like Hall, every contributor to the text was a marxist. There was no lecture. The teacher proceeded in Socratic fashion to guide the students page by page, and paragraph by paragraph, through the textbook assigned. It was like a science course based on an accepted body of knowledge, where a single class textbook is the norm.

Except that this norm was the discredited intellectual tradition of marxism. I looked over at the text of the student next to me and asked what the acronym ACS, which was staring out of the page, stood for. She said "Advanced Capitalist Society." I noticed another acronym MIBTC and was told it stood for "Military-Industrial-Bureaucratic-Technocratic-Complex." The teacher was admonishing the students to pay attention to the main points in the authors' arguments and to take note of the way they grounded them—whether in authorities or facts. Then she had the class break up into small groups, each of which was to apply this technique to a different section and assess whether the author of that section satisfactorily proved his point.

My group was assigned a little section on American militarism (seriously). The question put by the text was whether militarism emerged out of the capitalist economic structures of ACS, or whether once it emerged it became systemic. There was no question, of course, whether American society could reasonably be described as "militarist." One young woman in my group wondered aloud whether the author had proved there was an MIBTC merely by pointing out that cell phones made by AT&T were used by the army in the Gulf War. (I stepped out of my role as observer to assure her he had not.)

Subsequently, I bought *Modernity* from Amazon.com and found that the passage was typical. The viewpoints in the text ranged from classical marxism to feminist marxism to postmodernist marxism. There were no opposing views introduced except to be refuted. In the book's index there was not a single reference to Hayek. On the other hand, there were plenty of discussions of obscure marxists like Nicholas Poulantzas, who wrote a book on the "ruling class" in the 1960s before jumping out a window at age twenty-nine.

After the class, I went up to the teacher and said that I admired her pedagogy in advising the students that she was not there to tell them *what* to think, but to teach them *how*. On the other hand, I thought that assigning an ideological marxist tome as the course's only text worked at cross-purposes with that goal. At once the smile disappeared from her face. She said: "Well, they get the other side from the newspapers." Education like this costs Bates parents thirty thousand dollars each year in tuition alone.

This was not to be the end of my auditing adventure, however. Afterwards, the lecturer complained about me to the dean, who had ignored me until then. The dean called me up at my apartment to tell me I should have gone through his office if I wanted to sit in on a class. I explained the circumstances that had led me to the class, the encouragement of the departmental administrators, the pleasure with which the lecturer herself had welcomed me, and the reason for her change of heart. But to no avail. Obviously she had given him a hard time, and there was no way he was going to sympathize with me. I realized that this intimidation was similar to the intimidation over the advertisement and his invitation to me. It served a purpose, and served it effectively: to minimize the contact between professors and students and conservatives like myself.

That was no doubt why attendance at the little reception with faculty he arranged for me before my talk was limited to the handful of older professors at Bates who shared my views, or at least were not ideologically repelled by them, and who were protected by tenure. I nonetheless admired their courage in attending my event: I knew that even in the darkest days of the McCarthy era communist faculty were not threatened with ostracism by their peers as are politically incorrect academics by the reflexive McCarthyism of the tenured left.

I gave my speech to about sixty students, among whom seven or eight formed a very unhappy contingent of campus leftists. Had I not been officially invited, it is more than likely that even these few would not have been there. I spoke about the religious ideas that had led to the destruction of one hundred million people in our century, killed by progressive missionaries in order to realize their impossible dreams. Revolutionary leftists were modern Manichaeans, who believed that the world was ruled by alien powers of darkness. Even democracies were not free societies, but were dominated by these powers, which Marx called "ruling classes," against whom all those who believed in social justice were at war.

Even though these marxist fantasies had led to unprecedented ruin for all the societies that eventually came under their sway, their currency was evident throughout the curriculum. Now the alien powers were called the "patriarchy," or the "white male oligarchy," or more obliquely, "institutional racism." But they were just as fantastic, and belief in them inspired passions potentially as destructive as the passions of classical marxists. No one, I said, was oppressed in America (except perhaps children by abusive parents). To even suggest as much was to enter the realm of the absurd.

I give the leftist students credit for waiting until the end of my talk to vent their outrage over the blasphemies I had uttered. One young woman got so emotional she decided to leave the building to save herself from further contamination. Another young woman stood up and with tremendous urgency sputtered, "But what about the hierarchies? You didn't mention the hierarchies!"

She was referring, of course, to the hierarchies of race, gender, and class that were the staples of her Bates education and the modern-day equivalents of Marx's boogey man. Her professors had undoubtedly schooled her in the idea that these hierarchies oppress people of color, women, and wage-slaves in America. In America! In the year 1999!

Of course, I had actually "mentioned" the hierarchies (though not by name) to dismiss them as left-wing illusions, no more substantial than the idea that somewhere behind the Hale-Bopp comet a space ship was waiting to take the enlightened to heaven. So I tried another tack. "Let me ask you this question," I said. "Where do you put Oprah Winfrey in your hierarchies?" I knew that Oprah Winfrey was at the bottom of any oppressive hierarchy conceived by leftists. A woman born in Mississippi to a black sharecropper and a victim of sexual abuse, she was the oppressed of the oppressed. But in the real world Oprah had risen by dint of her own intelligence, effort, and talent to become a mother-confessor and authority figure to millions of lower-middle-class white females who had never passed through a sensitivity training course. The fortune she has been able to amass through these efforts casts her among the super-rich of America's ruling class as one of the *Forbes* four hundred, with a net worth of 550 million dollars *before* the recent stock-market boom.

"She's a token," the young woman said.

"Sorry, she's not a token," I replied. "Cornel West is a token."

Cornel West, an intellectual of modest talents whose skin color has catapulted him into academic stardom with a six-figure income at Harvard, is indeed a token. The contemporary American university is a feudal institution, run somewhat like the Communist Party, where the elect raise people to the heights by exercising the same kind of arbitrary *droit de seigneur* that was the privilege of rulers in pre-democratic and pre-capitalist times. There was no tenure committee or central committee, however, to lift Oprah out of the societal mud—to say, for example, to Phil Donahue, "Move over Phil, we need a person of color to put in prime time for diversity's sake." The power Oprah Winfrey has been able to accumulate refutes every cliché of the political left. Her psychological power over her mainly white audience has made her the first individual in history able to create a best-seller by fiat and the millions in revenues that go with it. She is a film-making industry in herself. She has shown that the barriers of race, class, and gender are not insuperable obstacles to advancement in America any more than residual anti-Semitism or prejudice against the Irish create impenetrable "hierarchies" of oppression to bar those groups' ascent.

But, of course, such a perspective is politically incorrect at places like Bates, so dangerous that the faculty commissars are constantly on guard to prevent students from too much contact with such dangerous thoughts. The relatively good behavior of my audience at Bates is not always in evidence. The campus norm when conservative ideas are expressed is a kind of intellectual fascism which makes such dissenting discourse improbable, and often impossible.

On the same trip, I spoke at the University of St. Thomas in Houston. When I got to the line "Nobody is oppressed in America," a very large African-American student stood up and began ranting in my direction, "You're a fascist! I can't listen to this anymore." Then he thrust his hand into the air in a Nazi salute, shouted "*Sieg Heil*," and walked out.

17

Calibrating the Culture Wars

A NEGATIVE ARTICLE in the *Los Angeles Times Sunday Book Review* on recent publications by two neo-conservative authors, Norman Podhoretz and Hilton Kramer, reveals how the culture war has become a dialogue of the deaf. In the article, the left-wing critic Russell Jacoby concludes that the "problem" with these neo-conservative writers "is less their positions than their delusions about them; they seem to think they represent lonely and beleaguered outposts of anti-Communism."

How could conservatives be beleaguered in an American culture that was itself conservative? Jacoby wanted to know. Referring to Kramer's *Twilight of the Intellectuals*, the more theoretical of the two books, Jacoby asserts: "Kramer refashions reality. . . . [He] writes as if he were a denizen of the former Soviet Union, where the party controls intellectual life and only a few brave souls like himself risk their lives and careers to tell the truth." The critic focuses on Kramer's lament that "it was not the Western defenders of Communist tyranny who suffered so conspicuously from censure and opprobrium in the Cold War period but those who took up the anti-Communist cause." Incredulous, Jacoby asks, "What could he mean?" as though there were no plausible answer to the question.

But it is obvious to any reader of Kramer's book that he had in mind the emblematic figure of Whittaker Chambers, the subject of the first two essays in his powerful volume. Jacoby seems to have given the book an attention as cursory as his evident contempt for its author's conservative politics. In Kramer's view, Chambers was an "archetypal" ex-communist and his treatment in "the court of liberal opinion," which is coterminous with the literary culture, reflected its own attitude towards the anti-communist cause. Chambers did risk his life and career to expose one of the top Soviet spies in the American government, yet his status in America's literary culture ever after has been that of a renegade and a snitch. As a direct consequence of his patriotic deed, Chambers—one of the towering figures of the early Cold War and, in *Witness*, the author of an American classic—was fired from his job as a top editor at *Time* and brought to the brink of personal ruin. Despised in life, for forty years after his death in 1957 Chambers was a forgotten man. Indeed, when I had the occasion to ask some senior honors students at the University of California in the early 1990s if they had ever heard of Whittaker Chambers, they said they had not. But they knew the name "Alger Hiss" and that he was a "victim of McCarthyism."

Alger Hiss was, of course, the Soviet spy whom Chambers exposed. In contrast to Chambers, Hiss emerged through his ordeal as a political martyr to the liberal culture, a hero and a *cause célébre* among *Nation* leftists, who continued to champion his "innocence" long after his guilt was obvious. The convicted Hiss even had an academic chair named in his honor at a distinguished liberal arts college. Upon his death in 1996, he was eulogized in progressive magazines and by liberal television anchors as an "idealist," and (inevitably) as a long-suffering victim of the anti-communist "witch-hunt." As Kramer sums up this parable, "Hiss—convicted of crimes that showed him to be a liar, a thief, and a traitor—was judged to be innocent even if guilty, and Chambers—the self-confessed renegade who recanted his treachery—was judged to be guilty even if he was telling the truth. For what mattered to liberal opinion was that Hiss was seen to have remained true to his ideals—never mind what the content of these 'ideals' proved to be—whereas Chambers was seen to have betrayed them."

In this passage, Kramer identifies the central cultural paradox of the Cold War epoch in the West: the survival among American intellectuals of the very ideals—socialist and progressive—that led to the catastrophe of Soviet Communism. As Kramer puts it, "Liberalism, as it turned out, was not to be so easily dislodged from the whole morass of illiberal doctrines and beliefs in which, under the influence of marxism, it had become so deeply embedded, and every attempt to effect such a separation raised the question of whether . . . there was still something that could legitimately be called liberalism." Yet, Jacoby's only response to these seminal chapters and the questions they pose is that they make Kramer's book seem "musty." This despite Chambers's final vindication in the release three years ago of the Venona transcripts of Soviet intelligence communications, which definitively established Hiss's guilt.

For anti-communist conservatives, Whittaker Chambers is a political hero. But it took forty years from the time of his death for the publishing world to produce a biographical tribute in Sam Tannenhaus's worthy volume. And Chambers stands almost alone among anti-Communist heroes of the Cold War in finally receiving his biographical due. Elizabeth Bentley, Louis Budenz, Bella Dodd, Frank Meyer, Walter Krivitsky, Victor Kravchenko, Jan Valtin, once large figures of the anti-communist cause, along with countless less well-known others, are more typical in having virtually disappeared from cultural memory.

By contrast, to cite only one of many counterexamples, Abbie Hoffman, a political clown of the next radical generation but a hero to the left, has been the subject of three biographies within a decade of his death, not to mention a book-length exposition of his political "philosophy." There can be no question that the nostalgic glow around Hoffman's memory and the interest in his life are integrally connected to the fact that he was a stalwart defender of communist tyrannies in Cuba and Vietnam, and thus in the shared ideals of progressives who now dominate the literary culture and shape its historical judgments.

Russell Jacoby acquired his own credentials by writing a book called *The Last Intellectuals*, which bemoaned the vanishing "public intellectual." This was a label he gave to intellectuals who worked outside the academy, wrote lucid (instead of postmodernist) prose, and influenced the public debate. The very title of Jacoby's book, however, is an expression of progressive arrogance and the unwillingness of leftists like Jacoby to acknowledge their cultural success. What Jacoby really mourned was the disappearance of the *left-wing* public intellectual, a direct result of the conquest of American liberal arts faculties by the political left and its distribution of academic privilege to comrades among the politically correct. Jacoby is well aware that an important consequence of this takeover is that almost all contemporary conservative intellectuals are (of necessity) public intellectuals. Indeed, this fact is regularly used by leftists in their *ad hominem* attacks on conservative intellectuals as "bought" by their institutional sponsors. Jacoby himself cannot even mention Kramer's magazine the *New Criterion*, without adding that it is "funded by a conservative foundation." Of course, the *Nation* for which Jacoby himself writes regularly is funded by rich leftists and leftist foundations. So what?

The reason conservative intellectuals gravitate to think-tanks like Heritage, American Enterprise, and Hoover, and to magazines like *Commentary* and the *New Criterion* is *because* of their de facto blacklisting by the leftist academy. It is, in fact, the public influence of these conservative intellectuals that is the focus of Jacoby's lament in *The Last Intellectuals*. Academic intellectuals, he complains, write for a professional coterie instead of a broad public. Yet the pull of institutional security is so great that Jacoby himself has since succumbed to its lure. Since writing his assault on the "obscurantist" university, Jacoby has given up his own independent existence and accepted an appointment from his political comrades in the history department at UCLA.

While lack of self-reflection and self-irony are indispensable characteristics of the left in general, Jacoby's attack on Podhoretz and Kramer is an extraordinary specimen. Not only is his attack directed at two intellectuals who, for political reasons, were denied a platform in the *Times*, but they were also denied the very academic patronage that Jacoby himself now enjoys. "*What can he mean?*" Indeed.

Jacoby's attack was actually one of four nonfiction reviews the *Times* chose to feature on its cover. Three were of conservative books—all of which were attacked from the left. The fourth was a review of two books on Clinton, both written by leftists, both praised by reviewers from the left.

The issue of the *Times* in question happened to be May 9, 1999, but it could have been any date. In December 1997, the *Book Review* ran a year-end wrap-up, the "*Times*' 100 Best Books," compiled from previous *Times* reviews. Because some reviewers had written more than one notice, there were eighty-seven contributors in all. They were a familiar sampling of the literary left, and even of the true believing left (Saul Landau, Martin Duberman, Robert Scheer, and Ellen Willis, for example). Among them all, however, the only reviewer I could detect with the slightest claim to a conservative profile was an academic, Walter Lacquer, who has no obvious association with conservative politics comparable to the connection of the aforementioned leftists to radical politics.

I learned how the "100 Best Books" were picked shortly after the issue appeared, when I had lunch with Steve Wasserman, the newly appointed editor of the *Review*. I knew Wasserman as a former Berkeley radical and protege, in the 1960s, of a *Times* contributing editor, Bob Scheer, when Scheer was promoting the party line of Kim Il Sung and plotting to overthrow the American empire as a member of the Red Family. Scheer's present politics were still to the left of "Senator Bullworth," in whose film he had made a cameo appearance courtesy of his friend Warren Beatty. After the 1960s, Scheer had ingratiated himself with Hollywood's bolsheviks, married a top editor at the *Los Angeles Times*, and become a figure of influence in the paper's hierarchy, which enabled him to secure Wasserman his job.

I had defended Wasserman's appointment in print, at his own request, when journalist Catherine Seipp attacked him in the now-defunct *Buzz* magazine. In my letter to *Buzz*, I praised what I thought were Wasserman's good intentions of fairness, despite our political differences. The lunch we had arranged was an attempt to rekindle the flame of a relationship that had survived the 1960s. The mere fact that he would have civil contact with me, a political "renegade," seemed an auspicious sign—rare as such gestures of civility had been over the years from my former comrades-in-arms. It led me to assume (falsely) that Wasserman had some respect for my own odyssey and quest for the truth. Indeed, he had praised my autobiography, *Radical Son*, which some reviewers had flatteringly compared to *Witness*, and even thought the critical portrait I drew of Scheer "charming" and "accurate."

In fact, given the proper circumstances, Wasserman could himself be an artful critic of the left, within the stringent boundaries it normally set for itself. I say this because I have sometimes been accused of "lumping" leftists together and missing the spectrum of "progressive" opinions. The reverse would almost be more accurate. I have often given too much benefit of the doubt to people like Wasserman, in recognition of mild deviations they have been willing to risk and have failed to see the hard line coming before it smacked me in the face.

When I raised the issue of conservatives' exclusion from the pages of his magazine, Wasserman dismissed my concern out of hand as "bean counting." He compared it to feminist complaints of underrepresentation, even though there were plenty of feminists and feminist sympathizers on the *Review*'s list. I found myself wondering whether a leftist writer of reputation comparable to mine would have been invited to lunch by Wasserman and not asked to write a review for his magazine.

I should have known at the time that this was not going to be a long-lived reunion. It came to an end almost a year later when Wasserman finally did ask me to write for the *Review*. He wanted me to join a "symposium" on the sesquicentennial of the publication of the *Communist Manifesto*. My contribution was to be 250 words (which he promptly cut to 125). I made the mistake of assuming others's would be equally brief. When the issue came out, however, I saw that the symposium opened with a three–thousand-word illustrated spread celebrating Marx's genius and continuing relevance. This mash note was written by Eric Hobsbawm, a member of the Communist Party until 1990 (!) and a recidivist marxist. Hobsbawm's most recent book had been a five hundred-page defense of the pro-Soviet left in the Cold War, which I had taken on in a lengthy review in the *Weekly Standard*. Hobsbawm's apologia for Marxism was an insult to the historical record and to everything that people like Chambers and I had stood for. In featuring this travesty, Wasserman had revealed the standard by which he lived (and his real opinion of me). Why not ask David Duke to write a paean to *Mein Kampf* on *its* anniversary, I asked, in an acidic note I sent him.

But I could not let the matter rest there, and decided to take it up with the top editors at the *Times*. Both of them were men of the left as well, who listened politely and ignored my concern. I also wrote a letter to the *Times*'s newly appointed publisher and CEO, Mark Willes, previously an executive at General Mills. I had met

Willes at a *Times* Christmas Party which was held at the Hancock Park mansion of its editorial page editor, Janet Clayton, an African-American woman whose living room was tellingly adorned with an iconic portrait of Jesse Jackson. Except for the passage of thirty years, the *Times* party could have been organized by *Ramparts*, the radical magazine Scheer and I edited in the 1960s. Clayton's living room was soon filled with the glitterati of the Los Angeles left. Scheer was there, gnashing his teeth at me because of what I had written about him in *Radical Son*. Tom Hayden came too, along with the ACLU's Ramona Ripston and black extremist (and *Times* contributor) Earl Ofari Hutchinson. In fact, the only person not of the left I encountered that whole evening, was Paula Jones's spokeswoman Susan Carpenter McMillan.

It occurred to me to make an appeal to Willes because he had already made a few gestures that seemed to indicate his intention to introduce some balance at the *Times*. He had even demoted several left-wing editors who had climbed the affirmative action ladder to the top of the paper, among them Scheer's wife. In my letter, I challenged the rationale behind pitching the book section of a major metropolitan newspaper to what was essentially a *Nation* audience. I made it clear that I had no problem with the representation of left-wing authors in the paper. It was the exclusion of conservatives that concerned me.

But I had misjudged Willes, whose reason for demoting the editors was related more to the *Times*'s poor economic performance than its sometimes extreme political postures. Like many businessmen, Willes showed little political sense when it came to the issues of left and right. Shortly after my appeal, for example, Willes was publicly embarrassed by a leaked internal memo in which he demanded that *Times* reporters include ethnically diverse sources in all articles, regardless of subject matter or context. This was too much even for the quota-oppressed *Times* staff and its politically correct editors. Instead of answering my letter, Willes handed it over to its target, Wasserman, whose reply was understandably terse and revealed that our relationship was effectively over.

In my discussions with Wasserman and the *Times*'s editors, I had raised another issue: the exclusion of conservative writers from the annual *L.A. Times* Festival of Books. This was an event normally attended by a hundred thousand readers and five hundred authors flown in from all over the country, eager to show up because of the opportunities for publicity and validation that an appearance entailed. At the previous festival, the only conservative authors I had been able to identify were celebrities Charlton Heston and Arianna Huffington.

I was made aware of the festival as a result of my own exclusion when my autobiography *Radical Son* was published. Like any author with a new book, I had been looking for venues in which to promote it. Given the liberal bias in the general media, securing an audience was already problematic for a conservative author. Although I had co-authored best-sellers with Peter Collier, and in *Radical Son* had a dramatic story of murder and intrigue to tell, I found my book blacked out in the review sections of most of the major metropolitan papers. A chance to have *60 Minutes* do a segment on the book's untold story of Black Panther murders was blocked by its chief investigative producer, Lowell Bergman, a veteran Berkeley radical. I had enough experiences like this to know I needed the book festival venue. As a well-known author based in Los Angeles, it seemed odd to me that I should not be invited. When I brought this up to Wasserman, however, he just brushed me off. "There are lots of authors," he said. To his credit, he did then try to get me invited but was unsuccessful because my request for inclusion had come too late.

That was last year, before the Marx fracas. This spring I answered my phone and to my surprise Wasserman was on the other end inviting me to the festival. We had not spoken for nearly a year, and his voice sounded strained and not particularly friendly as he made the offer. "I want to thank you, Steve," I said, accepting. "I know how hard this must be for you." The conversation was so short I never found out exactly how I had earned the invitation, or exactly who had decided I should get it.

The festival was held on the UCLA campus and was a capsule demonstration, with a cast of thousands, of why conservatives like Hilton Kramer and Norman Podhoretz harbor the "delusion" that the culture is controlled by the party of the left. As in previous years, the festival headliners were leftists like Alice Walker and Betty Friedan—and even Sister Souljah—who had drawn thousands of their dedicated fans to the event. There was no Tom Clancy, no Tom Wolfe, no Thomas Sowell, and no Robert Bork to draw a similar conservative crowd. Among the hundreds of authors, in fact, I counted only a handful (actually, five) who were conservative, all locals. None was flown in like Walker, Friedan, and Sister Souljah as marquee attractions. As a tribute to his own lack of self-irony, Wasserman had appointed himself chair of a panel called "The Ethics of Book Reviewing."

I amused myself by walking around and bumping into former comrades, who seemed omnipresent. Among them were *Nation* editor Victor Navasky and *Nation* writers Todd Gitlin and Bob Scheer. I especially enjoyed the encounter with Scheer, who was in company with Navasky and Gitlin, but who made an end run around the other two in order to avoid having to shake my hand. Later I came upon Christopher Hitchens showing his parents around the event. Christopher greeted me cordially and thanked me for defending him in *Salon* when he had come under attack from the left. When I told him how Scheer had run away, he smiled. "Yeah, he's not speaking to me."

I had been scheduled for the second of three serial panels on the 1960s, called "Second Thoughts," although in fact I was the only panelist who had had any. The panels were recorded for later showing on C-SPAN and were held in Korn Auditorium on the UCLA campus. When I arrived, the room was packed with five hundred graying and scraggly-faced leftists, many in message T-shirts and *Nation* baseball hats. I counted thirteen panelists in all for the three 1960s discussions, every last one but myself a loyalist to the discredited radical creed. Hayden and Scheer were on a panel together. Russell Jacoby was there, too.

The other panelists at my event were Maurice Zeitlin and Sara Davidson. A third leftist had failed to show. Davidson was the author of a 1960s memoir of sexual liaisons entitled *Loose Change* and the chief writer for the politically correct television series *Dr. Quinn, Medicine Woman*. Her politics could be gleaned from her latest book, *Cowboy*, about her affair with a man who was intellectually her inferior and whom she had to support with her ample television earnings, but who gave great sex. The book celebrated this affair as a triumph of feminism.

The panel moderator, Maurice Zeitlin, was a sociologist at UCLA and had written books with titles like *American Society, Inc.* and *Talking Union*. Maurice and I had been friends in Berkeley at the beginning of the 1960s, when the two of us, along with Scheer, were part of a radical circle that produced one of the first magazines of the New Left, called *Root and Branch*. Maurice and Scheer had co-authored one of the first favorable books on Fidel Castro's communist revolution, which I had edited. Although we lived in the same city, I had seen Maurice only once, by accident, in the last thirty-five years.

While waiting for the panel to begin, I thought about the dilemma the whole scenario presented. I owed Wasserman a thank-you for being there at all, but at the same time I could not ignore the outrage unfolding before me. A leftist political convention was being held under the auspices of one of the most important press institutions in America, and was being promoted to a national television audience under the pretense that such select and resentful voices somehow represented American culture.

I resolved my dilemma by thanking Steve and the *Times* editors "for allowing me to crash this party," and then remarked that it was a national disgrace that a major press institution would stage a "symposium" on the 1960s stacked thirteen-to-one in favor of the radicals. Later in the discussion, I pointed out that the UCLA venue reflected the same unconscionable bias. A politically-controlled hiring process at American universities had resulted over time in the systematic exclusion of conservatives from the liberal arts faculties of UCLA and other prestigious schools. In contrast, even non-academic leftists were regularly appointed to university faculties by their political cronies. Jacoby was one example. Scheer, who had been made a professor of journalism at USC's Annenberg School by its dean, a former Clinton Administration official, was another.

I focused my speech on the way in which 1960s leftists had betrayed their own ideals by doing an about-face on civil rights and supporting race preferences, by abandoning the Vietnamese when they were being murdered and oppressed by communists, and by helping to crush the island of Cuba under the heel of the Castroist dictatorship. I also described my experiences with the Black Panther Party, a gang led by murderers and rapists whom the left had anointed as its political vanguard and whose crimes leftists continue to ignore to this day. I thought it interesting that a left that had supported international criminals during the Cold War was now supporting criminals like Mumia Abu Jamal and the inhabitants of what one of their leaders, Angela Davis, called the "prison-industrial complex" at home. These crusades against law enforcement, so characteristic of the left, hurt the poorest and most vulnerable citizens of our cities, particularly blacks, who are the chief victims of the predators the left defends. While the ideas and programs of leftists were seductive, their implementation had been an unmitigated human disaster. Which is why I had become a conservative.

As was common in my experience on similar platforms, the debate turned out to be a non-event. Adopting a standard tactic of the left I had encountered in the past, Sara Davidson simply ignored the challenge of my remarks and opened hers by saying that she saw the 1960s "in a wider, bigger context than just the Black Panthers." Then she commented, "My challenge is not to revise the Sixties, to re-analyze and reinterpret it, but to get back in touch with the essence and the spirit of that time." This was the kind of thoughtless arrogance one can expect from people inhabiting a cultural universe which they effectively control and in which, therefore, no challenge can threaten their hegemony or require a serious reply.

Stepping in for the no-show panelist, Maurice gave a speech, which could easily have been made in 1964, about the "silent generation" and American imperialism in Vietnam. He concluded with a flourish about the movement and how it was inspired by the idea of social justice. Maurice's eloquence about this commitment and about Vietnam was not tempered by a single fact that had been revealed since the end of the war: not, for instance, the two-and-a-half million Indo-Chinese slaughtered by the communists after America's forced withdrawal, not the interviews with North Vietnamese leaders that showed how the support of American radicals for the communist cause had helped to prolong the war and make the bloodbath possible. Nor did he bother to explain the silence of the crusaders for social justice during the long night of Vietnam's oppression by its leftist liberators.

As the discussion grew heated during the rejoinder period that followed, the audience got into the act. There was lots of heckling, making it difficult for me to complete a sentence. Shouts of "racist" were audible. A member of the audience rubbed his fingers in the air as though holding a wad of bills, while he and several others accused me of selling out for money. It was a moment familiar to me from almost all my university appearances, when the importance of being a "public intellectual," beyond the control of the tenured left, was made eminently clear. For if I were inside an academic institution and dependent on it for my livelihood, my career would certainly be destroyed if I spoke out as I had.

Name-calling and *ad hominem* assaults, as I had come to appreciate, were indispensable weapons in the arsenal of the left. Fear of them was what kept people in line. "Over the whole of this worthy enterprise," Hilton Kramer writes of modern "liberalism," "there hovered a great fear—the fear of being thought 'reactionary,' the fear of being relegated to the Right. . . . The very thought of being accused of collaborating with 'reaction,' as it was still called, was a liberal nightmare, and there was no shortage of Stalinist liberals (as I believe they must be called) to bring the charge of 'reaction' . . . at every infraction, or suspected infraction, of 'progressive' doctrine." That was why at universities like UCLA, while private professional polls showed faculties to be evenly divided over race preferences, only a handful of professors have dared to publicly voice their opposition.

Maurice was embarrassed by the heckling and, to his credit, spoke in my defense. He recalled how as a young teaching assistant at Princeton at the end of the 1950s his own students had signed a petition to get him fired because of his views on the Vietnam War. He told the UCLA audience that they were engaged in the same type of behavior. Referring to me as "one of the most trenchant critics of the left," he advised them that when they were groaning at my remarks they couldn't hear what I had to say (as though that would bother them!). "It is precisely this," he added, "that David turns into a characterization of The Left, as though there really is such a monolith."

Here Maurice had hit the absolute center of the blind spot that has kept the left innocent of its effects. If there was no left, how could it do any of the things conservatives have accused it of doing? How could it dominate the culture or exclude conservatives even more effectively than McCarthyism had excluded leftists in the past? Obviously, it could not. This assumption (that there really is no left) explains why Jacoby and so many others could think such an idea incomprehensible.

Of course the left is not a monolith. But then it never has been—not even in the days of Lenin and Stalin. Today, the left includes civilized social democrats like Maurice Zeitlin, but also ideological fascists who will shout down a conservative speaker and threaten opponents with verbal terrorism and even physical violence. Ward Connerly, a trustee of the University of California who has led the fight against racial preferences, has been prevented by left-ist gangs from speaking at several major universities. These acts of incivility have been abetted by cowardly administrators who do not share the witch-hunting mentality of the demonstrators, but are unwilling to stand up to them. There is not a conservative faculty member lacking tenure at an American university who does not live in fear of possible termination for politically incorrect views. While Maurice can admirably chastise uncivil passions at a public forum, he nonetheless acquiesces in a political hiring process at his own university that ensures that conservatives will remain virtually invisible. Steve Wasserman may be a nuanced radical whose socializing generously includes political pariahs like myself, but he will still enforce their marginality in the pages of his own magazine, or at festivals he organizes. And Russell Jacoby may be capable of composing book-length critiques of his fellow leftists, but writing in the pages of the *Los Angeles Times*, he will casually dismiss as a paranoid delusion the view of one of America's leading conservative thinkers that he inhabits a culture that is controlled by hostile forces.

V

Looking Backward

18

Telling It Like It Wasn't

T HE YEAR 1998 was a time for the nostalgia artists of the left to remember their glory days of thirty years before, and the magic of a moment that many of them have never left. It was a time in their imaginations of lost innocence, when impossible dreams were brutally cut off by assassination and repression. For them, it was a time of progressive possibility that has left them stranded on the shores of a conservative landscape ever since.

A summary expression of such utopian regrets is found in Steve Talbot's PBS documentary, "1968: The Year That Shaped A Generation." Talbot's narrative is shaped by radicals of the era like Todd Gitlin and Tom Hayden, whom he interviews on camera. The choice of Gitlin and Hayden as authorities on the era is predictable for someone like Talbot, himself the veteran of a movement that promotes itself as an avatar of "participatory democracy" but closes off debate within its own ranks in a way worthy of the Communist regimes it once admired. Thus the *auteur* of "The Year That Shaped A Generation" excludes from this cinematic paean to his revolutionary youth any dissenters from inside the ranks of those who were there.

I myself am one such veteran who does not share Talbot's enthusiasm for 1968, nor his view of it as a fable of Innocents At Home. One explanation may be that I am ten years older than Talbot, and therefore know firsthand the state of our "innocence" then. Yet Gitlin and Hayden are also pre-boomers. An age gap cannot really explain the different views we have of what took place. Naturally, I would prefer to recall the glory days of my youth in a golden light, just like Gitlin and Hayden. For me, however, the era has been irreparably tarnished by actions and attitudes I vividly remember, but they prefer to forget.

The myth of innocence in Talbot's film, begins with President Lyndon Johnson's announcement in March 1968 that he would not run for reelection. Talbot was 19 years old and draft-eligible: "We were all like Yossarian in *Catch-22*," he recalls in an article written for *Salon* magazine reprising his documentary film. "We took this very personally. 'They' were trying to kill 'us.' But now Johnson had abdicated. We were free. It felt, quite simply, like a miracle." The miracle, of course, was the democratic system, which the left had declared war on, but which had responded to the will of the people all the same. In 1968, radicals like us were calling for a "liberation" that would put an end to the system. For us the "system" was the enemy. But contrary to what Hayden, Gitlin, Talbot, and all the rest of us were saying at the time, the system worked. Looking back, we should all have defended it, and worked within it, instead of what we did do, which was to try to tear it down. Gitlin and Hayden have hedgingly (and *sotto voce*) acknowledged this fact but without judging their past actions accordingly. Talbot does not notice the difference. Nor does he reflect on the contradiction between what he and his comrades advocated then, and what everyone recognizes to be the case now.

The "they" Talbot refers to, and by which he means the government and the social establishment, were assuredly not trying to kill "us" in 1968. (Even in its retrospective voice, the narcissism of the boomer generation is impressive.) The attention of Lyndon Johnson and Richard Nixon were actually not on us but on the fate of Indochina. They had committed American forces to prevent the communist conquest of South Vietnam and Cambodia, and the bloodbath that we now *know* was in store for their inhabitants, should the communists win the war. As a result of the communist victory (and our efforts to make America lose), more people—more poor Indo-Chinese peasants—were killed by the marxist victors in the first three years of the communist peace than had been killed on all sides in the thirteen years of the anti-communist war. This is a fact that has caused some of us veterans of those years to reconsider our commitments and our innocence then. But not Talbot or the other nostalgists he has invited to make his film.

For them, the moral innocence of their comrades and themselves remains intact to this very day. According to them, their innocence was brutally ambushed when forces inherent in the system they hated conspired to murder the agents of their hope: Martin Luther King and Bobby Kennedy. And it was *only* that murder that caused them to become radicals at war with America. The year was 1968.

"I experienced King's assassination as the murder of hope," writes Talbot, speaking for them all. In the film, Gitlin, whose history of the 1960s first announced this theme, remembers his similar thoughts at the time: "America tried to redeem itself and now they've killed the man who was taking us to the mountaintop." This is a false memory and there is something extremely distasteful in the fact that it is proposed by a historic participant like Gitlin. For, as Gitlin well knows, in the year 1968 neither he nor Tom Hayden, nor any serious New Left radical, thought of themselves as a liberal reformer or was still a follower of Martin Luther King.

One indicator of the self-conscious dissociation of radicals like Gitlin and Hayden from reformers like King is that neither of them, nor any other white student activist, sds leader, or anti-war spokesman was in Memphis for the demonstrations King was organizing in 1968 at the time he was killed. In fact, no one in the New Left (at least no one who mattered) could still be called a serious supporter of King in the year before he was assassinated. The new black heroes of the New Left were prophets of separatism and violence, like Stokely Carmichael, H. Rap Brown, Huey Newton, and the martyred Malcolm X. King had been unceremoniously toppled from the leadership of the civil rights movement two years before. The agendas of the radicals who pushed King aside were "black power" and revolutionary violence, and they had already replaced King's pleas for nonviolence and integration in the imaginations of the left.

Like other New Left leaders, Todd Gitlin was far from the idealistic liberal he impersonates in his book or Talbot's film. And like practically all in the New Left, Gitlin had (by his own admission) stopped voting in national elections as early as 1964 because, as the SDS slogan put it, "the revolution is in the streets." To Gitlin and other New Leftists, the two parties were the Tweedledum and Tweedledee of the corporate ruling class. Activists, who saw themselves as revolutionaries against a "sham" democracy dominated by multinational corporations, were not going to invest hope in a leader like King whose political agenda was integration into the system, and who refused to join their war on the Johnson Administration, its imperialist adventures abroad and "tokenist" liberalism at home.

In Talbot's film, Hayden, too, embraces a doctrine of original innocence, but his disingenuous presentation of self involves fewer flat untruths than Gitlin's. He relies on subtle shadings and manipulations of the truth, a style of deception that became his political signature: "At that point," Hayden says of the King assassination, "I had been so knocked out of my middle-class assumptions that I didn't know what would happen. Perhaps the country could be reformed and Robert Kennedy elected president. Perhaps we would be plunged into a civil war and I'd be imprisoned or killed."

The reality is that any "middle-class assumptions" held by Hayden—or any prominent SDS activists—had already been chucked into the historical dustbin years before. Three out of four of the drafters of the famous 1962 Port Huron Statement were "red diaper babies" or marxists. The fourth was Hayden himself, who by his own account in his autobiography, *Reunion*, learned his politics in Berkeley in 1960 at the feet of children of the Old Left. (Hayden names Michael Tigar and Richard Flacks, in particular, as his mentors.) By 1965, SDS president Carl Oglesby was proclaiming publicly, in a famous speech, that it was time to "name the System" that we all wanted to destroy. The name of the system was "corporate capitalism," and it was analyzed by SDS leaders in pretty much the same terms as in party texts read by the communist cadres in Moscow, Havana, and Hanoi.

Hayden was already calling the Black Panthers "America's Vietcong," and planning the riot he was going to stage at the Democratic convention in Chicago that August. This pivotal event is described conveniently, but inaccurately, as a "police riot" in Talbot's film, Gitlin's book, and Hayden's own memoir which singularly fails to acknowledge his efforts to produce the eruption that ensued. Civil war in America was not something that was going to be imposed on the SDS revolutionaries from the outside or above, as Hayden disingenuously insinuates. Civil war was something that radicals—Hayden foremost among them—were trying to launch themselves.

Talbot continues his mythologizing of the spring of 1968 and the period just prior to the Chicago Riot by romanticizing the political ambitions of Bobby Kennedy, and mis-remembering how the left reacted to them: "Out of the ashes of the riots in the wake of King's murder, new hope came in the form of Bobby Kennedy, who had undergone a profound transformation from Vietnam hawk and aide to Sen. Joe McCarthy to dove and spokesman for the dispossessed."

It is true, of course, that Bobby Kennedy made a feint in the direction of the anti-war crowd and more than one gesture on behalf of Cesar Chavez. It is also true that Hayden attended Kennedy's funeral and even wept a tear or two. But those tears had little to do with Hayden's political agendas at the time, which were more accurately summed up in Che Guevara's call to create "two, three, many Vietnams" inside America's borders. Hayden's tears for Kennedy were personal, and he paid a huge political price for them among his revolutionary comrades who were not overly impressed by Kennedy's sudden political "transformation." After the funeral, SDS activists wondered out loud, and in print, whether Hayden had "sold out" by mourning a figure whom they saw not as the great white hope of the political struggle that consumed their lives, but as a Trojan horse for the other side.

With King dead in April and Kennedy in June, the stage was set for what Talbot calls "the inevitable showdown" in Chicago in August. And here he allows a glimmer of the truth to enter his narrative: "Both sides, rebels and rulers, were spoiling for a confrontation." But just as quickly he reverts to the mythology that Hayden and his cohorts first created and that leftist historians have since perpetuated: "Chicago's Mayor Richard Daley made it possible. He denied permits for protesters at the Democratic Convention." The denied permits made confrontation inevitable.

In fact, the famous epigram from 1968—"Demand the Impossible"—which Talbot elsewhere cites, explains far more accurately why it was Hayden, not Daley, who set the agenda for Chicago, and why it was Hayden who was ultimately responsible for the riot that ensued. The police behaved badly, it is true—and they have been justly and roundly condemned for their reactions. But those reactions were entirely predictable. After all, it was Daley who, only months before, had ordered his police to "shoot looters on sight" during the rioting after King's murder. In fact, the predictable reaction of the Chicago police was an essential part of Hayden's choice of Chicago as the site of the demonstration in the first place.

It was also why many of us did not go. In a year when any national "action" would attract one hundred thousand protestors, only about ten thousand (and probably closer to three thousand) actually showed up for the Chicago blood-fest. That was because most of us realized there was going to be bloodshed and did not see the point. Our ideology argued otherwise as well. The two-party system was a sham; the revolution was in the streets. Why demonstrate at a political convention? In retrospect, Hayden was more cynical and more shrewd than we were. By destroying the presidential aspirations of Hubert Humphrey, he dealt a fatal blow to the anti-communist liberals in the Democratic Party and paved the way for a takeover of its apparatus by the forces of the political left, a trauma from which the party has yet to recover.

One reason the left has obscured these historical facts is that the nostalgists do not really want to take credit for electing Richard Nixon, which they surely did. As a matter of political discretion, they are also willing to let their greatest coup—the capture of the Democratic Party—go unmemorialized. Instead they prefer to ascribe this remarkable political realignment to impersonal forces that, apparently, had nothing to do with their own agendas and actions. Talbot summarizes: "While 'the whole world (was) watching,' [Daley's] police rioted, clubbing demonstrators, reporters and bystanders indiscriminately. The Democratic Party self-destructed." Well, actually, it was destroyed by the left's riot in Chicago.

When the fires of Watergate consumed the Nixon presidency in 1974, the left's newly won control of the Democratic Party produced the exact result that Hayden and his comrades had worked so hard to achieve. In 1974, a new class of Democrats was elected to Congress, including anti-war activists like Ron Dellums, Pat Schroeder, David Bonior, and Bella Abzug. Their politics were traditionally left as opposed to the anti-communist liberalism of the Daleys and the Humphreys (Abzug had even been a communist). Their first act was to cut off economic aid and military supplies to the regimes in Cambodia and South Vietnam, precipitating the bloodbath that followed. Though it is conveniently forgotten now, this cut off occurred two years *after* the United States had signed a truce with Hanoi and American troops had been withdrawn from Vietnam.

"Bring The Troops Home" may have been the slogan of the so-called anti-war movement, but it was never its only goal. The slogan was designed by its authors to bring about a "liberated" Vietnam. Within three months of the cut-off of military aid, the anti-communist regimes in Saigon and Phnompenh fell, and the genocide began. The mass slaughter in Cambodia and South Vietnam from 1975 to 1978 was the real achievement of the New Left and could not have been achieved without Hayden's sabotage of anti-communist Democrats like Hubert Humphrey.

While Talbot forgets this denouement, he does get the significance of the war right: "The war in Vietnam and the draft were absolutely central. I remember a cover of *Ramparts* magazine that captured how I felt: 'Alienation is when your country is at war and you hope the other side wins.'" This is a softened version of what we actually felt. As the author of that cover line, let me correct Talbot's memory and add a detail. The *Ramparts* cover featured a picture of a Huck Finn-like seven-year-old (it was our art director Dugald Stermer's son) who was holding the Vietcong flag—the flag of America's enemy in Vietnam. The cover line said: "Alienation is when your country is at war and you *want* the other side to win." This represented what we actually believed—Hayden, Gitlin, Steve Talbot, and myself. What lessons my former comrades draw from our service to the wrong side in the Cold War is not that important to me. I just wish they would have the decency to remember the events the way they happened.

I also wish they would have the good grace not to claim retrospectively sympathies for the struggle against communism, a struggle they opposed and whose true warriors and champions—however distasteful, embarrassing, and uncomfortable this must be for them—were Richard Nixon and Ronald Reagan, and the political right they hate and despise. Go over the fifty years of the Cold War against the Soviet empire and you will find that every political and military program to contain the spread of this cancer and ultimately to destroy it was fiercely resisted by those who now invoke the "spirit of '68" as their own.

"Assassinations, repression and exhaustion extinguished the spirit of '68," Talbot concludes his story. "But like a subterranean fire, it resurfaces at historic moments." Citing the socialist writer Paul Berman, the originator of this ultimate myth, Talbot argues that "the members of '68 . . . helped ignite the revolution of 1989 that brought liberal democracy to Eastern Europe and ended the Cold War." The distortion of this memory is one thing for Berman, who at some point joined a miniscule faction of the left that was indeed anti-communist, while still hating American capitalism almost as much. (How much? In Berman's case, enough to support the Black Panthers—"America's Vietcong"—in the 1970s and to praise the secret police chief of the Sandinista dictatorship in the 1980s as a "quintessential New Leftist.") But this attempt to hijack the anti-communist cause for a left that abhorred it, is particularly unappetizing in Talbot's case. Talbot, after all, made films into the 1980s celebrating communist insurgents who were busily extending the Soviet sphere in Africa. America, bless its generous heart, has already forgiven Steve Talbot for the indiscretions of the past. So why lie about them now?

Of course, New Leftists were critical of the policies of the Soviet Union (as, at various times were Khrushchev, Castro, and Ho Chi Minh). But their true, undying enemy was always democratic America—their hatred for which was never merely reactive (as is sometimes suggested), never truly innocent, and remains remarkably intact to this day. The worldview of this left was aptly summarized by the adoring biographer of the journalist I. F. Stone, who approvingly described Stone's belief that "in spite of the brutal collectivization campaign, the Nazi-Soviet Pact, the latest quashing of the Czech democracy and the Stalinist takeover of Eastern Europe . . . communism was a progressive force, lined up on the correct side of historical events."

Berman, Gitlin, and now Talbot have mounted a preposterous last-ditch effort to save leftists from the embarrassments of their deeds by attempting to appropriate moral credit for helping to end a system that the left aided and abetted throughout its career. It may be, as Berman and Talbot claim, that East European anti-communists drew inspiration from anti-government protests in the West. But this was a reflection of their admiration for a democratic system that embraced dissent and promoted freedom, not the anti-western agendas of the New Left demonstrators. Even in its best moments, the western left disparaged the threat from the communist enemy as a paranoid fantasy of the Cold War right.

The unseemly attempt to retrieve an honorable past from such dishonorable commitments might be more convincing if any of these memorialists (including Berman) were able to come up with a single demonstration against communist oppression in Vietnam, or the genocide in Cambodia, or the rape of Afghanistan, or the dictatorships in Cuba and Nicaragua. Or, if one veteran leader of the New Left had once publicly called on the Soviets to tear down the Berlin Wall, as Ronald Reagan actually did. Support for the anti-communist freedom fighters in Afghanistan and Africa and Central America during the 1980s came largely from Goldwater and Reagan activists on the right, like Jeanne Kirkpatrick, Grover Norquist, Elliot Abrams, Dana Rohrabacher, and Oliver North, whom progressives—for this very reason—passionately despise.

It would have been nice if the thirtieth anniversary of the events of 1968 had been used to end the cold war over its memories and start restoring a sense of the tragic to both sides. But to do that, the nostalgists of the left would first have to be persuaded to give up their futile attempts to re-write what happened, and start telling it like it was.

19

Two Goodbyes

1. ELDRIDGE CLEAVER'S LAST GIFT

LDRIDGE CLEAVER (1935–1998) was a man who made a
a significant imprint on our times, and not for the best. But
I mourn his passing nonetheless.

I first met Eldridge when he was *Ramparts* magazine's most famous and most bloodthirsty ex-con. "I'm perfectly aware that I'm
in prison, that I'm a Negro, that I've been a rapist," he wrote in a
notorious epistle that *Ramparts* published. "My answer to all such
thoughts lurking in their split-level heads, crouching behind their
squinting bombardier eyes, is that the blood of Vietnamese peasants has paid off all my debts." This nihilism became an icono-
graphic comment for the times, a ready excuse for all the destructive
acts radicals like us went on to commit.

No one doubted that Eldridge was the most articulate and col-
orful tribune of the Panther vanguard. But what he represented
most was a limitless, radical rage. Eldridge was indeed a rapist and
possibly a murderer as well (he boasted to Timothy Leary, whom
he held hostage in his Algerian exile, that he had a private grave-

yard for his enemies). It was Eldridge who accused Panther leader Huey Newton of betraying the radical cause when Newton reversed his famous summons to "pick up the gun" and begin the revolution. In protest against Newton's "kinder, gentler" Panthers, Eldridge split the party and became spiritual godfather to the Black Liberation Army and other violent revolutionary factions.

But in the 1970s and 1980s Eldridge had a change of heart, or rather many changes of heart. He became a Moonie, and then a Christian, and then a Republican, backsliding to political street hustler in between. Those of us who knew him saw these various incarnations as attempts to secure new support systems for an extraordinary individual who lacked a moral center. Still, it took a certain courage and integrity to tell even a part of the truth, as he did. It meant, for example, detaching himself from the radical gravy train, as others were just beginning to cash in on their criminal pasts. His Panther comrades David Hilliard, Bobby Seale, and Elaine Brown were busily taking advantage of a national false memory syndrome that recalled the Panthers not as the street thugs they were, but as heroes of a civil rights struggle they had openly despised. (To be fair, the public misperception of this past was heavily fostered by former radicals who now occupy editorial positions at ABC, the *New York Times*, and other institutions of cultural authority.) In their heyday, Panther leaders liked to outrage their white supporters by referring to Martin Luther King as "Martin Luther Coon." But now they were ready to pretend that the civil rights movement had been as much their achievement as his, to join the mainstream, and reap its rewards. On well-paid campus lecture tours, in Hollywood films, and in a series of well-hyped books lauded by reviewers in the *New York Times*, the *Los Angeles Times*, the *New York Review of Books*, and the *Washington Post*, the Panther survivors rewrote their histories to fit the revisionist legend.

Eldridge, however, chose the lonelier and more honest course of admitting what he had done. His most famous encounter with the law had been a shootout that followed the assassination of

Martin Luther King. In this episode, an eighteen-year-old Panther named Bobby Hutton had been killed. As Panther "Minister of Communications," Eldridge designed the propaganda campaign that portrayed the killing as a classic case of "police brutality." He was abetted in this by a white radical named Robert Scheer, now a national correspondent for the *Los Angeles Times*, who edited both of Eldridge's Panther books and saw to it that Eldridge's version of the Hutton incident received wide exposure in the nation's press. As a result, Hutton's death became a famous martyrdom for the entire New Left, an occasion to expose the "repressive, racist power structure" that victimized black militants like him. But in an interview with reporter Kate Coleman more than a decade after the events, Eldridge revealed that this was not a story of Panther innocence. On hearing the news of King's murder by a lone assassin, he had ordered party members to "assassinate" police in "retaliation" for King's death (but really to launch the war against America that the left was preparing for, but had been unable to carry out). Eldridge himself had participated in an armed ambush that left two San Francisco police officers wounded. This was the reason that the police were chasing a Panther vehicle containing Eldridge and Hutton that ended in Hutton's death. The courage that Eldridge's revelation took can be measured by the silence of other Panthers who know what happened and New Left radicals like Robert Scheer who have suppressed these facts ever since.

It was during his last televised interview on *60 Minutes* that Eldridge won my final respect. Quiet-spoken, as he had never been in his public life, sober, bespectacled and fully grey, he unburdened himself of what appeared at last to be truly felt convictions, not designed for anyone but himself. He said that when you looked at this country as compared to others, it had been remarkably good to people like himself, and to minorities generally, a fact he had not appreciated when he was young. He said, gravely, "If people had listened to Huey Newton and me in the 1960s, there would have been a holocaust in this country."

The interviewer hardly noticed this last remark, and its significance went unexplored. But I noticed. Here was the beginning of any understanding of what the New Left and its Black Panther vanguard were really about in the 1960s. They were attempting to launch a civil war in America that would have resulted in unimaginable bloodshed. At the same time, they had no sensible idea of how to make things better, as they claimed.

For coming to this understanding, and for having the courage to honestly confront what he did, Eldridge paid a profound price. In a world where it is so difficult to get a handle on the truth, and where so many would prefer that it be buried, we should all be thankful to him for providing us with the one he did.

II. ONE WHO WILL NOT BE MISSED

KWAME TURE, a k a Stokely Carmichael, is dead of prostate cancer at the age of fifty-seven. Jesse Jackson, who was with him in Africa at the last, claimed Carmichael for the radical 1960s. "He was one of our generation who was determined to give his life to transforming America and Africa," Jackson eulogized him. "He rang the freedom bell in this century."

The truth is otherwise. Kwame Ture was a racist and a lifelong friend of tyrants and oppressors. The world will not miss him. A West Indian immigrant to America, and a child of middle-class privilege, Carmichael hated his adopted country from youth to old age, and never bothered once to acknowledge the immense advantages and personal recognition it undeservedly gave him.

As Stokely Carmichael, his chief claim to fame was to lead young Turks in the civil rights movement in pushing Martin Luther King aside, while denouncing him as an Uncle Tom. In 1966, Carmichael emerged as the chief spokesman for the "black power" movement, which replaced King's goals of nonviolence and integration with agendas of political violence and racial separatism. In 1967, when Israel was attacked by six Arab nations, Carmichael announced that "the only good Zionist is a dead Zionist," and became the first prominent American figure since the Mississippi racist Senator Bilbo held forth in the 1940s, to spew anti-Semitic bile into the public square.

The following year Carmichael began a campaign to promote armed warfare in American cities and was briefly made "prime minister" of the Black Panther Party for his efforts. Ever the racist, Carmichael tried to persuade the Panthers to break off their alliances with whites, but failed. This led to his expulsion from the party and a ritual beating administered by his former comrades. Shortly thereafter, Carmichael left the United States for Africa.

In Africa, he changed his name to Kwame Ture, thereby honoring two dictators (Kwame Nkrumah and Sekou Toure) who caused untold misery to their own peoples. He took up residence as the personal guest of the sadistic Toure, Guinea's paranoid dictator, whose reputation was built on the torture-murders of thousands of his African subjects. Some 250,000 Guineans were driven into exile during Carmichael's stay there, without a protest from this New Left leader.

Returning to the United States in the late 1980s, he took to the lecture circuit as a racial hate-monger, attacking Jews, whites, and America to approving audiences of blacks and leftists on American university campuses, who paid him handsome fees for his efforts. In the end, he found a fitting refuge in the racial sewer of the Nation of Islam, to which he had been introduced at the end of the 1960s by the communist writer Shirley Graham. In his new religious home he proved an apt and loyal protégé of its Jew-baiting, America-hating, racist minister, Louis Farrakhan. Carmichael's parting shot at the country he victimized was to accuse "the forces of American imperialism" of causing the prostate cancer that would have killed him sooner had it not been for the creative medical contributions of scientists who were Jewish, white, and American.

20

Two Revolutions

THE ARREST IN ENGLAND of Chile's counter-revolutionary
General Augusto Pinochet just before the fortieth anniversary of the Cuban Revolution brought into focus two celebrated battles of the Cold War in which members of my generation had taken passionate sides. As one who went into these battles
on one of those sides and came out on the other, I found myself
reacting with mixed but ultimately clear emotions to this history
and the events that shaped it.

One source of this ambivalence, undoubtedly, was the residue
of feeling retained from my years on the left side of the political
struggle. To be on the left imbues one with a sense of righteousness, of having chosen the side of virtue in all such conflicts. Eventually, belonging to the camp of virtue becomes a second nature to
every "progressive" and provides compensation for the fact that most
of these battles are necessarily lost. As "revolutionaries" in the 1960s,
we would console ourselves with the idea that we were destined to
lose every battle but the last. We did not join the progressive cause
to support history's winners, but to stand up for its losers, the powerless and the victimized, the vulnerable and the oppressed. Our

political commitment was to put our weight on the side of social justice. It was a good feeling to have.

For this reason, when it came time to relinquish those political commitments, I found it far easier to identify what was wrong with the left than to move in the direction of the political right. So problematic was even the prospect of such a choice that I withdrew from all politics for nearly ten years before changing course.

When I stepped back from the left, it was because I was repelled by the crimes progressives had committed (and justified) and by the catastrophes they had produced. It turned out that winning the "last" battle could be worse than losing. But, as I made my choice, I had a nagging feeling about certain political events and about specific historical figures who had been associated with the battles I had fought and whose careers I had not yet reexamined. One of those figures was General Pinochet, and the revolution that brought him to power in Chile.

Chile had been rare among Latin American nations in boasting a fairly stable political democracy. Its democracy had produced a historical anomaly—a marxist who had actually been elected to power. We glossed over the fact, naturally, that in accomplishing this feat, Salvador Allende had received only 36 percent of the popular vote in a three-way election. Allende and his supporters seemed to gloss over this fact as well. Pushed by more radical forces on his political left, Allende began a program "to initiate socialism" at once.

A first law of revolutionary theory taught that ruling classes never gave up power without a fight. A first law of democratic theory would have taught that electoral minorities cannot force through revolutionary agendas and hope to survive. Sooner or later, a reaction can be expected. Latin American history taught that this would probably take the form of a military coup. The only question was when.

In thinking about these issues, at the time, we had our eye on our own government in Washington, which was the capital, as we would have put it, of global reaction. In political statements we made at the time, we invoked the cautionary memory of the Bay of Pigs, the failed CIA attempt to topple Fidel Castro during the second year of his revolutionary regime. In our eyes this act had betrayed the true of face of American power, the iron fist in the velvet glove. Policies that appeared to most Americans as democratic we knew to be orchestrated by corporate interests with high-stakes investments in the Third World. It was only a matter of time before these interests asserted themselves in Chile and provoked a civil war.

The coup against Allende came in 1973, when the army generals rose against the regime and toppled it. Allende committed suicide or was killed (as his partisans claim) in the heat of the military battle. The coup was led by Pinochet, who became the nation's new *caudillo*. In the measures imposed to "restore civil order," leftists were rounded up, and five thousand executed. The military dictatorship became the law of the land. Chile's once stable democracy was dead.

Of course, we "knew" the CIA was behind these events. President Nixon and his secretary of state, Henry Kissinger, were fighting a counter-revolutionary war in Vietnam and could not tolerate a second revolutionary example in the American hemisphere. The International Telephone and Telegraph Corporation (ITT) had a big investment in Chile, and the charts we drew to show the tentacles of power projected its influence far into the Nixon Administration and the American intelligence community. The entire episode was, in our view, straight out of Lenin.

When I defected from the left, I did not want to be any part of such developments, even in retrospect. It was one thing to reject the left; it was quite another to embrace what appeared to be this kind of right—one that trampled over defenseless people, making their lives even more miserable than they were. Moreover, there was no particular reason for me to do so, even with my new political second thoughts. It was perfectly possible for me to conclude that the schemes of the left were utopian and could result in great social disasters and grotesque crimes, without jumping to the opposite conclusion—that the sadism of right-wing dictators was a proper or even preferable alternative. No one among the conservatives I was familiar with, ever claimed that support for Pinochet was a *sine qua non* of conservative credentials, in the way support for Castro, for example, would have been for anyone on the left. (To be fair, as a leftist, one could be critical of the Castro regime in the 1970s, so long as one was careful to express even greater distaste for Washington and its Cuba policies.)

Another familiar reflex in the thought of progressives, which I retained during the early stages of my transition, was to avert one's eyes from bad news that came from the left. The enemies of promise would use every socialist failing to kill the socialist dream. It was important be on constant guard against these "reactionary" agendas. Every revolutionary enterprise was really a harbinger of human possibility. It was therefore often necessary to bury or repress (what the left regarded as) small or incidental truths, to keep the grand vision alive.

For reasons like this, I found myself paying as little attention as I could to the fate of this other revolution, the one that had actually inspired Allende to dream of a socialist Chile. This was Fidel's revolution in Cuba, whose launching in 1959 had been one of the primary inspirations for the American New Left. For many years now, even we realized that conditions in Cuba—both political and economic—had been degenerating under Castro's rule. Like my comrades, I was not unaware that Cuba was having problems, but I ascribed them—as I did Allende's pre-coup difficulties in Chile—to the machinations of external forces, emanating from two evil empires centered in Washington and Moscow.

At the end of the 1970s, however, I saw a documentary film about Castro's revolution, made by an Academy Award-winning Cuban filmmaker, Nestor Almendros, that changed my perspective.

Almendros had left the island in 1963 and gone on to a distinguished career as a cinematographer in Hollywood, where his credits included *Sophie's Choice, Kramer vs. Kramer,* and *Days of Heaven.* The documentary he had made about Cuba was called *Improper Conduct* and it focused on the Cuban government's brutal treatment of homosexuals as a metaphor for its treatment of all social and political deviants. It was a stunning indictment of what the revolution had become.

One characteristically striking scene in the film was an interview with a black Cuban exile on a street in New York's Harlem. The exile was a flamboyant homosexual, in his early twenties, dressed in a tangerine satin shirt open to the sternum and in white flared trousers. The interviewer asked him whether he liked the freedom he had found in America and in Harlem. Through ivory teeth he answered with a smile that, indeed, he did. The interviewer asked why. He responded: "I am free here. In Cuba I could be arrested just for being dressed like this, and put in jail for six months." The interviewer asked how old he was. "Twenty-three." And then: "How many times were you arrested." The Cuban answered: "Seventeen."

This was not a political person. This was one of those ordinary Cubans on whom history (along with the drama created by socialist intellectuals) was inflicted. If this was what the revolution represented to a Cuban like him, what did that say about the ideals to which I had been so devoted? Cuba now had a lower per capita income than it had in 1959, the year Castro took power. The political prisons were full. Hundreds of thousands had fled. Hundreds of thousands more were waiting to flee. Castro had turned his island into a national prison.

Pinochet had always justified his military rule as a temporary measure—in much the same way that Castro had defended his own revolutionary dictatorship. The suspension of liberties was necessary to defend the regime and restore stability to create the economic foundations of a true democracy. Ten years after I saw Almendros's film, the Pinochet dictatorship held an election. Pinochet had decided to end his military rule and restore Chilean democracy. The dictator was holding a national referendum to pronounce judgment on his own regime. Even the left was fielding a candidate under the ground rules that Pinochet had devised.

As it turned out, in Pinochet's Chile the claim of temporary expediency for the harsh measures was valid. Under the fifteen years of Pinochet's rule, Chile had prospered so greatly that it was dubbed the "miracle economy," one of the two or three richest in Latin America.

This economic success provided a stark contrast to Castro's achievement. In 1959, when he took power, Cuba was enjoying the second highest per capita income in Latin America. But in the thirty years that followed, Cuba had become one of the three poorest of the twenty or so Latin American republics. Food was scarcer than it had been within the memory of any Cuban alive, and even automobiles had vanished from Cuban streets. After Pinochet announced his referendum, Castro was approached by socialist supporters in Europe who appealed to him to hold a similar election to pave the way for democracy in Cuba. He refused.

The results of Pinochet's referendum were instructive. If the dictator had won, he would have become the new president of a democratic Chile. But Chileans rejected Pinochet, and elected a more moderate candidate who was not of the left. True to his word, Pinochet stepped down. His dictatorship had indeed been a temporary measure to restore Chile's stability, prosperity, and democracy. Moreover, after fifteen years of military dictatorship, Pinochet had still received a larger percentage of the popular vote than Allende had received to get elected in the first place.

These developments prompted me to take another look at Allende's decision to institute the radical programs that led to the coup and a mini-civil war. I had long since become suspicious of the idea that the CIA was a kind of deus ex machina that could explain these events. The CIA surely had a finger in the Chilean pot, but it had become clear over time that there were limits to what the CIA could accomplish. The CIA had not, for example, been able to overthrow Castro himself, despite his proximity to the United States, the relatively small population of Cuba, and its economic weakness. It could not even oust the marxist dictator of a ministate like Grenada, or a drug lord in its own employ like Panama's Noriega. These removals required military invasions. And Chile was not a tiny island or an isthmus nation, but a relatively large country, with a long-standing democratic tradition. Moreover, if Chileans themselves saw Pinochet as a creature of the CIA, it is unlikely he would have received a greater percentage of the vote than Allende.

Allende, however, was a radical, and to his left were forces more radical still. In 1970, when he came to power, these forces were inspired by Cuba's revolutionary example. They were impatient with the frustratingly slow processes of democracy, and quickly pushed Allende into measures designed to initiate a socialist regime, which was well beyond his electoral mandate and what Chile's constitution would allow. The result was an economic and political crisis that was soon out of his control. An article in the *Wall Street Journal* after Pinochet's arrest, summarizes what followed:

> Salvador Allende reached the presidency of Chile in 1970 with only 36 percent of the vote, barely forty thousand votes ahead of the candidate of the right. In Mr. Allende's one thousand days of rule, Chile degenerated into what the much-lionized former Chilean president Eduardo Frei Montalva (father of the current president) called a "carnival of madness." Eleven months before the fall of President Allende, Mr. Frei said: "Chile is in the throes of an economic disaster: not a crisis, but a veritable catastrophe. . . ." Shortly after those remarks were made, the legal ground beneath the Allende presidency

began to crumble. The Chilean Supreme Court, the Bar Association and the leftist Medical Society, along with the Chamber of Deputies and provincial heads of the Christian Democrat Party, all warned that Allende was systematically trampling the law and constitution. By August 1973, more than a million Chileans—half the work force—were on strike, demanding that Allende go. Transport and industry were paralyzed. On Sept. 11, 1973, the armed forces acted to oust Allende, going into battle against his gunslingers. Six hours after the fighting erupted, Allende blew his head off in the presidential palace with an AK-47 given to him by Fidel Castro.*

Forty years of history have left us with a fairly clear perspective on these two repressive regimes. Castro bankrupted his country, tyrannized its inhabitants, and is now the longest reigning dictator in the world. Pinochet presided over his own ruthless dictatorship for fifteen years, but created a booming economy and eventually restored democracy to Chile. If one had to choose between a Castro and a Pinochet, from the point of view of the poor, the victimized, and the oppressed, the choice would not be difficult. As an American conservative, however, I did not have to do that. It was Chileans, not Henry Kissinger or Richard Nixon, who made the real decision to put Pinochet in power. Unlike the American left, which passionately supported Fidel Castro and denied the realities of the oppressive state, the American right's sympathies for Pinochet were generally muted, and did not involve blindness to the stringency of his rule. In short, Pinochet's career does not compromise conservative expectations in the way that Castro's dictatorship compromises the visions of the left.

---

* A detailed study of Allende's three years in power and the causes of his fall can be found in Mark Falcoff's *Modern Chile* (New Brunswick, New Jersey: Rutgers 1989).

The imprisoning of Pinochet on a trip to London to seek medical help was a minor incident in the larger narrative. It is one of those bad ideas of progressives that will come back to bite them. Consider, for example, the prospect for Castro himself should he venture abroad for medical reasons. Yet, perhaps the idea does work from the partisan perspective of the left. What made Pinochet vulnerable to this kind of arrest is that he had voluntarily retired from his dictator's role. There is no danger of a Castro doing that.

21

Feminist Fibber

W HY DO POLITICAL "PROGRESSIVES" feel the need to lie so regularly about who they are? The question is an old one, but is newly prompted by a biography of feminist leader Betty Friedan, which establishes beyond doubt that the woman who virtually created modern feminism is a political imposter. In her path-breaking book, *The Feminine Mystique*, Friedan presented herself as a typical suburban housewife not "even conscious of the woman question" before she began work on her manuscript. But now Smith professor Daniel Horowitz (no relation) has shown that nothing could be further from the truth.* Under her maiden name, Betty Goldstein, the record reveals that Friedan was a political activist and professional propagandist for the communist left for nearly thirty years before the 1963 publication of *The Feminist Mystique* launched the modern feminist movement.

Betty Friedan's secret was shared by hundreds of her comrades on the left—though not, of course, by the unsuspecting American

---

* Daniel Horowitz, *Betty Friedan and the Making of the Feminist Mystique* (Amherst, Mass.: University of Massachsetts Press, 1998).

public—who went along with her charade presumably as a way to support her political agenda. As Horowitz's biography makes clear, Friedan, from her college days and until her mid-thirties, was a Stalinist marxist (or a camp follower thereof), the political intimate of leaders of America's Cold War fifth column, and for a time even the lover of a young communist physicist working on atomic bomb projects with J. Robert Oppenheimer. Not at all a neophyte when it came to "the woman question" (the phrase itself is a marxist construction), she was certainly familiar with the writings of Engels, Lenin, and Stalin on the subject and had written about it herself as a journalist for the official publication of the communist-controlled United Electrical Workers union. These newly disclosed facts suggest that the histories of feminism, including some written by other veterans of the communist movement like Eleanor Flexner and Gerda Lerner, apparently another Party alumna, need to be reexamined just to get the record straight.

The antecedents of Friedan's version of feminism also bear revisiting in light of the new information. Her infamous description of America's suburban family household as "a comfortable concentration camp," in *The Feminine Mystique*, probably had more to do with her marxist hatred for America than for her own experience as a housewife and mother. Her husband, Carl, also a leftist, once complained to a reporter in 1970 that, far from being a homebody, his wife "was in the world during the whole marriage, either full time or free lance," lived in an eleven-room mansion on the Hudson with a full-time maid, and "seldom was a wife and a mother." Of course, no one paid much attention to the family "patriarch" when he supplied these interesting details, because as a male he was deemed guilty before the fact.

One indication that Goldstein-Friedan has not liberated herself entirely from the Stalinist mentality that shaped her views is the fact that she still feels the need to lie about her identity. Although her biographer is a sympathetic leftist, Friedan refused to cooperate with him once she realized he was going to tell the truth. After Horowitz published an initial article about Friedan's youthful work as a "labor journalist," Friedan publicly maligned him. Speaking to an American University audience, she remarked: "Some historian recently wrote some attack on me in which he claimed that I was only pretending to be a suburban housewife, that I was supposed to be an agent."

This was both false and unkind because Friedan's professor-biographer bends over backwards throughout his book to sanitize the true dimensions of Friedan's past. Thus he describes Steve Nelson as "the legendary radical, veteran of the Spanish Civil War, and Bay area party official." In fact, Nelson was an obscure radical but an important party apparatchik (later notorious for his espionage activities in the Berkeley Radiation Lab), who would be a legend only to other communists and who was in Spain as a party commissar to enforce the Stalinist line. The professor also bends over backwards to defend Friedan's lying, excusing it as a response to "McCarthyism." In her attack on him she claimed, absurdly, that he was going to use "innuendos" to describe her past. This was based on the fact that he had asked questions about what she actually believed at the time, based on his examination of her published articles. Horowitz's response to what might be called Friedan's "right baiting" is all-too understanding or would be seen as such by anyone outside the claustrophobic circles of the left. "Innuendos," he explains, is a word often used by people "scarred by McCarthyism." Indeed.

Reading these passages called to mind a c-span *Booknotes* program on which Brian Lamb asked the president-elect of the American Historical Association, Eric Foner, about his father, Jack. The younger Foner claimed that his father was a man "with a social conscience" who made his living through public lectures and who, along with his brothers Phil and Moe, was "persecuted" during the McCarthy era. When Lamb asked Foner why they were persecuted,

Foner responded disingenuously that his father was a political dis-
senter and had supported the loyalist side in the Spanish Civil War.
(He repeated this misleading charade in a similar exchange with a
reporter from the *Chronicle of Higher Education*.*) Even in the
McCarthy 1950s, no one was persecuted simply for siding with the
Spanish Republic in the Spanish Civil War.

The Foner brothers, in fact, were fairly well-known communists,
one a party labor historian and another a party union organizer. It
is a historical fact that, communist-controlled unions in the CIO, on
orders from Moscow, sought to block the Marshall Plan effort to
rebuild Western Europe. This was a plan, it should be recalled, that
was in part designed to prevent Stalin's empire from absorbing
Western Europe which had been the fate of the new satellites in
Eastern Europe. That is why socialists like Walter Reuther purged
the union "reds" from the CIO and also why communists like Foner's
uncle came under FBI scrutiny—that is, why they were "persecuted"
in the McCarthy era. They were potential fifth column agents for
the Soviet state.

That communists, like the Foners, lied at the time was understandable. They had something to hide. But why are their children lying to this day? And why are people like Betty Friedan lying,
long after they have anything to fear from McCarthy committees
and other government investigators?

Surely no one seriously believes that people who reveal their
communist pasts in the Clinton era are going to be persecuted by
the American government. The folk singer, Pete Seeger, a party

---

* October 23, 1998: "His father, Jack D. Foner, and his uncle, Philip Foner, were
both leftist historians blacklisted during the McCarthy era for their alleged Communist activities ('like supporting the Spanish Civil War,' Mr. Foner says dryly).
'I grew up in a family where we were well aware of the gap between the rhetoric
and the reality of freedom—and where we were willing to challenge it.'" This is
how the DeWitt Clinton Professor of History at one of the nation's most prestigious schools describes his Stalinist family's political opinions.

puppet his entire life, is a nationally celebrated entertainer and was honored at the Kennedy Center with a Freedom Medal by President Clinton himself. Angela Davis was once the Communist Party's candidate for vice president and served the police states of the Soviet empire until their very last gasps. Her punishment for this career is to have been appointed "President's Professor" at the state-run University of California, one of only seven faculty members on its nine campuses to be so honored. Nationally, she is a living academic legend, officially invited to speak on ceremonial occasions at exorbitant fees by college administrations across the country and memorialized with rooms and lounges named in her honor—this despite the absence of any notable scholarly contributions on her part and a corpus of work that is little more than ideological tripe.

Nor does the amnesty extend merely to members of the Communist Party. In the midst of the Vietnam War, New Left icon Jane Fonda incited American troops to defect in a broadcast she made from the enemy capital over Radio Hanoi. She then returned to the United States to win an Academy Award and eventually become the wife of one of America's most powerful media moguls. In this capacity she oversaw a twenty-two-hour CNN series on the Cold War equating McCarthyism with the Soviet gulag. This travesty is now an "educational" tool destined for use in classrooms in every state in the nation. Bernadine Dohrn, leader of America's first political terrorist cult, who once officially declared war on "Amerika" and personally set a bomb in the nation's Capitol, and who has never conceded even minimal regret for her crimes or hinted at the slightest revision of her views, was appointed by the Clinton Administration to a Justice Department commission on children. Her husband and equally unrepentant fellow terrorist, Billy Ayers, is a professor of early child education at Northwestern University. The idea that America relentlessly punishes those who betray her is laughable, as is the idea that leftists have anything to fear from their government if they tell the truth about what they did fifty years ago.*

So why the continuing lies? The reason is pretty obvious: the truth is embarrassing. To *them*. Imagine what it would be like for Betty Friedan (the name actually is Friedman) to admit that as a Jew she opposed America's entry into the war against Hitler because Stalin told her that it was just an inter-imperialist fracas? Imagine what it would be like for America's premier feminist to acknowledge that well into her thirties (and who knows for how long after?) she thought Stalin was the Father of the Peoples and that the United States was an evil empire. Or that her interest in women's liberation was just the subtext of her real desire to create a Soviet America. Now, *those* explanations would demand a lot from anyone.

Which is why it probably seemed easier to lie about all of it at the time, apparently until after her death, when her papers would be unlocked. The problem with this solution, however, is that lying can't be contained. It begets other lies, and eventually becomes a whole way of life, as President Clinton himself could tell you. One of the lies that the denial of the communist past begets is an exaggerated view of McCarthyism. Fear of McCarthyism quickly becomes an excuse for everything. The idea advanced by people like Friedan, that McCarthyism was a "reign of terror," as though thousands lost their freedom and hundreds their lives while the country remained paralyzed with fear for a decade, is simply false. McCarthy's personal reign lasted but a year and a half, until Democrats took control of his committee. The investigation of domestic

---

* In fact this was even the case in 1955, when the left-wing journalist Murray Kempton published his book about the 1930s, *Part of Our Time*. Kempton felt at ease enough to recall that he had been a member of the Young Communist League. The difference was that Kempton was an anti-Stalinist and anti-communist in the 1950s, even though he was still on the left. Unlike Friedan he had nothing to hide from his readers about his politics.

communism, which needs to be separated from McCarthy's own underhanded tactics, is another subject altogether. Ultimately, however, being an accused communist on an American college faculty in the 1950s was only marginally more damaging to one's career opportunities than the accusation of being a member of the Christian Right would be on today's politically correct campus, dominated as it is by the tenured left. Bad enough, but a reign of terror, no.

The example of Betty Friedan should be a wake-up call. If we are going to restore civility and honesty to public discourse about these issues, and integrity to intellectual scholarship, it is necessary to insist on candor from people about their political commitments and from intellectuals about what they know. And it is important to call things by their right names. Without such a resolve, we will continue to be inundated with books from the academy with ludicrous claims like this: "In response to McCarthyism and to the impact of mass media, suburbs, and prosperity, a wave of conformity swept across much of the nation. Containment referred not only to American policy toward the USSR but also to what happened to aspirations at home. The results for women were especially unfortunate. Even though increasing numbers of them entered the work force, the Cold War linked anti-communism and the dampening of women's ambitions."

This is the commentary of Friedan's biographer and the kind of ideological hot air that passes for analysis in the contemporary academy. It is the same nonsense that Friedan has sold to American feminists: "With *The Feminine Mystique*, Friedan began a long tradition among American feminists of seeing compulsory domesticity as the main consequence of 1950s McCarthyism." Well, if the new biography is correct, perhaps it is not American feminists to whom Friedan has sold this bizarre version of reality so much as American communists posing as feminists in Women's Studies Departments, along with the unsuspecting young people whose understanding of the past comes from tenured leftist professors.

22

Professor Rorty's Left

For years, Richard Rorty has been holding court as the foremost left-wing intellectual in America. Recently, he published a book that is a heartfelt lament about the state of his party, which he describes as anti-American, programless, and politically irrelevant. Damning as this indictment might seem, *Achieving Our Country* is not a work of political "second thoughts." Rorty has no intention of abandoning a movement in whose causes he has toiled as a lifelong partisan. When all his complaints are registered, the left remains in his eyes the "party of hope," the only possible politics a decent, humane, and moral intellectual like himself could embrace. This irreducible air of invincible self-righteousness, coupled with a tone of worldly lament, make Rorty's book at once a desperate and revealing specimen, an emblem of the impossible quandary in which the American left now finds itself.

Rorty's own career as a philosophical pragmatist is based on an American skepticism hostile to the grand theorizing and absolute certitudes characteristic of marxism. Yet Rorty's background is rooted firmly in the marxist tradition. His parents, by his own account, were "loyal fellow-travelers" of the Communist Party, breaking with their comrades in 1932 when they realized how completely the party was dominated by Moscow. Rorty's father became a leader of American Trotskyism and was lampooned in a 1935 *Daily Worker* cartoon that portrayed him as a trained seal reaching for fish thrown by William Randolph Hearst. In this environment the young Rorty grew up as an "anti-communist red diaper baby"—supporting America's Cold War against the Soviet empire abroad, while keeping the socialist fires burning at home—a postmodernist *avant la lettre*. With the passing of Irving Howe, Rorty is now one of the last of the breed, godfather to a small but influential remnant of self-styled "social democrats" huddled around Howe's magazine *Dissent*. While Rorty sometimes seems to understand the profound real-world failure of the socialist fantasy, he stubbornly clings to an idea of socialism as (in Irving Howe's phrase) "the name of our desire."

Rorty begins his diagnosis of the American left by comparing national pride to individual self-esteem, declaring it a "necessary condition for self-improvement." This introduces his central concern, which is the emergence since the 1960s of a left that despises America and hates everything it stands for. When this left speaks of America, according to Rorty, it does so only in terms of "mockery and disgust." When it thinks of national pride, it is thinking of a sentiment "appropriate only for chauvinists." The left associates American patriotism with the endorsement of atrocities against Native Americans, ancient forests, and African slaves.

In Rorty's view, it was not always so. There was once a progressive left in America, whose pride in country was "almost religious" and whose aspirations were summarized in Herbert Croly's famous title *The Promise of American Life*. It was a left that believed in an organic development of this country into the nation that it *should* be; it believed, therefore, in a politics of piecemeal reform. Into this radical Eden, according to Rorty, there came first the serpent of marxism and then the trauma of Vietnam. Instead of reformism, the left embraced marxism, which was chiliastic in its ambitions and absolutist instead of skeptical in its epistemological assumptions. Instead of aiming at realistic improvements to our benighted condition, marxists aimed at a totalizing revolution that would transform the world we know into something radically other. This apocalyptic vision made piecemeal reform irrelevant and even dangerous, since reforms might co-opt the revolutionary spirit and dampen its zeal. Negativism is the principal weapon of revolutionary intellectuals committed to this totalitarian faith. In their hands, social criticism is a corrosive acid since, in order to create a new socialist order, the old slate of existing institutions has first to be wiped clean. But, in the absence of a social catastrophe that would provide it with fertile political ground, this negativism, according to Rorty, merely leads to political isolation.

Rorty views the Vietnam War as the decisive event converting the American left to the marxist revolutionary paradigm. He describes the war as "an atrocity of which Americans should be deeply ashamed." Along with the "endless humiliation inflicted on African-Americans," the war persuaded the New Left, which had previously recognized the "errors" of marxism, that something was "deeply wrong with their country, and not just mistakes correctable by reforms." As a result, they became neo-marxists and revolutionaries.

In Rorty's view, that revolutionary vision is now irretrievably dead, killed by the failures of twentieth-century utopias and the nonmarket economies on which they were based. The fall of communism made marxism untenable. Rorty is realist enough to recognize this truth, but remains leftist enough to believe that rather than vindicating its capitalist opponents, its death offers new opportunities for the left to advance its socialist agendas. With communism no longer an issue, the previously divided factions of the left can now unite in a new version of the old Popular Front, the anti-fascist coalition between Stalinists and liberals of the 1930s. According to Rorty, it is time to dispense with distinctions like "Old

Left," and "New Left," which once reflected differing attitudes towards the Soviet bloc. It is also time to erase the distinction between socialists and liberals, since it is easy to see that the two share similar egalitarian goals, once the (metaphysical) idea of overthrowing capitalism is abandoned.

Just how far Rorty is willing to take this reconciliation is revealed by the roster of icons he selects as representative of his progressive front: "A hundred years from now, Howe and Galbraith, Harrington and Schlesinger . . . Jane Addams and Angela Davis . . . will all be remembered for having advanced the cause of social justice," he writes, apparently forgetting that for Angela Davis the cause of social justice was the communist gulag itself. "Whatever mistakes they made, these people will deserve, as Coolidge and Buckley never will, the praise with which Jonathan Swift ended his own epitaph: 'Imitate him if you can; he served human liberty.'" Elsewhere, Rorty comments: "My leftmost students, who are also my favorite students, find it difficult to take my anti-communism seriously." His readiness to embrace apologists for police states like Angela Davis, while dismissing such defenders of liberty as William F. Buckley, shows why.

The attempt to resurrect a popular front of the left is threatened, however, by internal factors, specifically the emergence of what Rorty calls the "cultural left." Its commissars, as Harold Bloom and others note, have disquietingly reproduced the political modalities of 1930s fascism and Stalinism on American campuses. It is a left that Rorty describes as "spectatorial, disgusted, mocking," and politically correct. His chief complaint about the cultural left is not that it has purged conservative viewpoints from the academy using methods that even McCarthy did not, but that its nihilism is so total that it has no practical political agenda to offer. After reading works by prominent tenured radicals like Frederic Jameson, comments Rorty, "you have views on practically everything except what needs to be done."

There are overlaps between these "postmodernists" and the Old

Left. Rorty himself notes that Jameson, an armchair Maoist, thinks that "anti-communists are scum." To Rorty, this is an amusing quirk rather than a nasty political orientation. Indeed, elsewhere, Rorty himself has referred to anti-communist politicians like Ronald Reagan, in almost identical terms.

In distinguishing between the two incarnations of the left, Rorty characterizes the older economic vanguard as intending to purge society of "selfishness." The new "cultural left," in his view, aims rather to purge America of "sadism." As Rorty tells it, this agenda has been marked by "extraordinary success." According to Rorty, the speech code and sensitivity enforcers of the academic left "have decreased the amount of sadism in our society. Especially among college graduates, the casual infliction of humiliation is much less socially acceptable than it was during the first two-thirds of the century. The tone in which educated men talk about women and educated whites about blacks is very different from what it was before the Sixties. . . . The adoption of attitudes, which the Right sneers at as 'politically correct,' has made America a far more civilized society than it was thirty years ago."

In such statements, the intellectual bubble inside which leftists like Rorty conduct their ruminations is revealed in all its parochial glory. Perhaps it is true that the tone in which "educated" men talk to women, and whites to blacks, has improved under pressures from the left. But what about the tone in which women talk to men and blacks talk to whites, and in which both talk to males who are also white? What about the ritual punishments meted out daily in these havens of cultural sensitivity and concern to those who deviate from the leftist party line?* To those who are the subject of political grading and hiring, or who suffer general ostracism and reflexive hatred as a result of their unpalatable politics, race, gender, or religious orientation?

---

* See Alan Kors and Harvey Silverglate, *The Shadow University: The Betrayal of Liberty On America's Campuses* (New York: Free Press, 1998).

The poisons of atavistic prejudice have simply been redirected by the left, although a case could easily be made that they have also been intensified (since prior to the advent of the cultural left the liberal academy was not at all the scene of such sadism). Now faculty and student bigotry is aimed at religious Christians—and at Jews, who have been the subject of more virulent forms of anti-Semitic assault by black supremacists and Arab fundamentalists, egged on by progressives, than at any time since the liberation of Auschwitz.

How is one to account for these lacunae in the perceptions of so intelligent a man as Richard Rorty? Would it be so far-fetched to suppose that Rorty has become the intellectual prisoner of his own commitment to a movement whose younger generations he is loathe to alienate?

While writing mash notes to the politically correct, Rorty shrewdly punctures their revolutionary illusions: "The cultural Left has a vision of an America in which the white patriarchs have stopped voting and have left all the voting to be done by members of previously victimized groups, people who have somehow come into possession of more foresight and imagination than the selfish suburbanites. These formerly oppressed and newly powerful people are expected to be as angelic as the straight white males were diabolical. If I shared this expectation, I too would want to live under this new dispensation. Since I see no reason to share it, I think that the Left should get back into the business of piecemeal reform within the framework of a market economy."

A conservative could not have said it better. Yet Rorty keeps returning in his text to the idea that a way can be found to achieve the socialist fantasy despite what he knows. This acceptance of conservative truths while avoiding conservative conclusions marks the intellectual cul de sac in which the left finds itself in the post-communist era. In order to preserve his radical faith, Rorty constantly finds it necessary to demonize the conservative right, and to do so in a manner as ham-fisted as his cultural comrades' demonization

of white males and America itself. Here is how Rorty characterizes conservatives who are his intellectual peers:

> It is doubtful whether the current critics of the universities who
> are called "conservative intellectuals" deserve this description.
> For intellectuals are supposed to be aware of, and speak to,
> issues of social justice. But even the most learned and
> thoughtful of current conservatives ridicule those who raise
> such issues. They themselves have nothing to say about
> whether children in the ghettos can be saved without raising
> suburbanites' taxes or about how people who earn the mini-
> mum wage can pay for adequate housing. They seem to re-
> gard discussion of such topics as in poor taste.

Can it be that Rorty is ignorant of the work of James Q. Wilson, Marvin Olasky, Peter Mead, Glenn Loury, John DiIulio, Robert
Woodson, or any of scores of other conservative intellectuals who
have thought long and hard about the problems of poverty, and have
done so from a perspective of concern? One might suppose that
this caricature of conservatives as mean-spirited and lacking in basic
human instincts is so extreme as to be self-discrediting. On the
other hand, the purge of academic conservatives by Rorty's political allies has been so thorough, that in making such indefensible
statements he need hardly worry about being held to account.

Rorty's myopia (if that is all it is) extends to his characterization of the left, which he calls the "party of hope," while dismissing conservatives as defenders of the status quo: "The Right . . .
fears economic and political change, and therefore easily becomes
the pawn of the rich and powerful—the people whose selfish interests are served by forestalling such change." This is simplistic
nonsense worthy of the 1930s Stalinists who attacked Rorty's father, and as far removed from the reality it seeks to describe. It is
not even worth pausing to ask why the interests of a Bill Gates or
a Marc Andreessen, or a Larry Ellison or their community of su-

per-rich Silicon revolutionaries, or the 70 percent of American millionaires who are self-made, would be interested in "forestalling" economic and political change.

The other half of Rorty's marxist formula—that political conservatives are defenders of the status quo—is equally vacuous. Consider what the political right has accomplished of late: It has exploded the socialist empire, liberating its inhabitants and inaugurating the political and technological future across the globe. In America, it has stemmed the flow of government red ink that promised to drown future generations in an ocean of debt, and it has begun the long unraveling of the welfare bureaucracy that for a quarter of a century has stifled personal and economic growth in the inner city. In Washington, the Republican right is, in fact, the party of reform, just as surely as the Democratic left, hopelessly addicted to its socialist nostalgias, has become a camp of reactionaries, clinging to the bankrupt past of welfare entitlements and government handouts.

When all is said and done, the true source of the left's negativism is its guilty recognition that the future it promoted for two hundred years killed tens of millions and impoverished billions and, in the end, did not work. *Achieving Our Country* is a disappointing book about the left by a man who should know better, but like so many other pundits of today's radical academy, is not acquainted enough with his intellectual opponents to argue with them effectively and does not have the intellectual grit to admit that he was wrong.

23

Defending Christopher

I SHOULD BEGIN by acknowledging the obvious: I am the last person an ideological leftist like Christopher Hitchens might wish to see defending him in his imbroglio with White House henchman and ex-friend, Sidney Blumenthal. This affair was triggered when Hitchens signed an affidavit providing evidence to House investigators that Blumenthal had lied to the federal grand jury in the Lewinsky scandal. Like Sidney and Christopher, the two of us were also once political comrades, though we were never quite proximate enough to become friends. But for nearly two decades we have been squaring off on opposite sides of the political barricades. I was aware that Christopher's detractors would inevitably use my support of him to confirm that he had lost his political bearings and betrayed them. But Christopher has not had second thoughts about the left, nor is he ever likely to join Peter Collier and me as critics of the movement to which he has dedicated his life. On the contrary, as everything Christopher has put on the public record attests, his contempt for Clinton and his decision to expose Clinton's servant as a liar and knave spring from his deep passion for the left and the values it claims to hold dear.

In two mordant and incisive articles in *Vanity Fair* before the Blumenthal episode, Hitchens demonstrated that the nation's commander-in-chief cynically and mendaciously deployed the armed forces of the greatest superpower on earth to strike at three impoverished countries, with no clear military objective in mind. Using the most advanced weaponry the world has ever seen, Clinton launched missiles into the Sudan, Afghanistan, and Iraq for only one tangible political purpose (as Hitchens put it): to "distract attention from his filthy lunge at a beret-wearing cupcake."

Hitchens's claim that Clinton's military actions were criminal and impeachable are surely correct. Republicans, it seems, were right about the character issue, and failed only to show how this mattered to policy issues the public cared deeply about. Instead they got themselves entangled in legalistic disputes about perjury and constitutional impeachment bars and lost the electorate along the way. In making his own strong case against Clinton, Hitchens has underscored how Republicans botched the process by focusing on criminality that flowed from minor abuses of power—the sexual harassment of Paula Jones and its Lewinsky subtext—while ignoring a major abuse that involved corrupting the office of commander-in-chief, damaging the nation's security, and killing innocents abroad.

Reading Hitchens's riveting indictment stirred unexpected feelings of nostalgia in me for the left I had once been part of. Not the actual left that I came to know and reject, but the left of my youthful idealism, when I thought our mission was to be the nation's "conscience," to speak truth to power in the name of what was just. This, as is perfectly evident from the book he has written, was Hitchens's own mission in exposing Blumenthal as the willing agent of a corrupt regime and its reckless commander-in-chief. Unfortunately, in carrying out this mission, Hitchens was forced to trip over the Lewinsky matter, specifically Blumenthal's effort to smear the credibility of the key witness to the president's bad faith. But that is because it was through Lewinsky that the Starr investigators had set up the character issue in the first place.

It is difficult to believe that a sociopathic personality like Clinton's could be compartmentalized to stop at the water's edge of sex, or that he is innocent of other serious accusations against him that Starr and the Republicans have been unable to prove. In fact, the same signature behavior is apparent throughout his administration (an idea aptly captured in the title of Hitchens's book about the president—*No One Left To Lie To*). The presidential pathology is evident not only in his reckless private dalliances (the betrayal of family and office), but also in his strategy of political "triangulation" (the betrayal of allies and friends), and in his fire sale of the Lincoln bedroom and advanced military technology to adversarial powers (the betrayal of country). Hitchens is quite right (if imprudent) to strike at the agent of the King, when the King is ultimately to blame.

Given the transparent morality of Hitchens's anti-Clinton crusade, it is all the more remarkable, and interesting, that so many of his comrades on the left, who ought to share these concerns, chose instead to turn on him so viciously. In a brutal display of comradely betrayal, they publicly shunned him in an attempt to cut him off socially from his own community. One after another, they rushed into print to tell the world at large how repulsed they were by a man whom only yesterday they still called "friend" and whom they no longer wish to know.

Leading this pack was Hitchens's longtime *Nation* colleague Alexander Cockburn who denounced him as a "Judas" and "snitch." Cockburn was followed by a second *Nation* colleague, Katha Pollitt, who smeared Hitchens as a throwback to McCarthy era informers ("Let's say the Communist Party was bad and wrong. . . . Why help the repressive powers of the state? Let the government do its own dirty work."). She was joined by a thirty-year political comrade, Todd Gitlin, who warned anyone who cared to listen that Hitchens was a social "poison" in the same toxic league as Ken Starr and Linda Tripp.

Consider the remarkable nature of this spectacle. Could one imagine a similar ritual performed by journalists of the right? Bob Novak, say, flanked by Pat Buchanan and William. F. Buckley, proclaiming an anathema on Bill Safire, because the columnist had called for the jailing of Ollie North during the Iran-Contra hearings? Not even North felt the need to announce such a public divorce. When was the last time any conservative figure (let alone a gathering of conservative figures) stepped forward to declare they were ending a private friendship over a political disagreement?

The curses rained on Hitchens's head were part of a ritual that has become familiar over generations of the left, in which dissidents are excommunicated (and consigned to various Siberias) for their political deviance. It is a phenomenon typical of religious cults, where purity of heart is maintained through avoiding contact with the unclean. To have caused the left to invoke so drastic a measure, Hitchens had evidently violated a fundamental principle of its faith. But what was it?

In fact, there seem to be at least two charges attached to Hitchens's transgression. On the one hand, he was accused of "snitching" on a political ally; on the other, he was said to have betrayed a friend. These are not identical. Nor is it obvious that the left as a matter of principle is generally outraged about either. Daniel Ellsberg, to cite one example, is a radical snitch who betrayed not only his political allies but his own government. Yet, Ellsberg is a hero to the left. David Brock, who also kissed and told, is not exactly persona non grata among leftists either. The left's standards for snitching on itself are entirely different from its standards for those who snitch on its enemies.

Hitchens's *Nation* editor, Victor Navasky, has written a whole volume about the McCarthy era called *Naming Names* on the premise that the act of snitching is worse than the crimes it reveals *because* it involves personal betrayal. On the other hand, the bond of comradeship, of loyalty, of belonging, is exactly the bond that every organized crime syndicate exploits to establish and maintain its rule.

There is an immediate reminder of these connections in the Paul Robeson centennial that progressives were observing at the time Hitchens and Blumenthal ceased to be friends. In a variety of cultural and political events held across the nation, the left was celebrating the life and achievement of one of its great heroes on the hundredth anniversary of his birth. Robeson, however, is a man who also betrayed his friend, in his case the Yiddish poet Itzhak Pfeffer, not to mention thousands of other Soviet Jews, who were under a death sentence imposed by Robeson's own hero, Stalin. In refusing to help them, despite Pfeffer's personal plea to him to do so, Robeson was acting under a code of silence that prevented communists like him from "snitching" on the crimes their comrades committed. They justified their silence in the name of the progressive cause, allowing the murderers among them to destroy not only millions of innocent lives, but their socialist dream as well.

In that same spring, the Motion Picture Academy honored Elia Kazan, a theater legend who had been blacklisted for nearly half a century by the Hollywood left. He, too, was called a "Judas" by leftist members of the Academy protesting his award. Kazan's sin was to testify before a congressional committee about fellow communists who were also loyal supporters of Stalin's monstrous regime, and who conducted their own blacklist of anti-Stalinists in the entertainment community. Kazan's most celebrated film, *On the Waterfront*, scripted by another disillusioned communist, Budd Schulberg, depicts a longshoreman who "snitches" to a congressional committee that is investigating organized crime, specifically a mob that controls his own union and exploits its membership. It is a thinly veiled commentary on Kazan's and Schulberg's experiences in the left.

"Snitching" is how the progressive mob regards the act of speaking truth to power, when the power is its own. The mafia calls its code of silence *omerta*, because the penalty for speaking against the mob is death. The left's penalty for defection (in those countries where it does not exercise state power) is excommunication from its community of saints. This is a kind of death, too.

Cognizant of these realities, I avoided informing on friends or even "outing" them, during my own journey out of the left many years ago. In fact, my first political statements opposing the left were made a decade after I had ceased to be an active participant in its cause and when the battles I had participated in were over. This did not make an iota of difference, however, when it came to my former comrades denouncing me as a "renegade," as though I in fact had become an informer. I was subjected to the same kind of personal betrayal Hitchens is experiencing now. With only a handful of exceptions, all the friends I had made in the first forty years of my life turned their backs on me, refusing to know me, when my politics changed.

This tainting and ostracism of sinners is, in fact, the secret power of the leftist faith. It is what keeps the faithful faithful. The spectacle of what happens to a heretic like Hitchens when he challenges the party code is a warning to others not to try it. This is why Alger Hiss kept his silence to the end, and why, even thirty and fifty years after the fact, the memoirs of leftists are so elusive and disingenuous when it comes to telling the hard political and personal truths about who they were and what they did. To tell a threatening truth is to risk vanishing in the progressive communities in which you have staked your life—and to risk vanishing in memory, too. Hitchens's crime is not the betrayal of friendship. It is the betrayal of progressive politics, the only bond the left takes seriously.

This is far from obvious to those who have never been insiders. Writing in the *Wall Street Journal*, the otherwise perceptive Roger Kimball described what has happened to Hitchens under the following caption: "Leftists Sacrifice Truth on the Altar of Friendship." But this presumes either that they were closer friends of Blumenthal than of Hitchens, or that friendship means more to them than politics. None of the denouncers of Hitchens even claimed a closer friendship with Blumenthal as a reason for their choice. Moreover, there is not the slightest reason to suppose that these leftists would remain friends of Blumenthal should he, in turn, reveal what he really knows about Clinton's obstructions of justice and the machinations of the White House crew.

To examine an actual betrayal of friendship one need go no further than Cockburn's *New York Press* column outing Hitchens as a compulsive snitch. Friends can take different political paths and still honor the life that was once between them, the qualities and virtues that made them friends. Alex was once closer to Hitchens than Blumenthal ever was. They knew each other longer and their friendship was deeper. Hitchens even named his own son "Alex" out of admiration for his friend. But in his column, Alex gratuitously smeared Hitchens (who is married) as an aggressive closet homosexual, an odorous, ill-mannered, and obnoxious drunk, a pervert who gets a sexual frisson out of ratting on his intimates. Not a single member of Hitchens's former circle, which include people who have known him as a comrade for thirty years, has stepped forward to defend him from the ugly slander.

What then inspires these auto-da-fés? It is the fact that the community of the left is a community of meaning and is bound by ties that are fundamentally religious. For the nonreligious, politics is the art of managing the possible. For the left, it is the path to a social redemption. This messianism is its political essence. For the left, the agenda of politics is ultimately not about practical options concerning which reasonable people may reasonably differ. It is about moral choices that define one as human. It is about taking sides in a war that will decide the future and whether the principle of justice will prevail. It is about *us* being on the side of the angels, and *them* as the party of the damned. In the act of giving up Blumenthal to the congressional majority and the special prosecutor, Hitchens put power in the hands of the enemies of the people. He acted as one of *them*.

Katha Pollitt puts it to Hitchens this way: "Why should you, who call yourself a socialist, a man of the left, help Henry Hyde and Bob Barr and Trent Lott? If Clinton is evil, are the forces arrayed against him better, with their 100 percent ratings from the Christian coalition, and their after-dinner speaking engagements at white supremacist clubs?" Of course, Katha Pollitt doesn't for a moment think that Clinton is evil. But Hitchens's new friends obviously are. Observe how easily she invokes the McCarthy stratagems to create the taint—the demonization of Hitchens's new "friends," the guilts by association that link him to them and them to the devil, the absurd reduction of the entire Clinton opposition to any of these links.

The casting out of Hitchens, then, was a necessary ritual to protect the left's myth of itself as a redemptive force. How could Blumenthal, who is one of them, who is loyal to their cause be connected to something evil, as Hitchens suggests? How could *they*? All of Hitchens's attackers and all fifty-eight members of the congressional Progressive Caucus—yesterday's vanguard opponents of American military power—supported the wanton strikes against the Sudan, Afghanistan, and Iraq, without batting a proverbial lash. Every one of them found a way to excuse Clinton's abuse of disposable women like Paula Jones, Kathleen Willey, and Monica Lewinsky. The last thing they would want to do is confront Blumenthal's collusion in a campaign to destroy one of Clinton's female nuisances because she became a political threat. After all, it is they who want the reprobate in power. In blurting out the truth, Hitchens slammed the left up against its hypocrisies and threatened to unmask their sanctimonious pretensions. This is the threat the anathema on Hitchens was designed to suppress.

Here is my own message for the condemned man: You and I, Christopher, will continue our disagreements on many important things, and perhaps most things. But I take my hat off to you for what you have done. For your dedicated pursuit of the truth in these matters, and for your courage in standing up under fire. The comrades who have left you are incapable of such acts.

24

A Proper Love of Country

THE FIRST COLUMN I WROTE for the Internet magazine *Salon* in 1997 was a piece about the director Elia Kazan, calling for an end to Hollywood's "longest blacklist." For more than twenty years it had been impossible to honor Kazan in Hollywood, although he was its greatest living film legend. I did not say so at the time, but I felt a kinship with Kazan in the fact that the invitation to write for *Salon* had ended a long exile for me from the literary culture, the result of a kind of graylist in force for ex-radicals like myself.

I had no idea the shunning of Hollywood's greatest living figure would come to an end only two years later, or that it would come as a result of an honor bestowed on him by the Academy of Motion Pictures itself. Ostensibly the anti-Kazan anger was over the original blacklist of communists that was introduced into the film industry by the Hollywood studio heads some fifty years ago. Abe Polonsky and Bernard Gordon, two minor film professionals who organized the anti-Kazan protest, had been among those blacklisted at the time. Their charge against Kazan was that he had been an "informer" for the blacklisters, had collaborated with witch-hunters, and had betrayed colleagues and friends. For these crimes, they argued, the film community should continue to shun him and not give him an award.

Let me make clear my own views of congressional investigations like the one with which Kazan cooperated. The only legitimate purpose of congressional investigations is to determine whether there should be legislation to deal with certain problems and how that legislation should be designed. It was as legitimate for Congress to hold hearings inquiring into the influence of an organization like the Communist Party in an important American industry like film, as it was for legislators to inquire into the influence of organized crime in the union movement and other areas of American life. The Communist Party was conspiratorial in nature and operated through concealed agendas. It infiltrated open organizations and set out to control them through systematic deception and political manipulation. Its own purposes were determined by the fact that it was financed and directed by a foreign dictatorial power, whom its members worshiped. Kazan deeply resented the way the Communist Party had infiltrated and taken control of the Group Theater, where he was an actor and director, to exploit it for its own political ends.

What was not legitimate in these investigations was for congressmen to use their hearings to expose the influence of communists (or gangsters, for that matter) to the public at large. Such public hearings were, in effect, trials without the due process protections afforded by courts of law. By opening testimony to the public, the committees, in effect, tried uncooperative witnesses who were called before them. The committees became juries, judges, and executioners all rolled into one, since the mere charge of being a gangster or a communist was enough to ensure a public judgment that was punitive.

By this standard, many congressional investigations that are open, whether they are of organized crime or of communists or of executive misdeeds, as in the Iran-Contra Hearings, have the potential for such abuses and are equally illegitimate, and qualify as witch-hunts. Oliver North had no more constitutional protections than did the communists in the McCarthy era when he appeared before the Iran-Contra committee and had to sit in the dock while Senators and congressman who enjoyed legal immunity denounced him as a liar and traitor to the entire nation. On the other hand, I do not remember protests issuing from liberals over the attempted public hanging of Oliver North and the other Iran-Contra figures. Perhaps that is because the political shoe was on the other foot. Yet the only way to avoid such abuses of congressional power would be to require that all such congressional hearings be closed.

There were other aspects of the Hollywood witch-hunt (and of Kazan's role) that were blurred in the ensuing Academy controversy. Every one of the communists Kazan named, for example, had already been identified as a communist by other witnesses. None of those he named even worked in the film industry, but were theater professionals in New York. In other words, Kazan's testimony destroyed no Hollywood careers. More importantly, it was not Congress that imposed the blacklist but Hollywood itself. This little fact, now forgotten, was dramatized by the way the blacklist finally came to an end. This was accomplished essentially through the action of one man, who was not even one of the studio heads who had initiated the process. The blacklist episode was put to an end by the actor Kirk Douglas when he decided to give Dalton Trumbo a screen credit for the film *Spartacus*. By putting Trumbo's name on the credits he legitimized those who had been hitherto banished and opened the doors to their return. What made the blacklist possible was Hollywood itself—the collusion of all those actors, writers, and directors (some of whom sat on their hands and scowled for the cameras the night Kazan's own exile ended) who went to work day and in a day out during the blacklist years, while their friends and colleagues languished out in the cold.

The anti-Kazan protest, in short, was entirely symbolic and contained large dollops of hypocrisy and amnesia. Ultimately, it was an attempt to re-fight the Cold War. And that is why the anti-Kazan forces lost.

Suppose the studio heads who met in 1951 to ban communists in Hollywood had instead announced that they were not going to employ nazis and racists, or members of the Ku Klux Klan. Would Abe Polonsky and Bernard Gordon and the other progressives who tried to deny Kazan his honor have come out to protest *this* black-list? Would they have regarded friendly witnesses against the Nazis and racists as betrayers of "friends?" Or would they have welcomed them as men who had come to their senses and done the right thing?

Many of those who defended the Kazan award invoked the quality of his art to overlook what he did politically. The director Paul Schrader was typical. Artistically, he told the *LA Weekly*, "Kazan is a giant. [But] that does not mitigate the fact that he did wrong things. I think evil things. But at the end of the day, he's an artist, and his work towers over that." Schrader explained that to say Kazan should not get an honorary Oscar was like saying that Leni Riefenstahl shouldn't be acknowledged because she worked under the heel of Hitler's propaganda machine. What Schrader (and others) conveniently overlooked was that it was Kazan's antagonists who volunteered to work for Stalin's propaganda machine, while Kazan went to the mat for America, for the democracy that had given him refuge, freedom, and unbounded opportunity.

I had the occasion to raise this issue, on a talk show, with Victor Navasky, editor of the *Nation* and author of a book on the McCarthy period that established him in the controversy as the most articulate defender of the Old Left. When I asked Navasky if he would have similar objections to a blacklist of Nazis, he said, "The difference is the Nazi Party was illegal. The Communist Party was legal."

This was an odd position for a New Left radical. Would it have been all right to inform on members of the civil rights movement because they broke laws? Should the Communist Party have been outlawed to make the hearings legitimate? (In fact, one of the purposes of the congressional hearings, as Navasky well knows, was to see if such legislation was warranted.) If Congress had decided to outlaw the Communist Party, wouldn't Victor Navasky and other progressives be pointing to this as an example of witch-hunting, evidence of an incipient American fascism at the time? Of course they would.

In fact, Navasky draws a sharp distinction between communists and nazis that has nothing to do with legalities. In a *Newsweek* column, he wrote, "[unlike nazis] the actors, writers and directors who joined the Communist Party . . . in the '30s started out as social idealists who believed that the party was the best place to fight fascism abroad and racism at home." But this is not a plausible argument for anyone familiar with the political realities of the time, let alone a lifelong partisan of the left like Victor Navasky. There were many organizations other than the Communist Party where one could fight fascism abroad and racism at home if one so desired. Indeed, during the Nazi-Soviet Pact, the Communist Party was hardly the place to fight "fascism abroad" at all.

What made the Communist Party distinctive for those who joined was its belief that the Soviet Union was the future of mankind, and that preparation for a Bolshevik-style revolution in the United States was the appropriate politics for anyone interested in a liberated future. People who joined the party were given secret names so they could function in the underground when the time came for such tactics and were introduced into an organization that was conspiratorial in nature because it fully intended to conduct illegal operations. That was what the revolution required, as they understood it. It was not for nothing that they thought of themselves as Leninists.

One of the famous incidents of the blacklist period was the Peekskill riot where anti-communists broke up a public concert by Paul Robeson, at the time the most famous figure associated with the party. The pretext for the riot was a recent public statement Robeson had made that revealed what every communist secretly knew: in the Cold War with Stalin's Russia, he or she was actively pulling for the other side. What Robeson said (and I paraphrase) was that American Negroes would not fight in a war between the United States and the Soviet Union. This was a crude exploitation of black Americans, but it accurately reflected the sentiments in Robeson's own heart and in the hearts of his comrades.

This is the missing self-perception that underlies the odd postures of the left during the Kazan affair, and indeed the postures of many post-communist leftists when they reflect on the Cold War years.

One such oddity is the way in which those who protested the Kazan honor were actually the aggressors in the entire episode, yet presented themselves as victims. Imagine what would have happened if a group of Hollywood figures had organized a protest over the honorary Oscar that the Academy gave to Charlie Chaplin some years ago. Suppose they had done so because forty years earlier Chaplin had been a communist fellow-traveler and given money and support to the Stalinist cause. Can it be doubted that cries of "red-baiting" and "witch-hunting" would issue from the left? Why was Kazan's case any different? Why didn't they see their own protest as a witch-hunt to deny an honor to someone who was on the other side of the political battle fifty years ago? Their only possible answer to this question would be: Who did Chaplin betray?

The centrality of this issue in all the responses of the anti-Kazan forces was brought home to me by a book I have been reading, called *Red Atlantis*, by the film critic for the *Village Voice*, J. Hoberman. The concluding chapter of *Red Atlantis* is a compilation of two pieces Hoberman wrote years ago on the controversy over the

Rosenberg case. Like the Kazan affair, the passions over the Rosenbergs still ran high at the time, despite the fact that here, too, the historical record is closed. Just as there is no secret anymore that virtually all the victims of the blacklist were also defenders of a monster regime that was America's sworn enemy, so it is clear that the Rosenbergs were actual spies for Stalin's Russia. Hoberman does not deny either fact, but so minimizes them that they become insignificant to his argument. The climactic passage of his text contains these judgments:

Q. Were Julius and Ethel guilty?
A. Affirmative. Guilty of wanting a better world.
Q. Does that mean they were traitors?
A. Negative. Negative. Negative. Negative. Negative...
Nega.... How could the Rosenbergs be traitors? Traitors! To whom?...The Rosenbergs never betrayed their beliefs, their friends. They kept the faith. They sacrificed everything—even their children. In a time when turning state's witness was touted as the greatest of civic virtues, the Rosenbergs went to their deaths without implicating a soul.

Here is the mentality that explains the oddities of the Kazan protest and the left's defense of itself during the Cold War era. For the argument proposed by Hoberman is absurd to anyone not committed to the progressive faith. Isn't it the case that even nazis think of themselves as wanting the better world? Don't we all? In other words, if Hoberman's proposition is true, doesn't wanting a better world become a license to tell any lie, perpetrate any crime, commit any betrayal? And how could he have overlooked the betrayals that the Rosenbergs did commit? If they sacrificed their children, as he admits, surely this was a betrayal. If they maintained their innocence to friends and comrades, as they did, surely this was a betrayal. If they pledged their faith to Stalin's evil regime, surely this was a betrayal of their own ideals. If they spied for the Soviet government, as Hoberman concedes they did, is there any question they betrayed their country?

It is their country and its citizens who are the missing elements in the consciousness of progressives like Hoberman, Navasky, and the anti-Kazan protesters. For them, collaborating with their own democratic government as it tried to defend itself against a mortal communist threat, is still more culpable than serving a totalitarian state and aiding an enemy power.

What is missing from these progressive hearts, after all is said and done, is a proper love of country, and therefore a sense of the friends, neighbors, and countrymen they betrayed. A proper love of country does not mean the abandonment of one's principles or the surrender of one's critical senses. It means valuing what you have been given, and what you have, and sharing the responsibility for nurturing and defending those gifts, even in dissent. The Old Left, the Stalinists, the people whom Kazan named, betrayed their country and the real people who live in it, their friends, their neighbors, and ultimately themselves. They may have betrayed their country out of ignorance, or out of misplaced ideals, or because they were blinded by faith. But they did it, and they need to acknowledge that now by showing humility towards those, like Kazan, who did not.

VI

FOREIGN AFFAIRS

25

Misdemeanors or High Crimes?

O N NEARLY TWO HUNDRED OCCASIONS in the three years before the breaking of the China scandal, including innumerable campaign appearances and three State of the
Union addresses, the president of the United States looked the
American people in the eye and assured them that, because of his
policies, "there are no more nuclear missiles pointed at any children in the United States."

If you are Bill Clinton, the truth of this statement probably
depends on what "are" means.

But to the rest of us who live in the shadow of a nuclear Armageddon, the president's statement is a morally repulsive and dangerous lie. The shred of truth out of which Clinton has woven his
politically useful deception is a meaningless, post-Cold War agreement between Russia and the United States not to target each
other's cities. But even if Russia were not a country in a state of
near dissolution, the stark military reality is that United States intelligence services normally have no way of telling what targets
Russia's leaders have actually chosen for their nuclear warheads. In
fact, it would take a mere fifteen seconds for Russian commanders

to re-target any of the hundreds of strategic missiles tipped with multiple nuclear warheads they have ready to go.

More important, the Russians are energetically planning for the possibility of nuclear war with the United States. And they are not alone. Thanks to technology transfers courtesy of the Clinton Administration, China and North Korea are also armed with long-range missiles capable of reaching the American mainland. And they are not parties to the non-targeting agreement. Thanks to six years of tenacious, dedicated opposition by the Clinton Administration to the Strategic Defense Initiative, moreover, America has no defense against incoming missiles and no prospect of deploying one for many years.

By every reasonable measure, the post-Cold War world is a dangerous one, perhaps even more dangerous than the world during the Cold War itself. That is the conclusion that any responsible commander-in-chief would draw and that is what he would tell the nation whose security depends on his political judgment. It is the assessment that any responsible administration would have acted on in the last seven years. But the actual response of the Clinton Administration during those years, as documented by the veteran military reporter Bill Gertz, in his disturbing new book, *Betrayal*, are different indeed:

- While the Clinton Administration has cut America's military by 40 percent and dramatically drawn down America's nuclear forces, the general in charge of Russia's rocket forces has publicly boasted that his are still at 90 percent of their combat effectiveness during the Cold War. The same general admits that his nuclear command and control systems are already stretched 71 percent beyond their life expectancy (and thus susceptible to unauthorized acts by rogue commanders).

- While threats from nuclear proliferation and nuclear terrorism continue to grow, Clinton has used his veto power to resist every effort by Republicans in Congress to authorize an anti-missile defense program. This opposition was mounted in the name of will-o'-the-wisp "arms control" agreements with the Russians (who have failed in the past to respect them) and under the assumption that there was no imminent threat of a missile attack to the United States. In pursuit of these chimeras, as Gertz has documented, Clinton was willing to go behind the back of his own Pentagon and collude with the Russians in blocking the development of a United States anti-missile system. This attitude only changed with the discovery of the wholesale nuclear spy leaks under the Clinton watch and the imminent publication of the *Cox Report*. Even then, the Clinton Administration refused to make a decision whether to implement such a program until June 2000, which ensured that the nation would remain defenseless in the face of a potential missile attack well into the future.

- While the Clinton Administration has stopped all development of nuclear weapons and is in the process of drawing down America's existing forces and while Clinton's Department of Energy chief (in charge of nuclear weapons development) publicly assailed America's "bomb building culture" and, for the benefit of potentially hostile powers, declassified information on 204 nuclear tests, Russia and China are engaged in a full-scale nuclear arms race to develop and expand their own arsenals. The express purpose of these large-scale nuclear buildups is to gain military superiority over the United States.

- While the United States has largely closed down its own underground military shelters, Soviet rulers are devoting massive resources (in a country on the verge of famine) to building an underground nuclear bunker the size of Washington, D.C.. The evident purpose of this bunker is to allow the Russian elite to survive a nuclear attack so that Russia can prevail in an all-out nuclear war. There is no country besides the United States that could qualify as an enemy in such a war. Meanwhile, Clinton is sending a billion dollars to Russia earmarked for its "nuclear disarmament program" even though the government's own General Accounting Office has already determined that millions of these dollars are going to Russian scientists working to *build* new nuclear weapons for the Russian military.

Now the Cox report has revealed that even while the Clinton Administration was steadfastly "engaging" China as a friendly power, the Chinese were systematically plotting to infiltrate the Democratic Party and current administration, subvert America's electoral process, and (with the help of the president himself) steal America's advanced weapons arsenal. The result is chillingly captured in the *Wall Street Journal's* summary of the bipartisan report: "The espionage inquiry found Beijing has stolen U.S. design data for nearly all elements needed for a major nuclear attack on the U.S., such as advanced warheads, missiles and guidance systems. Targets of the spying ranged from an Army antitank weapon to nearly all modern fighter jets. Most of the theft wasn't done by professionals, but by visitors or front companies. Lax security by the Clinton Administration is blamed in part, and satellite makers Hughes and Loral are criticized."

Loral and Hughes are the companies that provided the Chinese with the technology to deliver their nuclear payloads. They were able to accomplish this with indispensable assistance provided by the Clinton White House that allowed them to circumvent technology controls instituted for national security purposes by previous administrations. Loral and Hughes are large Clinton campaign

contributors. In fact, the head of Loral is the largest electoral contributor in American history.

Pennsylvania representative Curt Weldon, who is chair of the
National Security subcommittee on military research and development, and is fluent in Russian, has characterized the six years of
Clinton's administration as "the worst period in our history in terms
of undermining our national security." In May, Weldon traveled to
Russia, in company with ten other congressmen. On that trip, in
his presence, a Russian general threatened the assembled congressmen, warning that if the United States put ground troops in Kosovo,
Russia "could" detonate a nuclear device in the lower atmosphere
off the eastern United States. The resulting electromagnetic pulses,
he claimed, would "fry" every computer chip in the country, shut-
ting down phones, airplanes, electrical grids, and so on until the
country was thrown into absolute chaos. This threat was not made
during the Cold War by a ruler of the former Soviet Union. It was
made by a Russian general, in May 1999.

These revelations are disturbing enough, but in the initial reactions to the Cox report there was enough complacency and denial to add an ominous element to the mix. Before the report was
even issued, the Clinton cover-up squad had begun its famous spin
cycle. Spokesmen for the White House and congressional Democrats explained that the damage resulting from all the spying was
not that great because China only has eighteen missiles, while the
United States has six thousand. Well, that may be fine, temporarily.
But the theft has given China a twenty-year jump in its nuclear
weapons development—an eternity in terms of modern technologies. What happens five or ten years in the future when the Beijing
dictatorship has hundreds of missiles aimed at American cities and
decides that it wants Taiwan? What consolation would it be to
people in Los Angeles, who have already been threatened with a
nuclear attack over the Taiwan issue, should Beijing decide to launch
even one missile in their direction, given that their president has

denied them a missile defense? In the event of such an attack, would Washington be willing to trade seventeen American cities in a retaliatory nuclear exchange to defend Taiwan?

On the other hand, if historical experience is any guide, the communists just might. In Vietnam, the communists were willing to sacrifice two million of their own citizens (a figure comparable to seventy-two million deaths in the United States) against the prospect of victory, while fifty-eight thousand proved too great a sacrifice for Americans. The Chinese Communists have already killed an estimated fifty million of their own population in their pursuit of a revolutionary future. Why would they not risk another fifty million to achieve a goal their leadership deems worthy?

In addition to making the false and irresponsible claim that the thefts reported by the Cox committee were not so serious, Clinton and his spinners argued that they themselves were not really guilty because "everyone does it." Shame on Democrats who have gone along with this argument, as they did with similar mendacities during the impeachment process over the President's dalliance with Monica Lewinsky. This is not about a squalid presidential affair but about reckless and perhaps criminal behavior affecting the very lives of the American people. Yes, nuclear spying took place in previous administrations, and in every administration no doubt since the invention of the atom bomb. The difference is that previous administrations cared about such leaks and prosecuted the offenders—and had not accepted millions of dollars in illegal campaign contributions from the military and intelligence services of the foreign power that pulled off the theft. Previous administrations did not lift security controls that supplied the thieves with additional vital military technologies, after the thefts had been discovered. Or systematically disarm their own military forces while this was happening. Or vigorously oppose the development of necessary defenses in the face of the threat. But the Clinton Administration did.

One of the key technological breaks China received without having to spy to get it was the delivery of supercomputers once banned from export for security reasons. Supercomputers underpin the technology of modern warfare, and not only for firing and controlling missiles. A supercomputer can simulate a nuclear test and is crucial to the development of nuclear warheads. But, according to a *Washington Post* editorial on May 26, 1999, "In the first three quarters of 1998 nine times as many [supercomputers] were exported [to China] as during the previous seven years." This transfer was authorized three years after the spy thefts were detected. What rationale (besides stupidity, greed, or some treasonous motive) could justify this decision? What responsible president or official in any government would allow the massive transfer of national security assets like these to a dictatorship they knew had stolen their country's most highly guarded military secrets? And if they did do it, why did they?

Was this the reason for the Chinese cash flow to the Clinton-Gore campaign? If not, what *was* the payoff the Chinese expected? What *was* the payoff they received? And who in the administration is responsible for the cover-ups, the laxity, and the leaks that made the Chinese conspiracy work as effectively as it did? Is there, for example, any connection between this security disaster and the fact that Sandy Berger, the president's National Security Advisor was a lobbyist for Chinese companies before being appointed to his post? Or that he and other top Clinton officials responsible for this mess have been left-leaning skeptics about Communist threats in the past, and radical critics of American power?

In the immediate handling of the national security disaster, a profound disservice was done to the American people, in fact, by both political parties. Shell-shocked by Democratic attacks during the impeachment process, Republicans on the Cox Committee became complicit in an essential part of the cover-up in the name of bipartisanship. This was the decision to de-couple the spy scandal and the technology transfers from the Clinton money trail to Beijing. This removed a large potential area of conspiracy from the perspective of the Cox report. In all, 105 witnesses to the illegal funding of the Clinton-Gore campaign by people connected to the Chinese military and Chinese intelligence either took the Fifth Amendment or fled the country to avoid cooperating with investigators. They did this with the tacit acquiescence, if not active help, of the Clinton Administration. What were they hiding, and why the did Clinton Administration, at the very minimum, not care?

The entire debate has taken place in a surreal atmosphere of politics-as-usual: the partisan defense of the White House, the denial of the real magnitude of the nuclear danger, the political decoupling of the Chinese plot to infiltrate and influence the Clinton-Gore Administration, and the failure even to acknowledge that what is at stake is a probable massive betrayal of the American people's trust by its national security leadership.

Someday, the American people may want to revisit questions they disposed of during the president's perjury over an illicit affair in light of the unfolding national security drama. Is bad character an impeachable offense? Does reckless behavior and lying under oath make a leader unfit to be commander-in-chief? Whatever their answers, and whatever the results of the investigations in progress, one thing is certain: the already revealed facts will redraw the legacy of this presidency as the most reckless and dangerous in our lifetimes.

26

A Question of Loyalties

E VEN AS OFFICIALS WERE PREPARING to release the Cox report on how the communist dictatorship in Beijing had stolen the design information for America's nuclear weapons
systems, the Democratic National Committee was announcing the
appointment of its new "political issues director," Carlottia Scott, a
former mistress of the marxist dictator of Grenada and an ardent
supporter of America's adversaries during the Cold War. What
could the DNC have been thinking to make such an appointment at
such a political juncture? And what might this tell us about the
roots of the nation's security crisis, the dramatic erosion of its defenses and military credibility, and the theft of its nuclear arsenal
by an opponent the administration thinks of as a "strategic partner," while its communist leaders regard America as their "international archenemy"?

Carlottia Scott was for many years the chief aide to Congressman Ron Dellums, a Berkeley radical who, with the approval of the
congressional Democratic leadership, was first appointed to the
Armed Services Committee and then to the chair of its subcommittee on Military Installations, which oversees United States bases

worldwide. The Democratic leadership apparently detected no problem in the fact that every year during the Cold War with the Soviet empire, Congressman Dellums introduced a "peace" budget requiring a 75 percent reduction in government spending on America's defenses. Nor did they have any problem with Dellums's performance during the Soviet invasion of Afghanistan, which occurred on Jimmy Carter's watch. As Soviet troops poured across the Afghanistan border and President Carter called for the resumption of the military draft, Dellums told a "Stop the Draft" rally in Berkeley that "Washington, D.C. is a very evil place," and the only "arc" of a crisis that he could see was "the one that runs between the basement of the west wing of the White House and the war room of the Pentagon."

Among the government documents retrieved when the marxist government in Grenada was overthrown were Scott's love letters to Grenada's anti-American dictator Maurice Bishop. Scott wrote that "Ron has become truly committed to Grenada. . . . He's really hooked on you and Grenada and doesn't want anything to happen to building the Revolution and making it strong. . . . The only other person that I know of that he expresses such admiration for is Fidel." Bishop and Fidel were not the only communists in the Americas favored by Dellums. About the time these letters were retrieved, Dellums was opening his congressional offices to a Cuban intelligence agent organizing support committees in the United States for the communist guerrilla movement in El Salvador. Yet when Dellums retired, the Clinton Administration's Secretary of Defense, William S. Cohen, bestowed on him the highest civilian honor the Pentagon can award "for service to his country." After Dellums's retirement, Scott became chief of staff to Dellums's successor, Berkeley leftist Barbara Lee. I met Barbara Lee in the 1970s, when she was a confidential aide to Huey Newton, the "Minister of Defense" of the Black Panther Party, whose calling card was the "Red Book" of Chinese dictator Mao Zedong.

Also among the documents liberated from Grenada, were the minutes from a politburo meeting of the marxist government attended by Barbara Lee. The minutes state that "Barbara Lee is here presently and has brought with her a report on the international airport done by Ron Dellums. They have requested that we look at the document and suggest any changes we deem necessary. They will be willing to make the changes."

The airport in question was being built by the Cuban military and, according to United States intelligence sources, was designed to accommodate Soviet warplanes. The Reagan Administration regarded the airport project as part of a larger Soviet plan to establish a military base in this hemisphere, and administration officials invoked its construction as a national security justification for the invasion that followed. In an effort to forestall such an invasion, as head of the House subcommittee on Military Installations, Dellums made a "fact-finding" trip to Grenada and issued his own report on the airport, concluding that it was being built "for the purpose of economic development and is not for military use." Dellums's report also made the political claim that the Reagan Administration's concerns about national security were "absurd, patronizing and totally unwarranted." In other words, the captured minutes of the politburo meeting show that Ron Dellums and his aide Barbara Lee colluded with the dictator of a communist state to cover up that the Soviet Union was building a military airport that posed a threat to the security of the United States.

Despite this betrayal, and with the approval of her Democratic colleagues in the House, Barbara Lee is now a member of the House International Relations Committee, which deals with issues affecting the security of the United States. With equal disregard for national security the Democratic Party has appointed Scott to her new position. When I asked a leading Democratic political strategist, who is not a leftist, how it was possible that the leaders of the Democratic Party could appoint someone like Scott to such a post at such a time, he replied: "You have to understand that in the 1960s these people were chanting "Ho, Ho, Ho Chi Minh, the NLF Is Gonna Win!"

The left-wing culture that pervades both the Democratic Party and the Clinton Administration is at the heart of the current national security crisis. People who never conceded that the Soviet Union was an evil empire, who never grasped the dimensions of the Soviet military threat to the United States, who regarded America's democracy as an imperialist empire and as morally convergent with the Soviet state, who insisted (and still insist) that the ferreting out of Soviet loyalists and domestic spies during the early Cold War years was merely an ideological "witch-hunt," who opposed the Reagan military buildup and the development of an anti-ballistic missile system in the 1980s, and who consistently called for unilateral steps to reduce America's nuclear deterrent, could hardly be expected to take the post-Cold War threat from the Chinese Communist dictatorship seriously. And they have not.

In fact, the current national security crisis may be said to have begun when President Clinton appointed an anti-military, environmental leftist, Hazel O'Leary, to be Secretary of Energy in charge of the nation's nuclear weapons labs. O'Leary promptly surrounded herself with other political leftists and anti-nuclear activists, appointing them assistant secretaries with responsibility for the nuclear labs. In one of her first acts, O'Leary declassified eleven million pages of nuclear documents, including reports on nuclear tests, describing the move as an action to safeguard the environment and a protest against a "bomb-building culture." Having made America's nuclear weapons secrets available to adversary powers, O'Leary then took steps to relax security precautions at the nuclear laboratories under her control. She appointed Rose Gottemoeller, a former Clinton National Security Council staffer with extreme anti-nuclear views to be her director in charge of national security issues. Gottemoeller had been previously nominated to fill the post—long-vacant in the Clinton Administration—of Assistant Secretary of Defense for International Security Policy. The appointment was successfully blocked, however, by congressional Republicans alarmed by her radical disarmament views. The Clinton response to this rejection was to appoint her to be in charge of security for the nation's nuclear weapons labs.

The architect of America's China policy over the course of the current disaster has been another left-winger, Clinton's National Security Adviser Sandy Berger. Berger began his political life as an anti-Vietnam war protestor and member of the radical "Peace Now" movement which regards Israel as the aggressor in the Middle East. Berger first met Clinton as an activist in the McGovern for President campaign, the most left-wing Democratic presidential campaign in American history. Prior to his appointment, Berger was a lobbyist for the business arm of China's communist dictatorship. (The other root cause of the security breach was, of course, greed—a major factor in all its aspects, and on both sides of the political aisle.) Is it surprising that a political leftist and business lobbyist for China's rulers should take steps to lift the security controls that previously protected United States military technology? Or that, during his tenure, invitations to the White House should be extended to agents of Chinese intelligence and China's military, or that the appointment of Chinese intelligence assets like that of John Huang to posts with top security clearance should be considered reasonable? Or that Huang should be protected by Clinton's Justice Department who handed him a sweetheart deal, after he was exposed, protecting him from prosecution for serious crimes?

Is it surprising, given the politics of the Clinton managers, that the administration should place its faith in arms control agreements that depend on trustworthy partners, while strenuously opposing measures to develop anti-ballistic missile defenses that do not? Even after the revelations of China's thefts, Berger and the Clinton Administration still opposed the implementation of anti-ballistic missile defense programs, while pressing to keep China's most favored nation trading status.

Nor is it surprising that a Democratic Party, whose political culture is pervaded by left-wing illusions and deceits, should work so assiduously to obstruct the investigations of the debts of the Clinton-Gore campaign to the Chinese dictatorship, or should be so irresponsibly complacent in the face of the revelations of the Cox report. There was perhaps nothing more alarming for the prospects of the two-party system than the wall of denial that was hastily and irresponsibly erected around these issues by Democratic leaders like Tom Daschle in the wake of the Cox disclosures. To say, as the Senate Minority Leader did, that there was nothing really new in these revelations—as though previous administrations had dismantled vital security procedures, taken illegal monies from foreign intelligence services and then blocked investigations when the illegalities were revealed, presided over the wholesale evaporation of the nation's nuclear weapons advantage, abetted the transfer of missile technologies that could strike American cities to potentially hostile powers, and opposed the development of weapons systems that could defend against such attacks—is absurd.

At the heart of the crisis is, in fact, a White House that has loaded its administration with officials deeply disenchanted with, if not actively hostile to, America's character and purposes. This is a White House whose leader has spent enormous political capital apologizing to the world for America's role in it. Standing behind that leader and his many cover-ups is a party that lacks proper pride in America's national achievement and proper loyalty to America's national interests. This is a party that, even in the face of the most massive breach of security in America's history, took the position that, like Monica, "everybody does it." This is the legacy of the triumphs of the political left during the era of the Vietnam War, and its long march through the Democratic Party and the cultural institutions that support it.

27

The Manchurian President

WITH THE PUBLICATION of the Cox report we now know that seven years of the Clinton Administration have co-incided with the most massive breach of military security in American history. As a result of the calculated degrading of security controls at America's nuclear laboratories, Chinese Communists have been able to steal the designs for our arsenal of nuclear weapons, including our most advanced warheads. As a result of the 1993 Clinton decision to terminate the COCOM security controls that denied sensitive technologies to nuclear proliferators and potential adversary powers, Chinese Communists have been given the secrets of our intercontinental ballistic missile systems, along with previously restricted computer hardware. This allows them for the first time to target cities in the United States. In little over five years, the Chinese Communist dictatorship has been able to close a technology gap of twenty and to destroy a security buffer that had kept America safe from foreign attacks on its territorial mainland for more than a hundred years.

Throughout its entire history until 1957, the United States was protected from such attacks by the oceans, whose natural barriers have insulated it from potential aggressors. In 1957, the Soviet Union acquired an intercontinental missile technology that threatened to close that gap. Since then, the only real protection the United States has enjoyed has been its technological edge in developing more sophisticated warheads and more accurate missiles than its potential opponents. The edge provided a possibility that America might prevail in a nuclear war and discouraged preemptive strikes. The catastrophe that has occurred on the Clinton watch is summed up in the fact that this edge has now vanished, probably never to be regained.

America is now vulnerable to nuclear attack, not merely from China but, in the absence of an anti-ballistic missile defense which the Clinton Administration has steadfastly refused to develop, from every rogue state that China has chosen to arm. Along with Russia, China is the chief proliferator of nuclear, missile, and satellite technology to other governments. The governments it has chosen to benefit in this way are notorious stockpilers of biological and chemical weapons, and among the most dangerous and dedicated enemies of the United States: Libya, North Korea, Iraq, and Iran.

Yet, in the midst of the revelations that make up this grim prospect, the attitude of the Clinton Administration has been one of hear-no-evil, see-no-evil. The official line, ritually repeated by the Democratic leadership in the sickeningly familiar refrain of the Monica scandal is "everybody does it" and "it's no big deal," presumably because, at the moment, China only has a few nuclear weapons actually deployed. Far from acknowledging the catastrophe that has occurred or recognizing the dangers it creates, the Clinton White House has hurried to resume export sales of the same previously restricted technologies and to reassert the "strategic partnership" it promoted with the very dictatorship that has declared America its "number one adversary" and has stripped us of our military shield.

Indeed, the government's awareness of many of the losses dates back several years, during which the Clinton reaction was exactly the same: continue on the destructive course. According to Congressman Curt Weldon, who is a member of the Cox Committee, at least fifteen government officials have experienced the wrath of the Clinton Administration *because* they tried to protect America's secrets from being transferred to China. One notorious case was described in a recent *Wall Street Journal* article by a former security official, Michael Ledeen. According to documents obtained by Ledeen, a mid-level government arms-control bureaucrat was asked in 1997 to provide a memo supporting the administration's certification that China was not a nuclear proliferator and could be provided with advanced technologies. This request was made on the eve of a visit from China's communist dictator, Jiang Zemin. The bureaucrat refused and wrote that the agreement the Clinton Adminstration was about to sign "presents real and substantial risk to the common defense and security of both the United States and allied countries." The official added that China was actively seeking American secrets and that "China routinely, both overtly and covertly, subverts national and multilateral trade controls on militarily critical items." This patriot was immediately told by his superiors to revise his memo or lose his job. Sadly, he complied with the order and rewrote the document to state that the proposed Clinton trade agreement "is not inimical to the common defense or the security of the United States."

In keeping with its fierce defense of a suicidal policy, the Clinton Administration has failed to prosecute the very spies who have been identified as responsible for the most critical thefts of American military secrets, and has protected those whose wrists it has slapped. Wen Ho Lee, the man responsible for the most damaging espionage, is known to have downloaded millions of lines of computer codes revealing the designs of our most advanced nuclear warheads. But Wen Ho Lee today is a free man. Peter Lee, who gave Communist China our warhead testing techniques and the radar technology to locate our submarines (until then the most secure element of our nuclear deterrent), is also free, having served only a year in jail for his treason.

Wen Ho Lee was actually protected while performing his dirty work. When government agents requested a wiretap on Wen Ho Lee's phone, the request was denied by Clinton Justice. From its inception the Clinton Justice Department had never denied a wiretap request before. In explaining why it has not prosecuted Lee, the Clinton Justice Department claims that its evidence only shows that Lee downloaded the classified information onto a non-secure computer, from which others unknown may have picked it up. But, as Angelo Codevilla pointed out in the *Wall Street Journal*, "by this logic no one could be prosecuted for espionage for putting stolen documents into a dead drop, such as a hollow tree, for later pickup by foreign agents." Of course, the administration lacks even this transparent excuse in the case of Peter Lee, who did give the information directly to the communists.

Why is Bill Clinton furiously covering up for the Communist Chinese and protecting its leaders and their spies from the wrath that should surely follow their rape of America's most guarded secrets? Certainly not, as Clinton and his complicit Democratic defenders now claim because "everyone does it." Unlike China, for example, the state of Israel is a democracy and a proven ally of the United States. Yet when an Israeli agent named Jonathan Pollard was discovered stealing secrets whose dimensions did not even approach the seriousness of these thefts (no technologies, for example, were involved), he was given a life sentence amidst the most solemn anathemas from the officials of the government he betrayed.

The evidence is compatible with only one conclusion. The reason Bill Clinton is protecting China's spies and their communist masters is because in protecting them he is protecting himself. The China strategy is fully intelligible in the frame of Clinton's strategy on other matters: *the President has triangulated with China's com-*

munist government in pursuit of his own political interest at the expense of the United States. This is not about loyalties that Bill Clinton might have to communist ideology or communist dictators. On this, Bill Clinton's record is clear: he has no loyalties, except to himself. It is the solipsistic nihilism that we have come to know as the very essence of Bill Clinton that has made this treachery possible, even inevitable.

Clinton's triangulation with Communist China has been chillingly charted by two national security professionals (although they do not employ the term itself), with the help of the Thompson Committee investigations into illegal campaign contributions. In the *Year of the Rat*, Bill Triplett and Ed Timperlake show that the roots of the Clinton betrayal lie in relationships that go back to Arkansas, and the fact that Bill Clinton owes his political life to the Chinese Communists through their agents, business associates, and friends.

Year of the Rat begins with the authors' observation that the number one funder of the Clinton-Gore 1992 presidential campaign was an Arkansas resident and Chinese banker named James Riady, who has been a friend of Bill Clinton for twenty years. Riady is the scion of a multi-billion dollar financial empire which is a working economic and political partnership with China's military and intelligence establishment. The Riadys gave 450,000 dollars to Clinton's presidential campaign and another six hundred thousand dollars to the Democratic National Committee and Democratic state parties.

But the importance of the Riadys to Clinton's ascent is far greater than even these contributions suggest, and not merely because the Chinese network, in which the Riadys are only one important factor, extends through thousands of companies and individuals whose contributions no one has as yet attempted to track. Without the Riadys, Clinton would not have won the Democratic nomination in the first place, and would not have been in a posi-

tion to benefit from their later largesse. In the presidential prima-
ries of 1992, in fact, the Riadys were the absolutely crucial factor
that stood between Clinton and defeat. After losing the New
Hampshire primary, the candidate faced a crucial test in New York.
But he had also run out of money. At this critical juncture, James
Riady stepped in to arrange a 3.5 million dollar loan to the Clinton
campaign. New York proved to be the last real competition that
Clinton faced on his path to victory.

When the Arkansas governor stepped onto the national scene,
Clinton and Riady were not new acquaintances. They had met in
1978 when Clinton was attorney general and had not yet become
governor of the state. They were introduced by Clinton's chief
political backer, Jackson Stephens, the head of Stephens, Inc., one
of the largest private investment firms outside of Wall Street. "Thus
began a friendship," in the words of Timperlake and Triplett, "that
has lasted twenty years, and has spread a web of intrigue, financial
corruption, and foreign influence into American government."

James Riady had begun his American banking career earlier in
the 1970s as an intern at Stephens, Inc. Later they became partners in the Worthen Bank of Little Rock, the very same that subsequently experienced a mysterious fire which destroyed records
being sought by Kenneth Starr and other Whitewater investigators
in their inquiries into Hillary Clinton's Rose law firm activities. It
was through the Worthen bank that Riady arranged the 3.5 million
dollar credit to Clinton's failing primary campaign. The Riady relationship extended beyond the Clintons themselves to their friends
and to Hillary's associates at Rose, including its head, Joe Giroir,
and a White House aide named Mark Middleton, who later invoked
the Fifth Amendment when he was called before the Thompson
committee. It was the Riadys who provided a one hundred thousand dollar "job" for the indicted Web Hubbell, at the moment when
he had indicated to the Starr prosecutors that he might be ready to
talk. After the payment from Riady and others, Hubbell changed
his mind and chose jail instead.

Understanding the security disaster that has befallen the United States requires an understanding that the leakage of America's secrets proceeded along two parallel tracks. One track was espionage, the other was a political-economic track through the legal commercial activities of the United States government and in particular through its political oversight of these commercial activities, which in past administrations had included formal controls of sensitive technologies that the Clinton team systematically dismantled. Political contributors to the Clinton-Gore campaigns played key roles in promoting the dismantling process.

A central figure in the economic track of Chinese activities was the vice president and Far East area manager for the Worthen Bank, a Chinese-born American named John Huang, who was a friend of Clinton from Little Rock days. Triplett and Timperlake make a strong case that it was through the personal intervention of Hillary Clinton that in 1994 John Huang was made a top official in the Commerce Department, where he had access to all the information an agent would need to strip America of the supercomputer technologies vital to the development of advanced weapons systems. Huang has been identified by the CIA as a spy, but like Wen Ho Lee has been protected by Clinton Justice and is still free. Huang is the only person ever to have been given top security clearance in the Commerce Department, and he retained it when he left the government.

The decision to leave the government for a position at the Democratic National Committee was made for Huang at a meeting in the Oval office attended by the President, Huang, James Riady, Riady partner and former Rose law firm head Joe Giroir, and presidential aide Bruce Lindsey. This meeting took place three days after the president had decided on a strategy to rescue his failing political fortunes which had reached a nadir following the Democrats' historic defeat in the congressional elections of 1994 and Newt Gingrich's ascension to the Speakership of the House. It was the first Republican majority in the House in forty-eight years. Designed by the President's new political advisor, Dick Morris, the strategy involved a massive television advertising campaign, directed against Gingrich and the Republican House. The campaign has been directly credited with turning the political tide and ensuring the re-election in 1996 of the Clinton team. The chief fundraiser for this campaign was John Huang.

It should be evident from these facts (and they could easily be amplified with many more) that the alliance Bill Clinton has made with the Riadys and their China network is the pivot of his political career, and the absolute key to his survival. It has had consequences for American politics and security so vast that no brief summary can begin to describe them. In 1996, to pick an illustrative example, the Long Beach City Council granted a lease on the demobilized Long Beach Naval Station to a Chinese company named cosco, which is little more than the naval arm of the Chinese Communist Army and is a major arms supplier to dictators and terrorists. Its cargoes have included rocket fuel for Pakistan, helping to destabilize the Indian peninsula, and nuclear components for Iran, a volatile factor in the Middle East. In 1996, a cosco ship was seized in Oakland, California by U. S. Customs agents who discovered a cargo of two thousand assault weapons intended for sale to Los Angeles street gangs.

Why would the Long Beach City Council approve a lease to such a company, particularly if the relevant oversight officials in Washington had alerted them to the nature of the cosco enterprise? But the relevant oversight officials in Washington did not alert Long Beach to the danger posed by cosco. On the contrary, they encouraged the deal.

In the 1996 election campaign, Johnny Chung—another middleman for the China network and for cosco in particular—gave 366,000 dollars to the Democratic Party. It was subsequently returned after the campaign finance scandal surfaced and it was clear that it had come illegally from foreign sources. Among the sources was a Chinese intelligence officer, Lieutenant Colonel Liu Chaoying, the daughter of China's highest ranking military officer. On the eve of the 1996 elections, a White House official named Dorothy Robyn made a conference call to the Long Beach City Council and applied direct pressure on them to push the deal with cosco through. Robyn told the Council that the "national interest would best be served if the [cosco] plan proceeds." The chief competitor for the lease, whose application was denied by the White House pressure, was the U. S. Marine Corps.*

Nine months before the cosco lease was sealed, a crisis had developed in the Taiwan Strait. Elections were being held in Taiwan and the communist regime, which claims sovereignty over Taiwan, was launching intermediate range ballistic missiles with blank warheads in the direction of the island, an act of blatant intimidation. The Clinton Administration had interposed two aircraft carriers from the Seventh Fleet, ostensibly to remind the communists that Taiwan was an American ally. At that moment, an old Little Rock friend of Bill Clinton's appeared in Washington with a 460,000 dollar donation to the Presidential Legal Defense Trust that Clinton had set up to defray his legal expenses in the Paula Jones sexual harassment case. The friend also brought a message from one of China's top officials that if the United States interfered in this matter, a missile attack against Los Angeles would become a possibility. The friend also brought his own broken-English personal message: "Any negative outcomes of the US decision in the China issue will affect your administration position especially in the campaign year." The messenger was Charlie Trie, owner of the Fu Lin Restaurant in Little Rock. Trie was also a member of the "Four Seas" Triad, a billion-dollar Asian crime syndicate allied to Chinese military and intelligence agencies. Clinton's written reply to Trie's blackmail was addressed "Dear Charlie" and assured him (and

---

* In 1998 the Republican Congress killed the cosco deal.

his communist bosses in Beijing) that the interposition of the air-craft carriers was "not intended as a threat to the Peoples Republic of China," but as "a signal to *both* Taiwan and the PRC that the United States was concerned about maintaining stability in the . . . region" (emphasis added).

The network of businessmen, agents, and gangsters that links Bill Clinton to China's communist dictatorship is interwoven with every element of the greatest security disaster in American history. It as though the Rosenbergs were in the White House, except that the Rosenbergs were little people and naïve, and consequently the damage they were capable of accomplishing was incomparably less. It could even be said in behalf of the Rosenbergs that they did not do it for themselves, but out of loyalty to an ideal, however pathetic and misguided. Bill Clinton has no such loyalties—neither to his family, nor his party, nor his country. As is evident from the dis-closures that have already come to light, the damage he has done is without precedent and will dwarf even the legacy of national em-barrassment that he earned for himself in the Lewinsky affair. The wounds he has inflicted on this nation, and every individual within it, with consequences unknown for future generations, cannot be said to have been inflicted for ideological reasons or even out of some perverse dedication to a principle of evil. The destructive-ness of Bill Clinton has emerged out of a need that is far more banal—to advance the cause of a self-absorbed and criminal per-sonality.

A Political Romance

WHEN I WAS A LITERATURE STUDENT in college my Shakespeare professor drew our attention to the way the playwright turned to romance as he grew older, writing symbolic pastorals devoted to themes of redemption. According to my professor, this was a natural human progression, and he cited examples from other writers to prove his point. Youth is characterized by a hunger for information, he told us; age distills what it knows in parables, and returns to archetypal myths.

When Shakespeare wrote *The Tempest*, the most famous of his late romances and the very last of his plays, he was actually only forty-seven—more than a decade younger than I am now. Moreover, I have found my own experience to be exactly the opposite of what he predicted. Growing up in a progressive household in New York City (my parents were members of the Communist Party), I found myself enveloped in the vapors of a romantic myth not unlike that of Shakespeare's pastorals or the fairy tales that had been read to me as a child. In the radical romance of our political lives, the world was said to have begun in innocence, but to have fallen afterwards under an evil spell, afflicting the lives of all with great suffering and injustice. According to our myth, a happy ending beckoned, however. Through the efforts of progressives like us, the spell would one day be lifted, and mankind would be freed from its trials. In this liberated future, "social justice" would be established, peace would reign, and harmony prevail. Men and women would be utterly transformed.

Being at the center of a heroic myth inspired passions that informed my youthful passage and guided me to the middle of my adult life. But then I was confronted by a reality so inescapable and harsh that it shattered the romance for good. A friend—the mother of three children—was brutally murdered by my political comrades, members of the very vanguard that had been appointed to redeem us all. Worse, since individuals may err, the deed was covered up by the vanguard itself who hoped, in so doing, to preserve the faith.

If this personal tragedy had remained isolated, perhaps the romance itself could have survived. But the murder of my friend was amplified and reflected in numerous others. Most notably, the slaughter of millions of poor peasants in Southeast Asia by the "liberation fronts" my comrades and I had aided and defended, who were supposed to be the angels of progress, too. When all was said and done, there was no happy ending. If anything, in the liberated nations the injustice was even greater than before. In retrospect it was apparent to me that most of the violence in my lifetime had been directed by utopians like myself against those who would not go along with their impossible dreams. "Idealism kills," Nietzsche had warned before all the bloodshed began. But nobody listened.

As a result of my experience, I developed, in age, an aversion to romantic myths. Instead I was seized with a hunger for information—for the facts that would reveal to me the truth about the years I was a member of a heroic vanguard. The fall of the communist empire and the opening of its secrets have fed this passion. Preserved in the decoded communications between Soviet agents in America and their contacts in the Kremlin is the record of the truths we had denied, and whose denial made our romance possible. The truths revealed that we were just what our enemies had always said we were. There were spies among us, and cold-blooded agents for a tainted cause. And all of us, it could no longer be denied, had treason in our hearts in the name of a future that would never come.

In the battle of good and evil that formed the core of our romantic myth, we had enlisted—New Left and Old alike—on the wrong side of the historical conflict. We had set out as the proud harbingers of a progressive future. But what we had actually created were realities far worse than those we were seeking to escape. The enemies we scorned—patriots defending America—turned out to be the protectors of what was decent and pragmatically good, and had saved us from being consumed by our crimes.

It became clear to me that the world was not going to be changed into anything very different or better from what it had been. On this earth there would be no kingdom of freedom where lions would lie down with lambs. It should have been obvious when I began. Many things change, but people do not. Otherwise how could Shakespeare, or writers more ancient, capture in their creations a reality that we recognize and that still moves us today?

These revelations of experience had a humbling effect. They took my mind off the noble fantasies and forced me to focus on my ordinary existence. To see how common it was; how unheroic, ordinary, and unredeemed. The revelations that shattered my faith allowed me, for the first time, to look at my own mortality. I was not going to be born again in a New World; I was going to die like everyone else and be forgotten.

And that is when I realized what our romance was about. It was not about a future that was socially just, or about a world redeemed. It was about averting our eyes from this ordinary fact. Our romance was a shield protecting us from the terror of our common human fate. And that was why we clung to our dream so fiercely, despite all the evidence that it had failed. That was why we continued to believe, despite everything we knew. For who would ever want to confront such terror, unless forced to do so by circumstances beyond their control? Who would want to hear the voice of a future that was only calling them to their own oblivion?

And that is when I also realized that our progressive romance would go on. Some, like myself, might wake from its vapors under blows of great personal pain. But there would always be others, and in far greater number, who would not. A century of broken dreams and the slaughters they spawned would, in the end, teach nothing to those who had no reason to hear. Least of all would it cure them of their hunger for a romance that is really a desire not to know who and what we are.

Index

A Note on the Author

David Horowitz is the author of the best-selling autobiography *Radical Son* and co-author, with Peter Collier, of *Destructive Generation*. A leader of the New Left in the 1960s, he grew disillusioned with the consequences of radicalism in America and abroad, and by the 1980s his political about-face was complete. Mr. Horowitz lives in Los Angeles, where he is president of the Center for the Study of Popular Culture and editor of the journal *Heterodoxy*.

This book was designed and set into type
by Mitchell S. Muncy,
with cover art by Stephen J. Ott,
and printed and bound
by Quebecor Printing Book Press,
Brattleboro, Vermont.

The text face is Caslon,
designed by Carol Twombly,
based on faces cut by William Caslon, London, in the 1730s
and issued in digital form by Adobe Systems,
Mountain View, California, in 1989.

The index is by IndExpert,
Montpelier, Vermont.

The paper is acid-free and is of archival quality.

20